WINSTON-SALEM
THROUGH TIME

MICHAEL BRICKER

AMERICA THROUGH TIME®

AMERICA THROUGH TIME is an imprint of Fonthill Media LLC

Fonthill Media LLC
www.fonthillmedia.com
office@fonthillmedia.com

First published 2014

ISBN 978-1-62545-017-3

Typeset in Mrs Eaves XL Serif Narrow
Printed and bound in England

Connect with us:
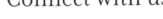 www.twitter.com/usathroughtime
www.facebook.com/AmericaThroughTime

AMERICA THROUGH TIME® is a registered trademark of
Fonthill Media LLC

INTRODUCTION

During the colonial period, the Piedmont section of central North Carolina was rugged and wild. Moravians, a Protestant sect, had come to America from the European region of Moravia by way of the Pennsylvania colony. Moravians were seeking a home where they could practice their religion in isolation and harmony. The North Carolina Piedmont was chosen and a 100,000-acre tract was purchased from Lord Granville. The landscape and climate suited the Moravians nicely, as the tract reminded them of their home countries' geography. After a long journey, the first Moravians arrived and named their settlement Bethabara in 1753. This was the temporary headquarters until the true town was built. Moravians had planned their central town before leaving Pennsylvania. The town was to be called Salem, which means peace. Salem was no ordinary town, but was the seat of the religious hierarchy of North Carolina, a village of trade and craftsmen. Salem was not a farming community; farms and industry were laid to the west of town, and with that, West Salem was born. Over 200 years ago, the new United States of America had a population of less than four million people. More than ninety out of one hundred of these people lived and worked on farms. Salem outlots and farms were the lifeblood of the congregational town. The Krueser and Brietz farm and plantation in Old West Salem spanned nearly 150 years. Presenting in photographs and texts such a farming experience of 150 years showcases the great impact farms had on American towns during the nineteenth and twentieth centuries. The creation of a town, Old Winston in 1849, came out of a need by the Salem Moravians. The evolvement of the 'string' Moravians and the 'wealth' of Winston built to prosperous towns, merging to become Winston-Salem, a 'City of Industry'. Combining the power of textiles and tobacco, the Hanes and Fries families in textiles and R. J. Reynolds in tobacco, along with trade, commerce, and technology, helped to create the city as a number two target by the Soviet Union during the Cold War after the Second World War. These histories and more will be presented in the following format; Old Salem, pages 5-20, Old West Salem, pages 21-44; Brietz farm and plantation, pages 45-64; Old Winston and merged Winston-Salem, pages 65-95. The map below shows growth over the years of the two towns. Now, let us begin our journey of *Winston-Salem Through Time*!

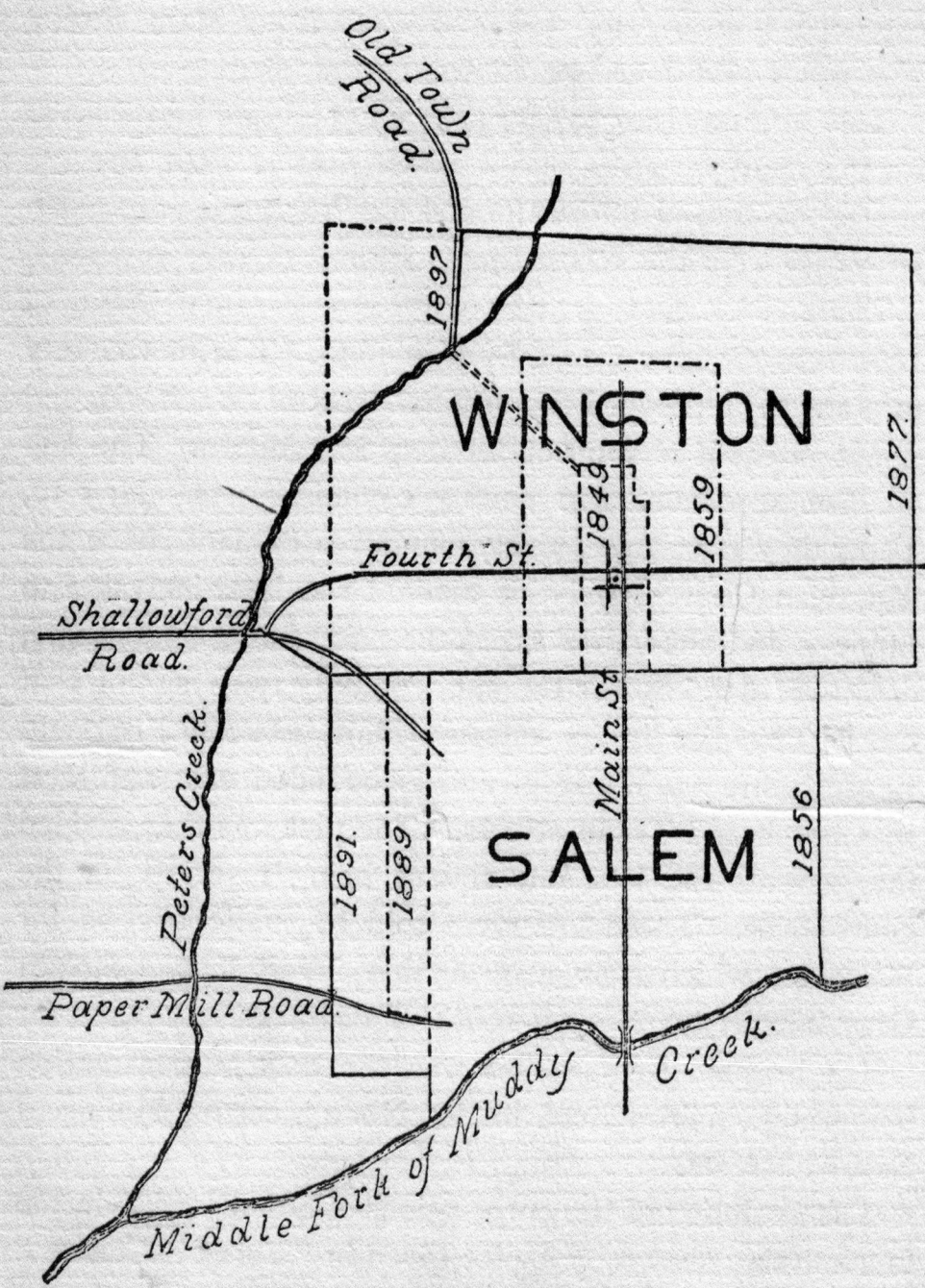

WINSTON AND SALEM CORPORATIONS

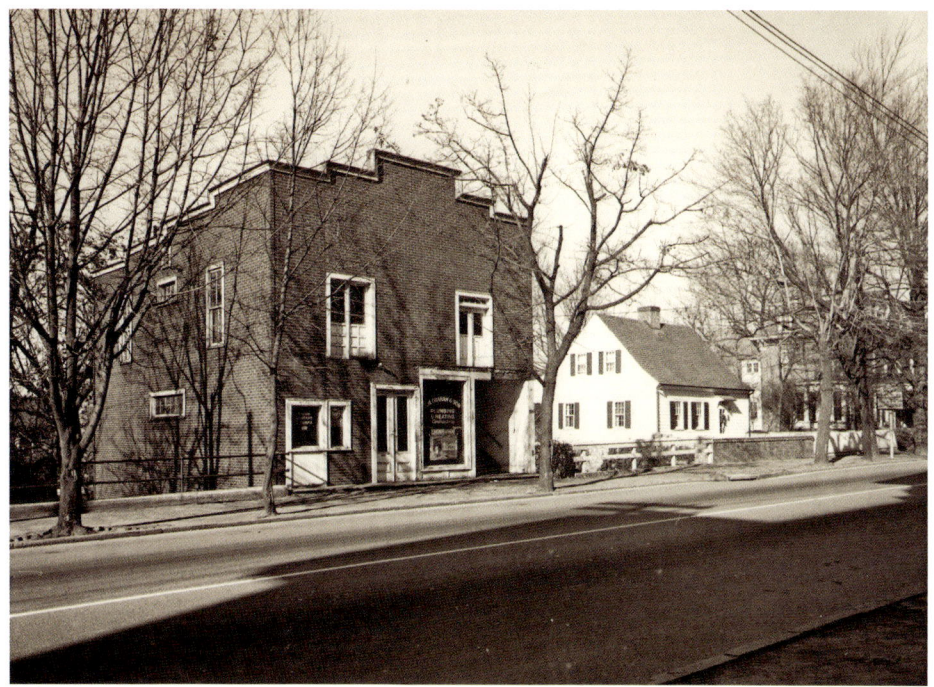

FIRST BLOCK OF HOUSES BUILT ON MAIN STREET: The site of the first constructed houses in Salem is shown *c.* 1950s. The white house was the fourth house built. The Graham & Sons plumbing and heating brick building is shown to the left. It replaced the fifth and third houses around 1900. Four of the five houses have been rebuilt and restored in this 2013 photograph.

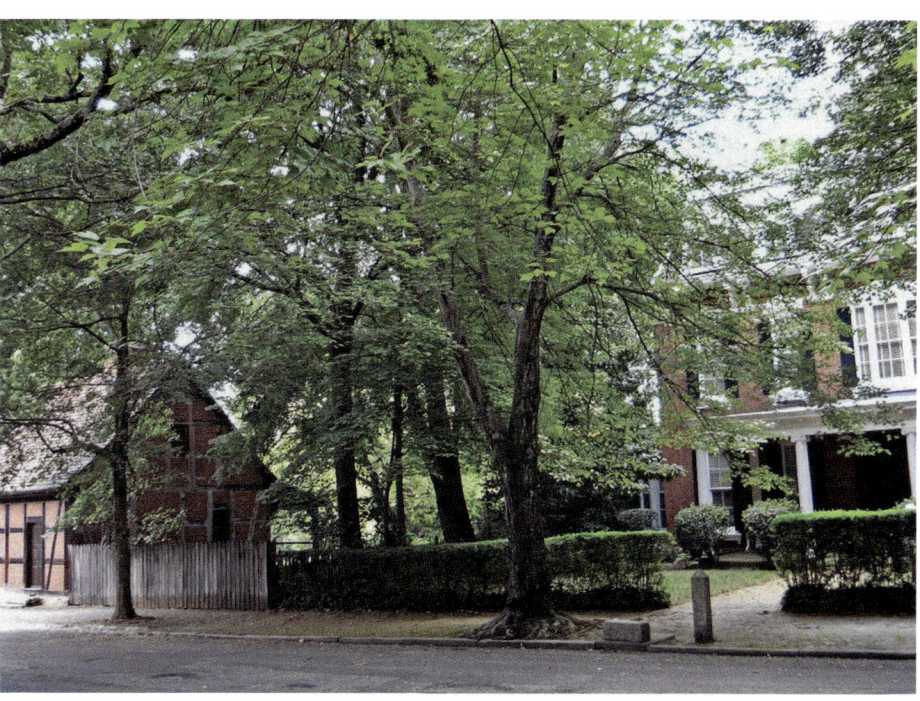

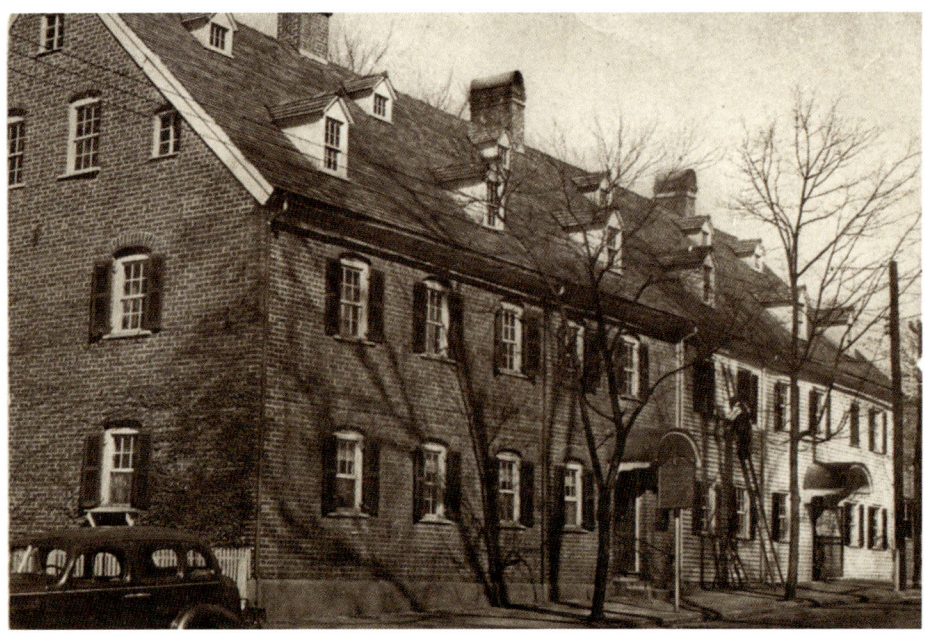

MAIN STREET AT ACADEMY STREET, NEW CENTER OF SALEM: After the first five homes were built, the Moravians decided to move the center of town south, two blocks on Main Street, to acquire a better flow of its water supply. The Single Brothers' House *c.* 1769 is the benchmark of restored Old Salem incorporated. The single men of the community learned their crafts and trades while taking residence in the building. Older residents resided here in a photograph *c.* 1940s. Today it is a tourist establishment.

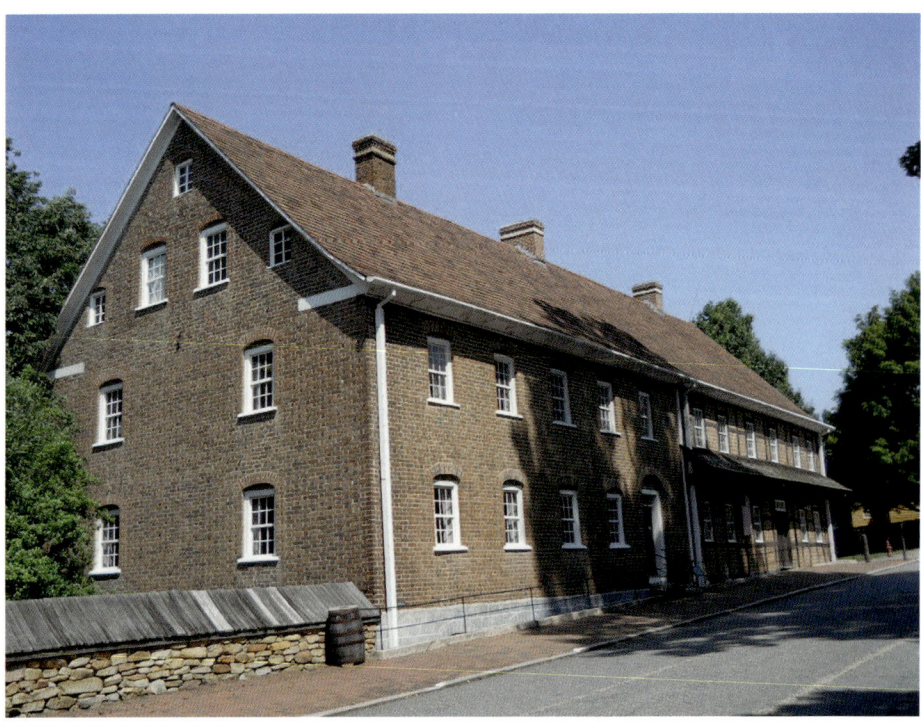

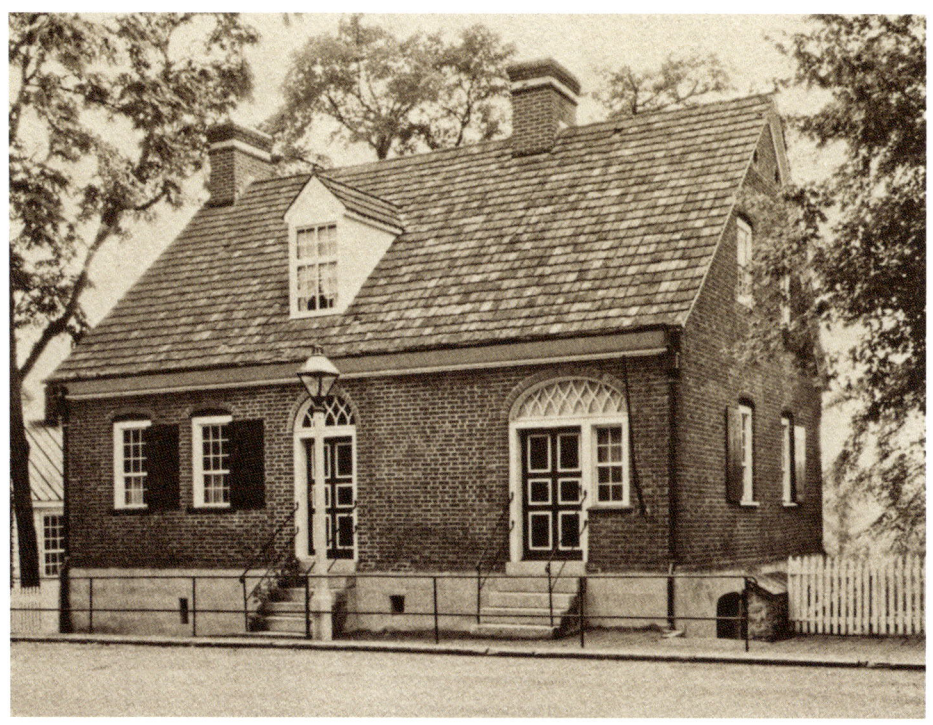

700 BLOCK OF MAIN STREET: The Christopher Vogler House was home to 'the gunsmith of Salem'. Shown is his residence to South and workshop to North (two entrances). His nephew, John Vogler, built next door in 1819 and became Salem's premier silversmith. The restored house appears today as it did in this photograph from the 1940s.

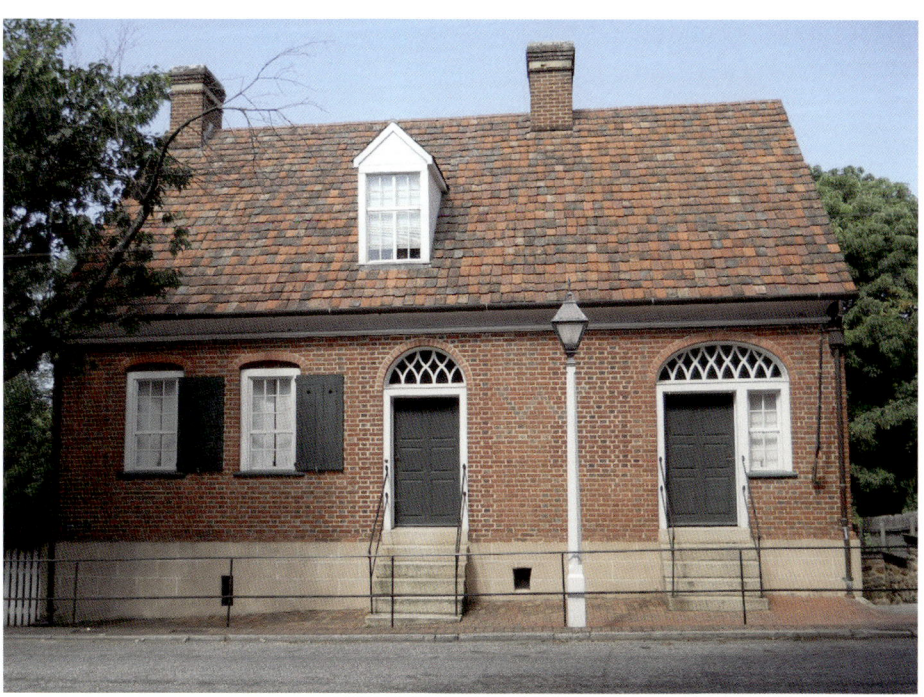

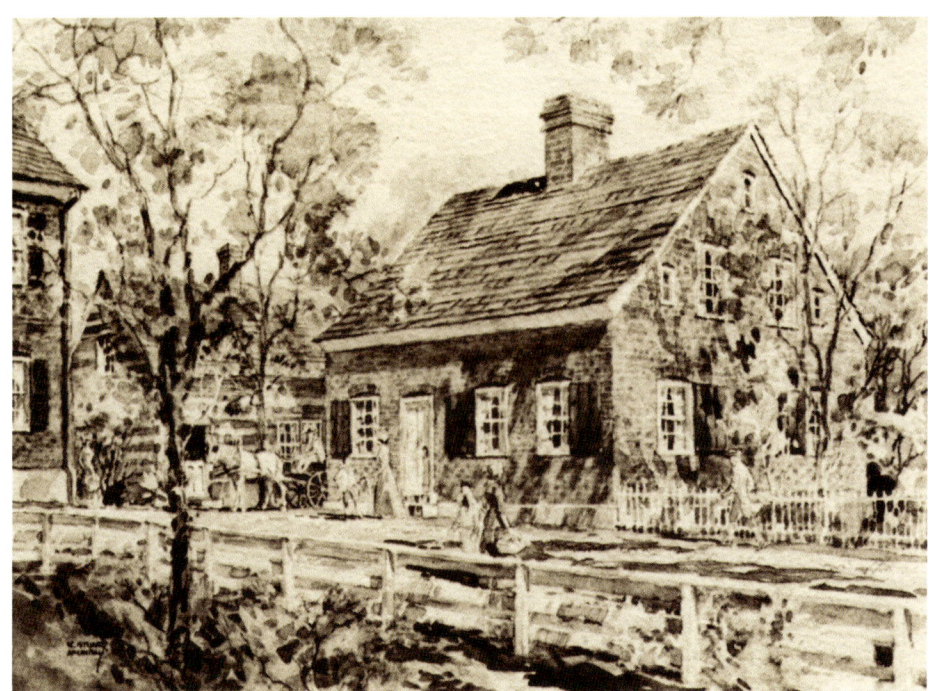

CORNER OF WEST STREET AT CHURCH STREET IN SALEM: Depicted in an early painting is the Gottlieb Schober House at the South corner of the Salem Square. Brother Schober was a major 'mover and shaker' in Salem between 1780 and 1830. A progressive by name, he founded a paper mill, served as the first postmaster of Salem, and represented the Moravians in the Continental Congress. He became a Lutheran Minister while remaining a Moravian elder and he also championed Sunday schools. These schools evolved into the modern grammar schools after the Civil War. His restored home appears complete in 2013.

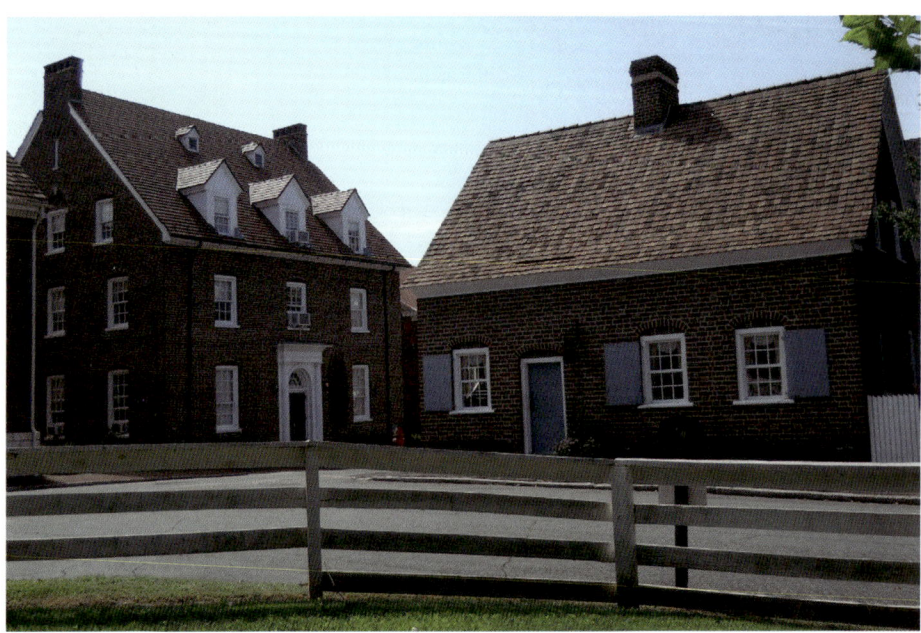

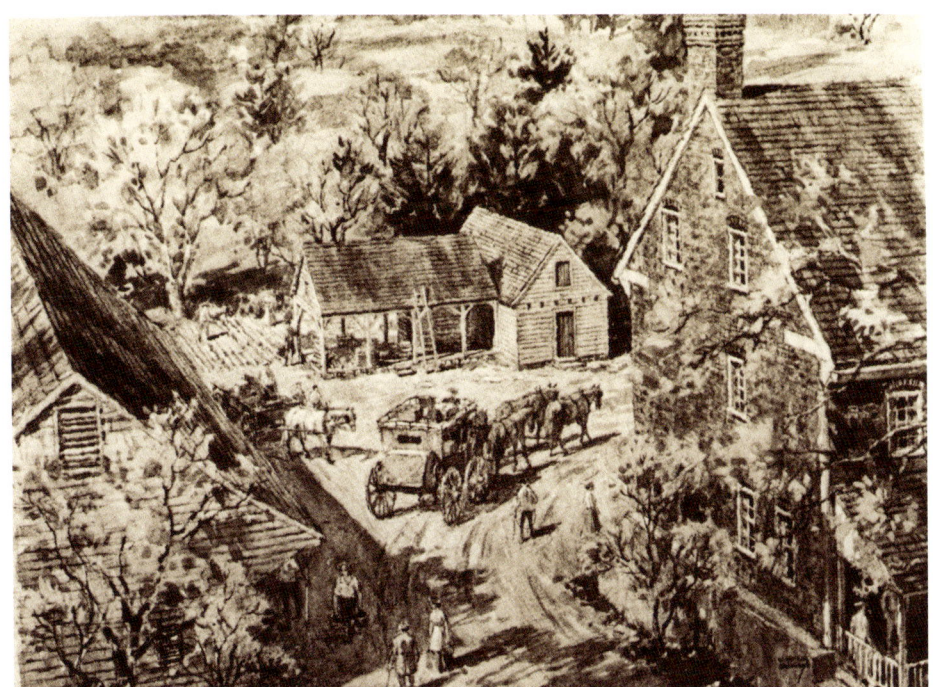

800 BLOCK OF SOUTH MAIN: This painting was used during the reconstruction of Old Salem beginning in 1950. The Salem Tavern *c.* 1784 to the right is original. To the left is found an outbuilding and barn constructed in 1740 and moved to Salem from the E. Beverly Jones Farm near Bethania, North Carolina. The Hattie Butner stage line from Clemmonsville, North Carolina was a regular visitor to early Salem. All are tourist attractions today.

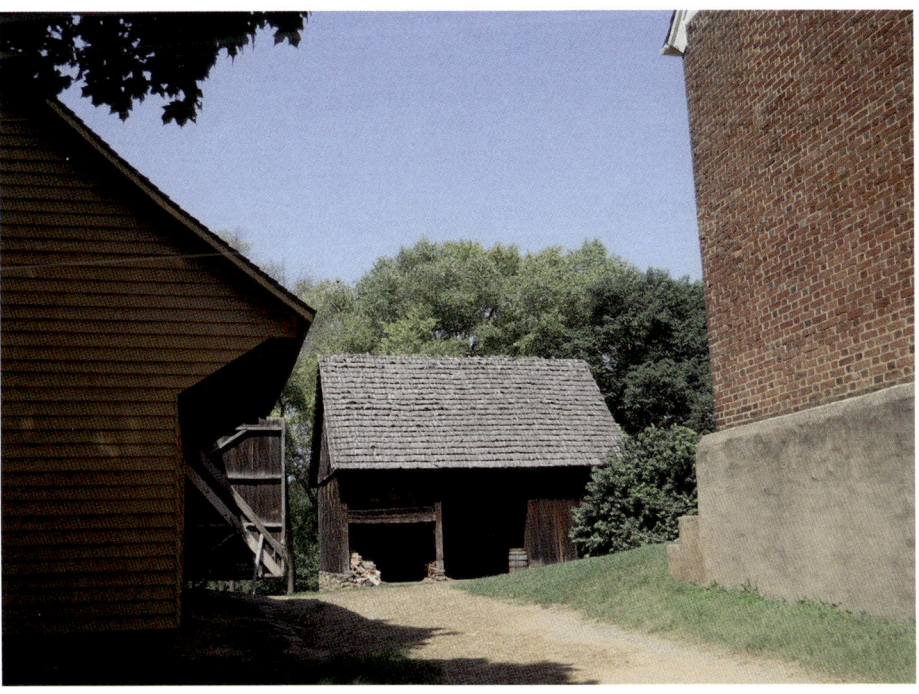

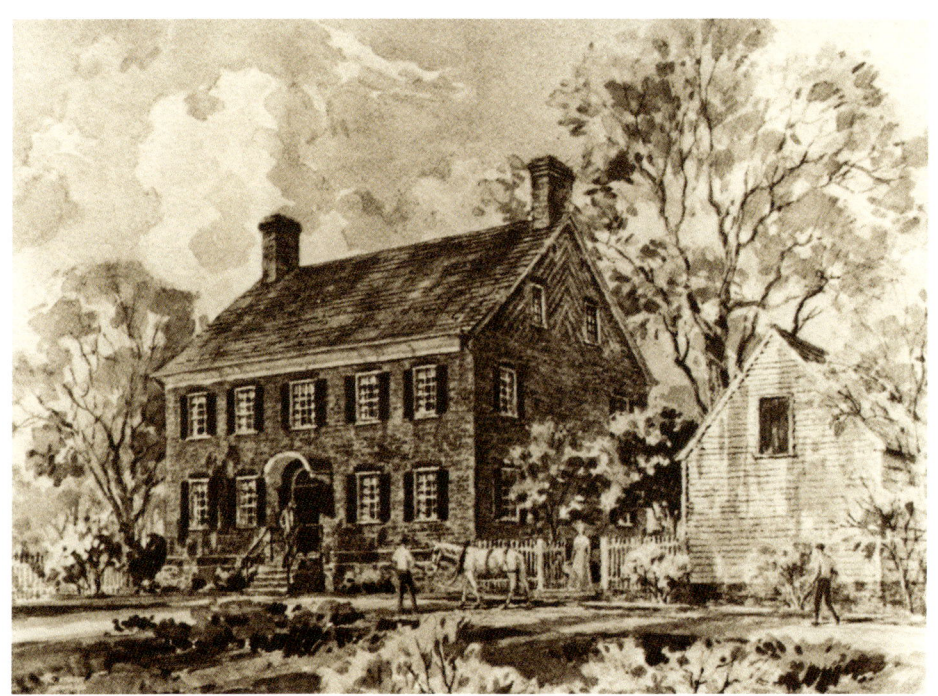

EDGE OF SALEM AT SOUTH CHURCH STREET: The Vierling House and Barn *c.* 1802 appears in another early painting of East Salem. Dr. Benjamin Vierling arrived from Berlin, Germany in 1790 and began a twenty-seven year career in Salem. As a doctor ahead of his times, he championed the first 'cowpox' vaccinations in the United States and the rehabilitation of his patients. The modern photograph shows another tourist gem of Salem.

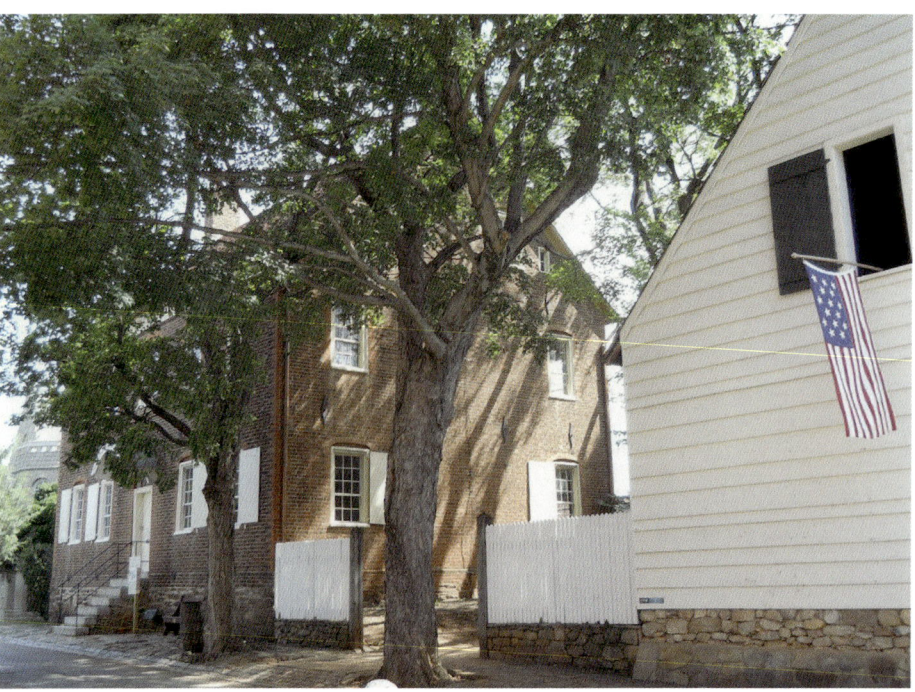

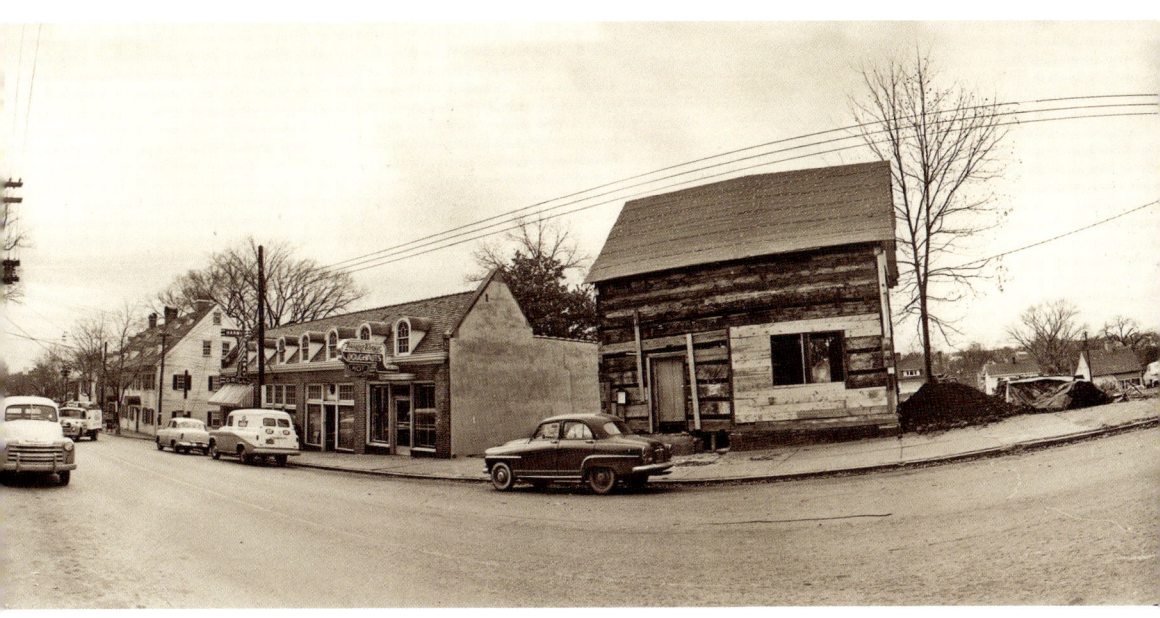

500 BLOCK OF MAIN STREET, TOBACCO AND DOUGHNUTS: Before the creation of Old Salem in 1950, Salem was a typical evolved Southern Town. In this 1950s era photograph a log house rises as a 'phoenix from the dust'. The 1771, Miksch Tobacco House existed alongside the 1920s era building of the Krispy Kreme doughnut shop. The completed project of Old Salem incorporated is shown today.

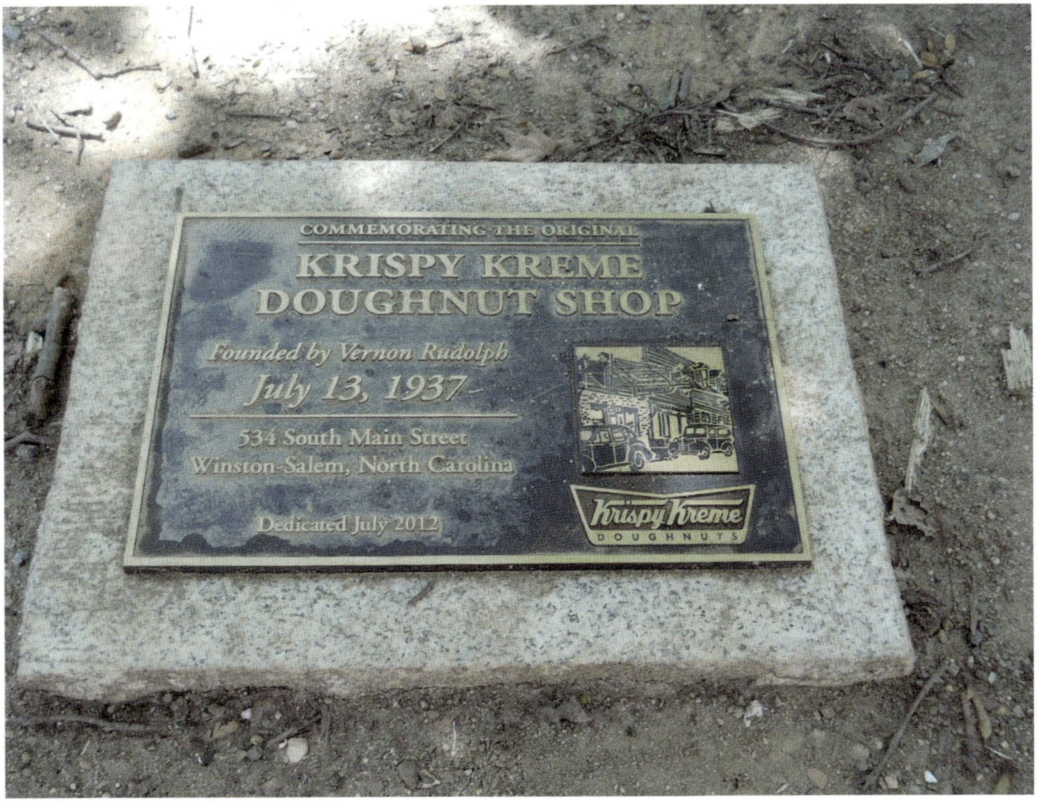

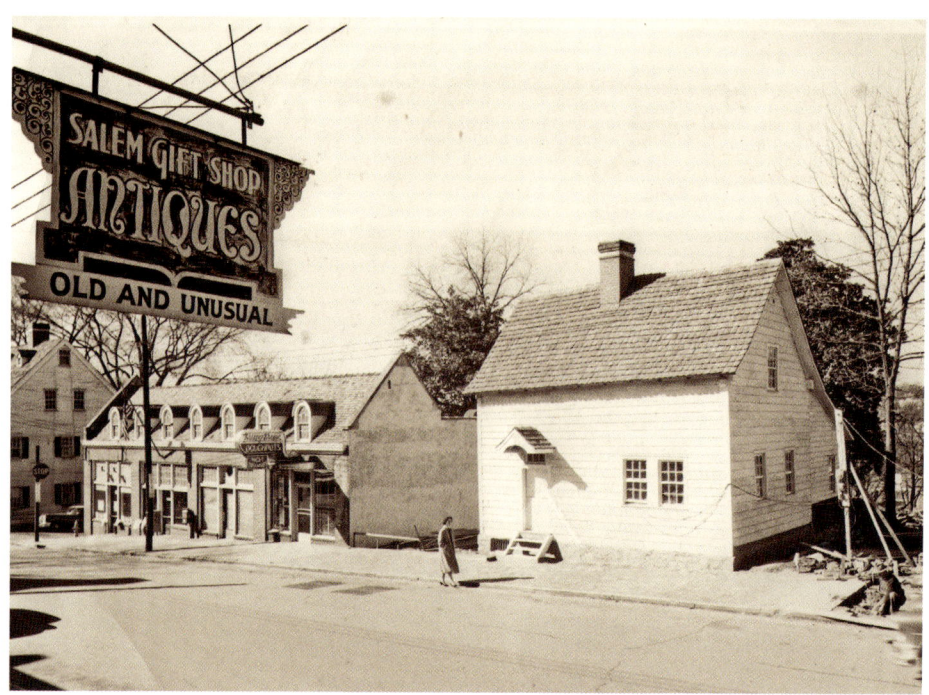

TOBACCO HOUSE NEARS COMPLETION ON MAIN STREET: With the completion of another restored building the Old Salem collection of restored and rebuilt homes total in excess of fifty structures. Unfortunately, the loss of structures outside of the Old Salem time period of expression saw the demise of the 1930s Krispy Kreme location as shown today. Even historic preservation comes with a price.

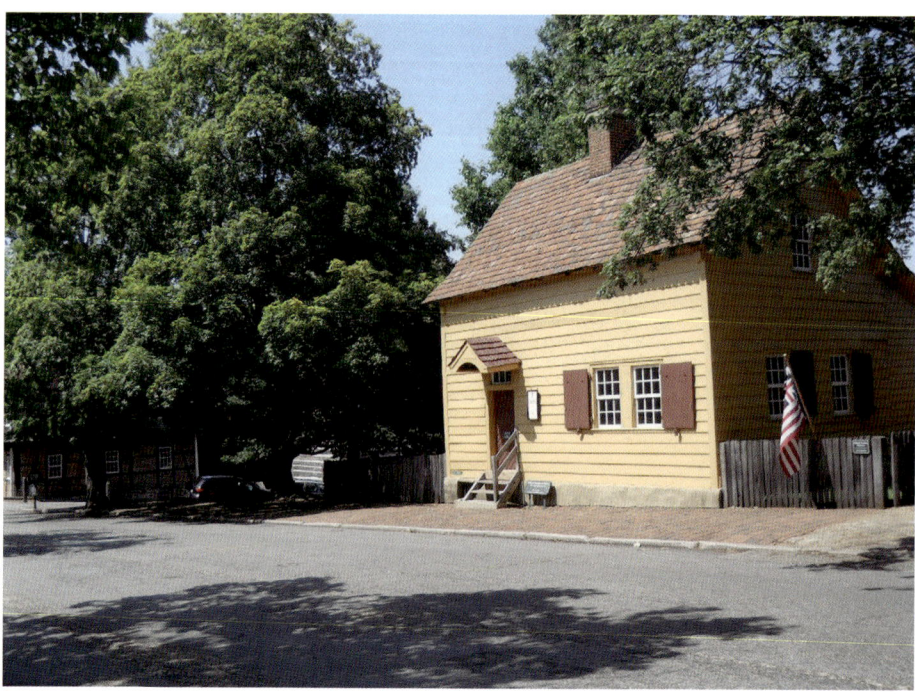

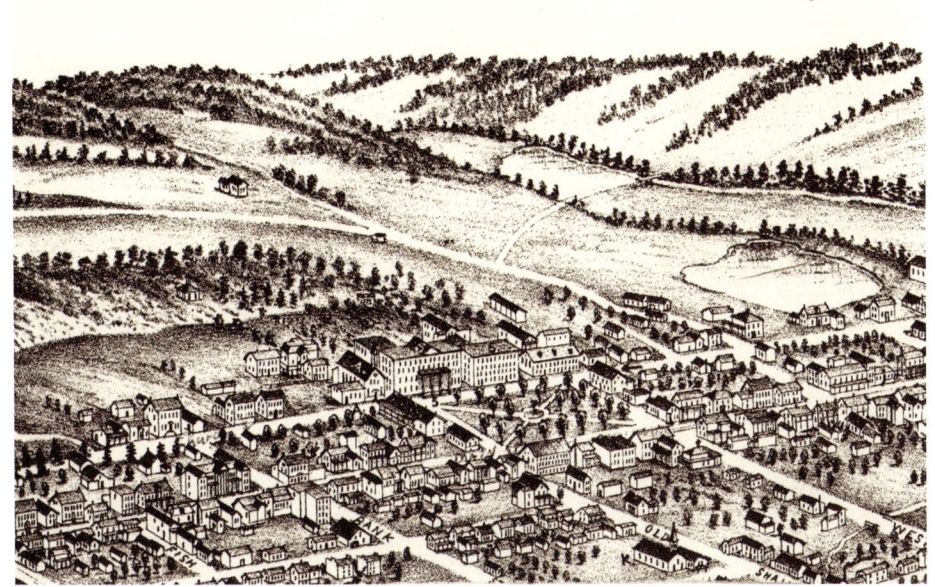

BIRD'S EYE VIEW MAP OF SALEM: The Bird's eye view image map was created by the Stoner & Ruger mapping company in 1891. Most of the major towns in the US used Stoner and Ruger maps as promotional advertisements for their individual towns. This portion of the map presents the center square surrounded by the rest of East Salem. The central building *c.* 1900 houses the post office next to the Welfare Drugstore (restored Miksch Tobacco House today). The wrecking ball also found the Krispy Kreme building as well.

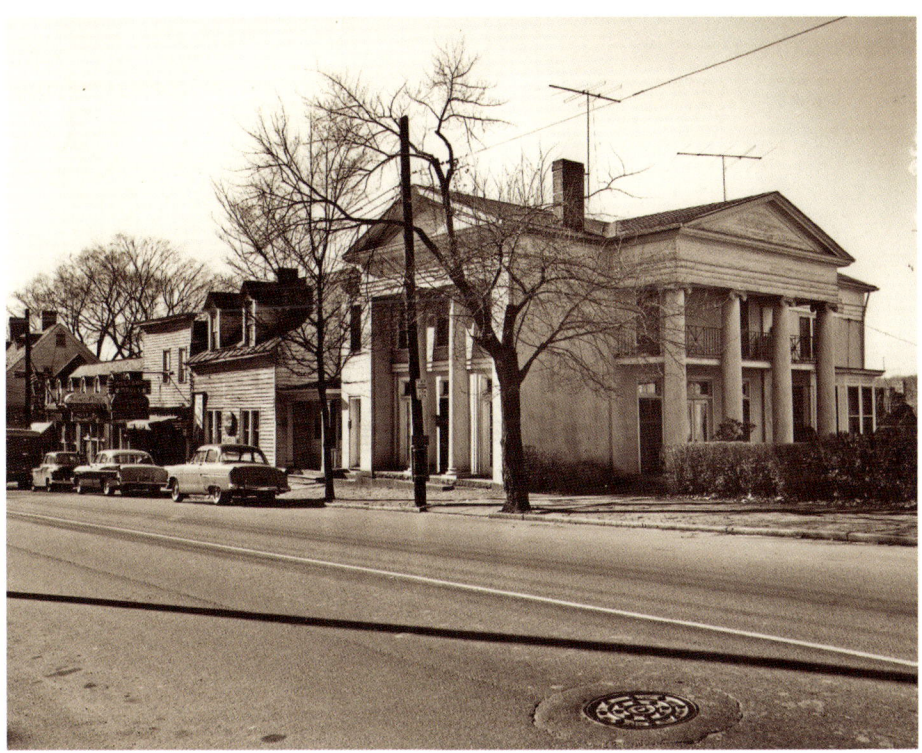

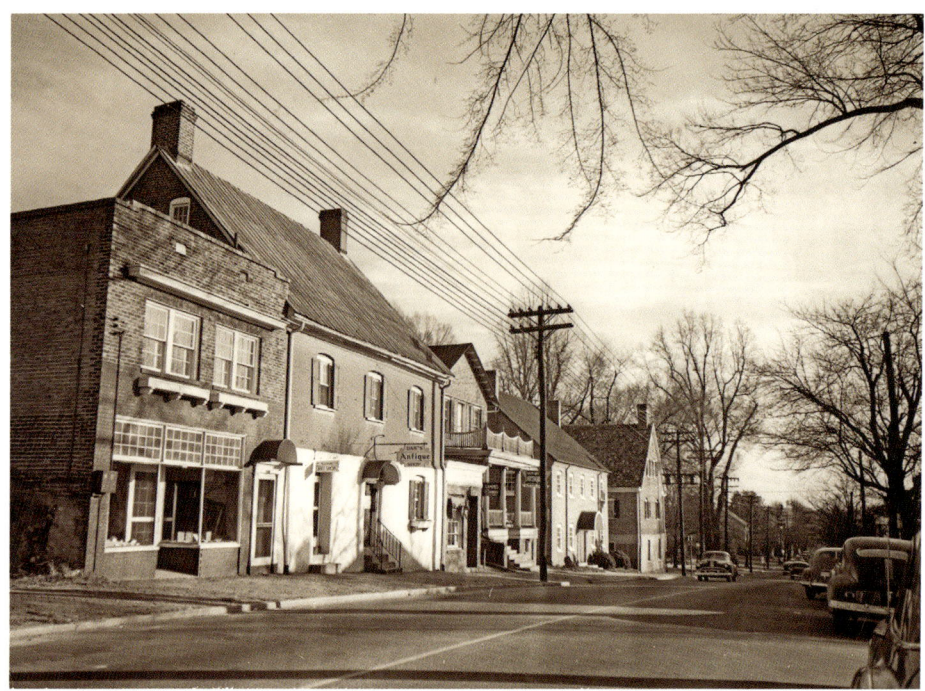

EAST SIDE; 500 BLOCK OF MAIN STREET: Across the street from the Welfare Drugstore and Krispy Kreme doughnut shop contained this 1940s row of businesses. The buildings from left to right contain a photographer's shop, Salem Knit Shop, Dan's Antique Shop, Lammis Cleaners and Salem Gift & Antiques. In today's landscape can be found the restored Winkler Bakery *c.* 1800. All others have been razed by Old Salem Incorporated.

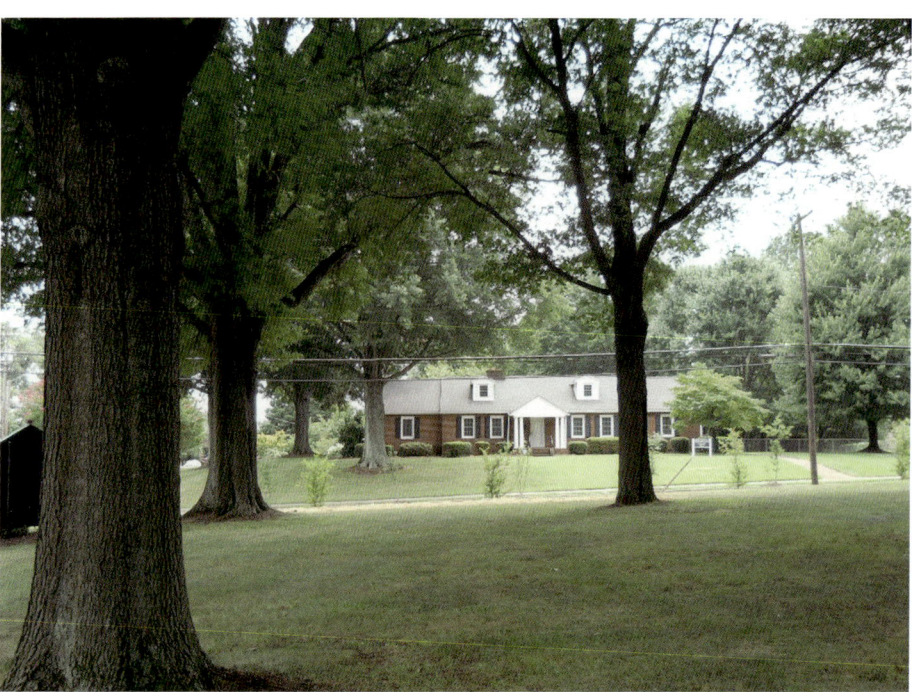

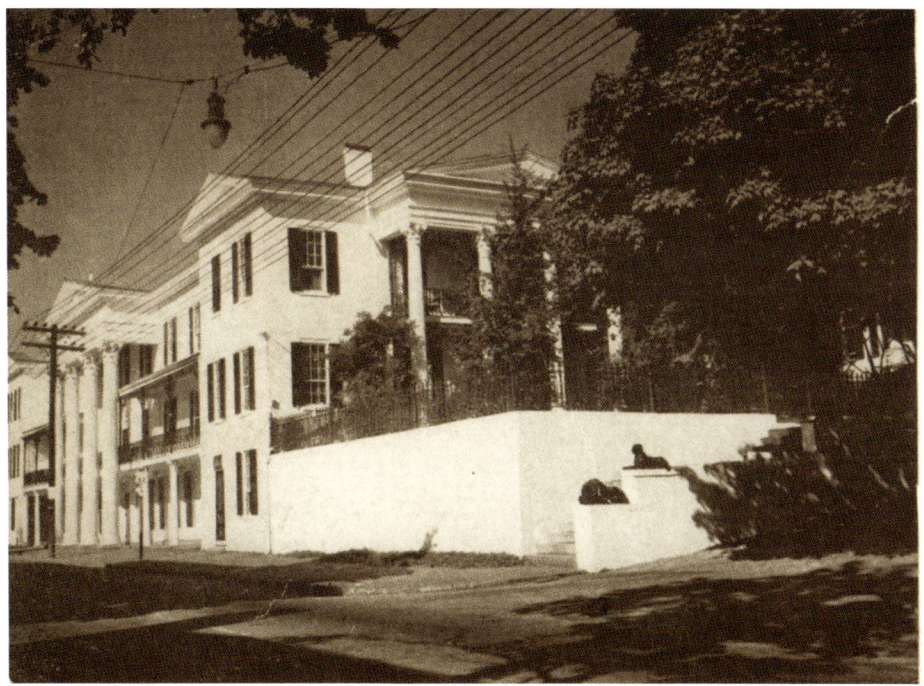

East Side of 400 Block of Main Street: Across the street from the first five houses built, existed the *ante bellum* style and largest homestead in Salem. Known as the Belo Home *c.* 1863, it was built by Edward Belo who began the construction in the 1850s. With the advent of the Civil War years and the loss of many sons the home took nearly ten years to complete. Belo's foundry business is showcased with the animal sculptures, a lion and two dogs on steps. The *c.* 1900 photograph corresponds greatly with the 2013 model.

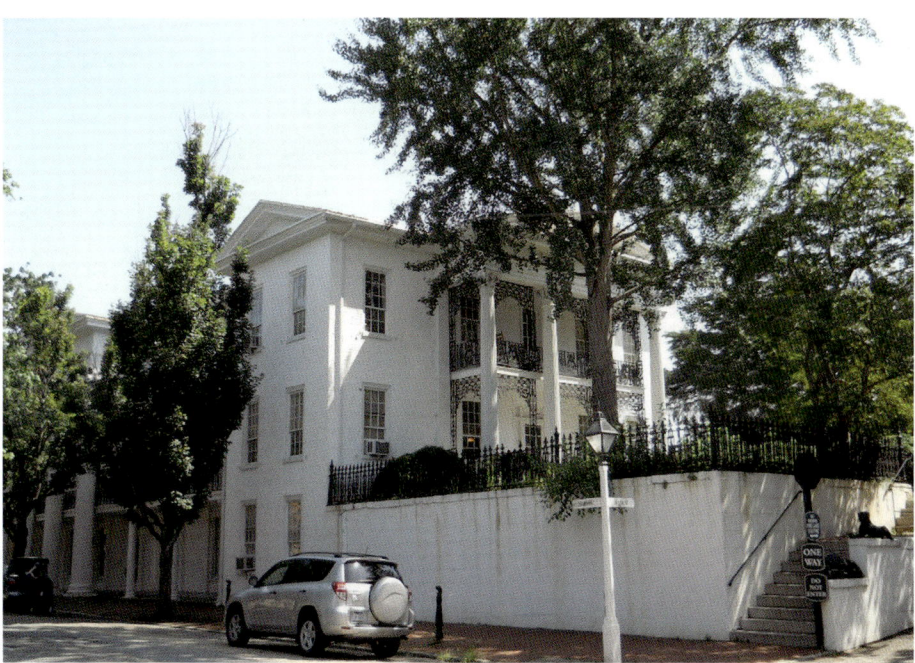

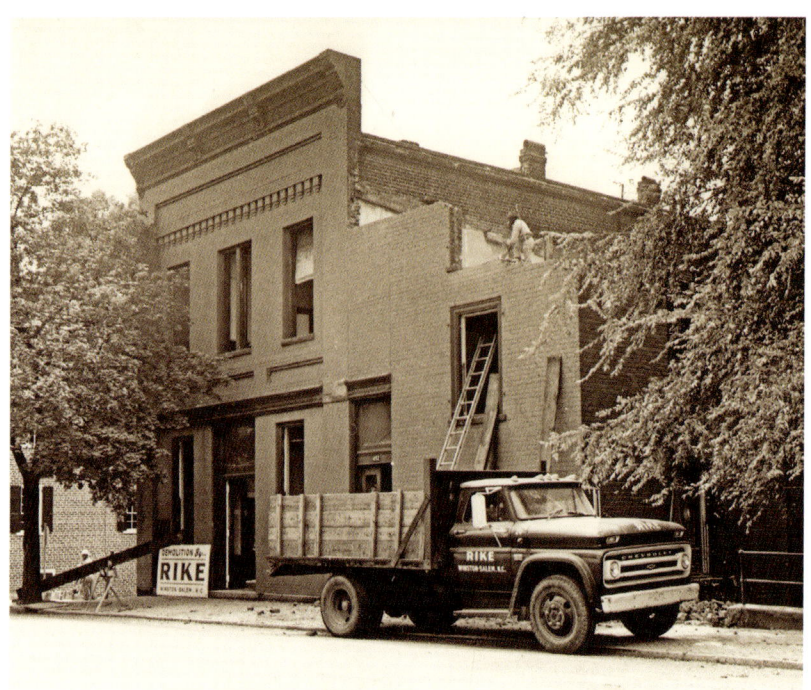

WEST SIDE 400 BLOCK MAIN STREET AND BANK STREET: This early twentieth-century building, which is being razed, had served as a mortuary and apartment building. The site was across from the Belo home and was also the site of the second house of Salem. The second house was the only two-story house of the first homes *c.* 1767. During the Revolutionary War the house served as a hospital for wounded soldiers. Today the site is shown bare, with the hopes of future restoration of the two-story house.

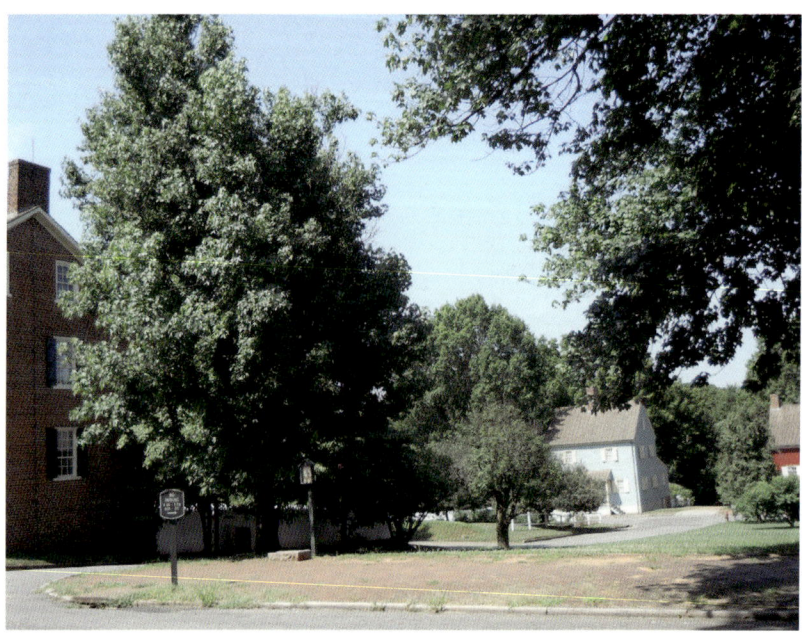

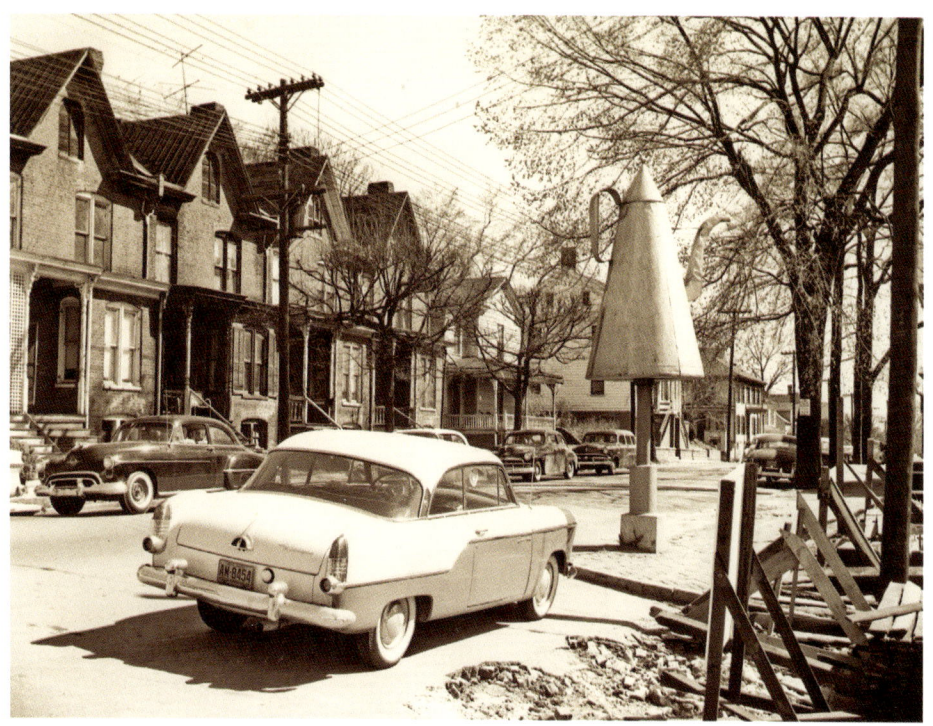

INTERSTATE 40 BRIDGE EAST SIDE OF MAIN STREET: The Mickey Tinsmith Shop was a fixture on Main Street at Belews Street beginning before the Civil War. The Salem Tea Pot was an advertising agent for Samuel Mickey. The photograph c. 1956 shows the Western side of the Tea Pot razed, not by Old Salem, but the arrival of the Interstate 40 Highway System. As far as the eye can see in this photograph, all structures were razed as shown in the current view.

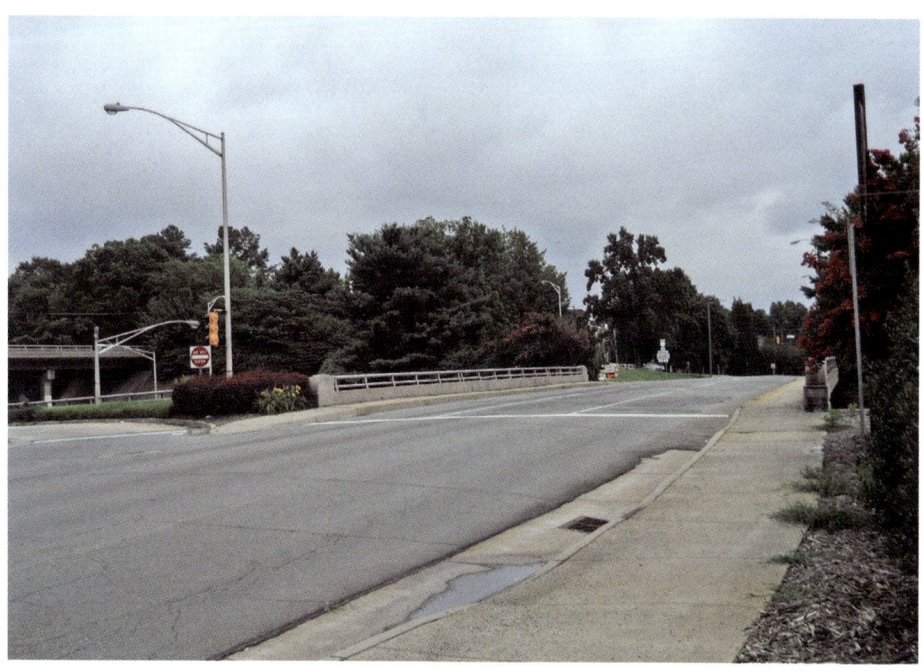

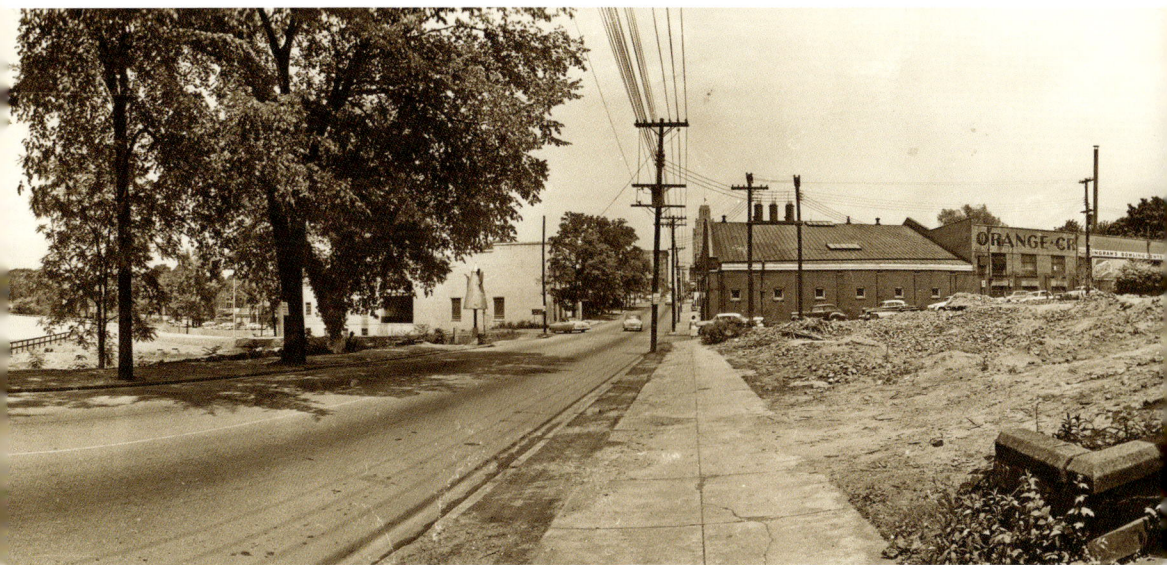

EAST AND WEST SIDE OF MAIN STREET AT INTERSTATE 40: All homes and businesses to the south for several city blocks ending at Cemetery Street can be seen in this 1956 photograph. The Tea Pot stands as a testament to life. All other structures between these two points, Vogler's Funeral Home and Cemetery Street, are gone. The Tea Pot, a new symbol of Winston-Salem, was moved south on Main Street where it resides today.

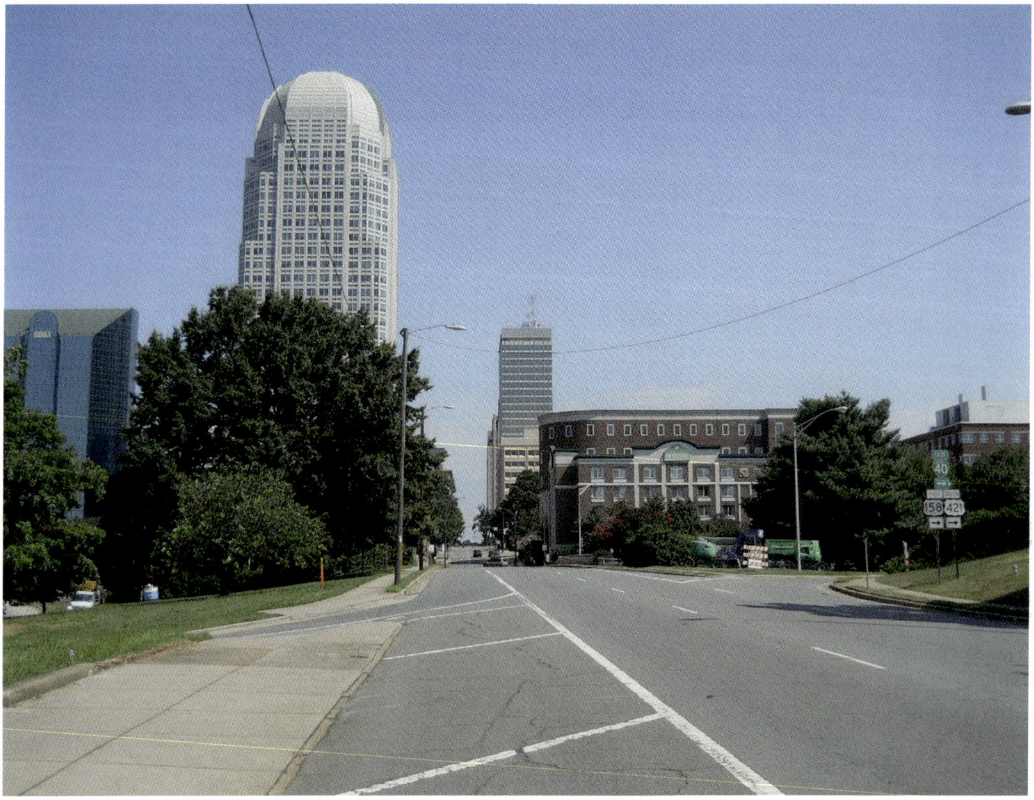

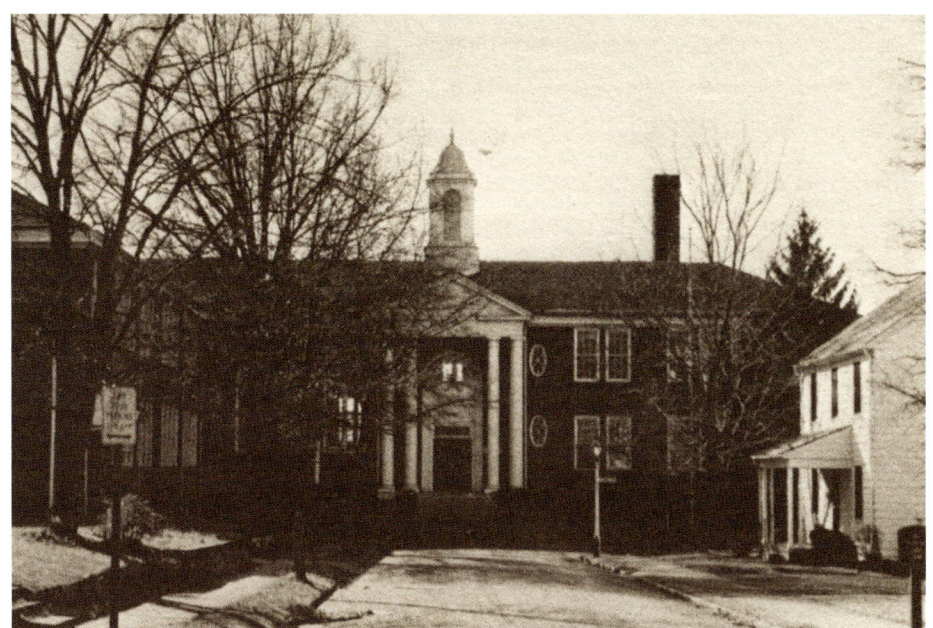

SOUTH MAIN STREET ENDS AT RACE STREET: After the second boys' school *c.* 1893 located on North Church Street across from the Vierling House and Barn became inadequate, the new Central Graded School opened in 1922. Along with Grandville Graded School the two schools served both of the neighborhoods of East Salem and West Salem. Today the site appears without the razed school, but with a new addition on the left of photograph is the rebuilt and restored Saint Philips Moravian Church *c.* 1822. This was the first African-American church built by the Moravians in the United States.

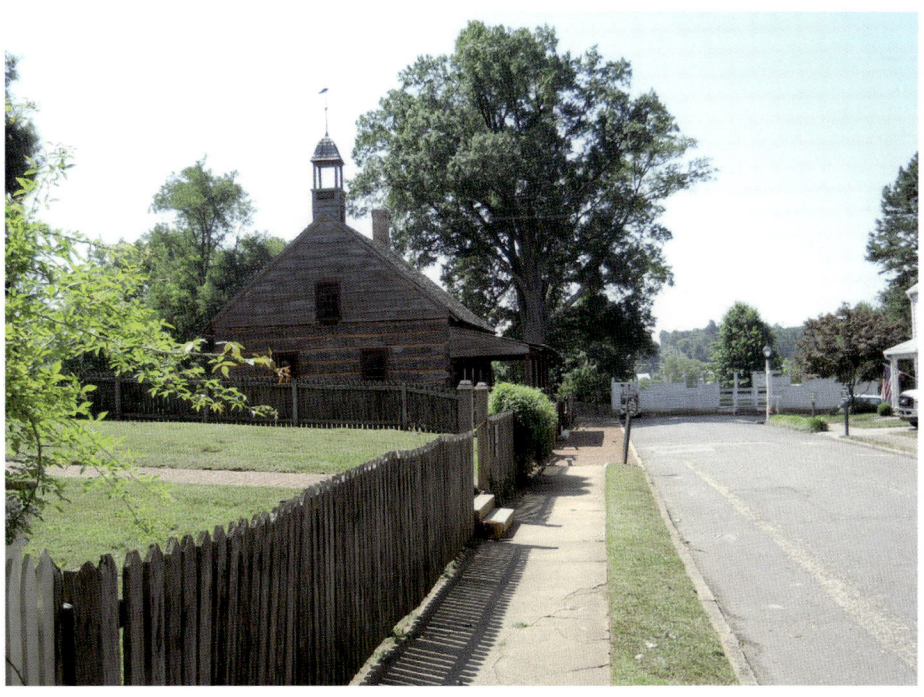

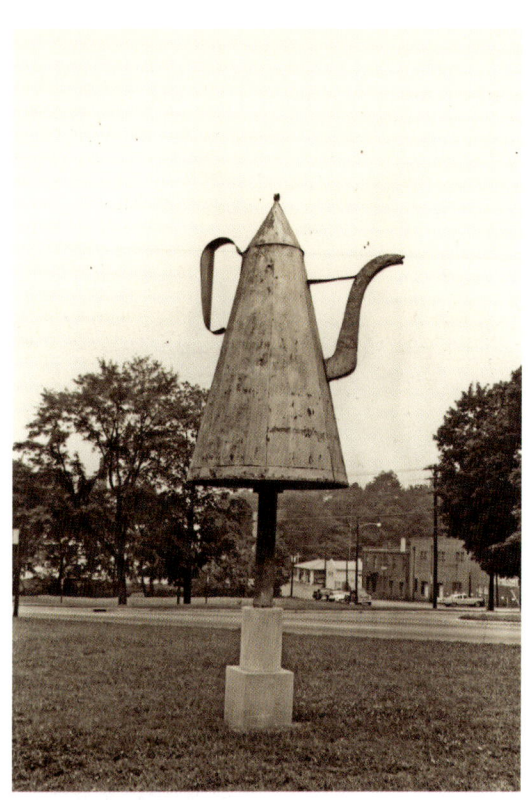

EAST OF MAIN AT BROOKSTOWN AVENUE:

The final resting place of The Salem Tea Pot was a few blocks South on Main Street at the newly constructed Salem Bypass. This bypass road keeps the majority of traffic outside of the historic district of Old Salem. In the background is found the remnant buildings of the Fries Woolen Mill. During the Civil War Confederate uniforms were made here. Currently, the Tea Pot makes an excellent tourist photograph.

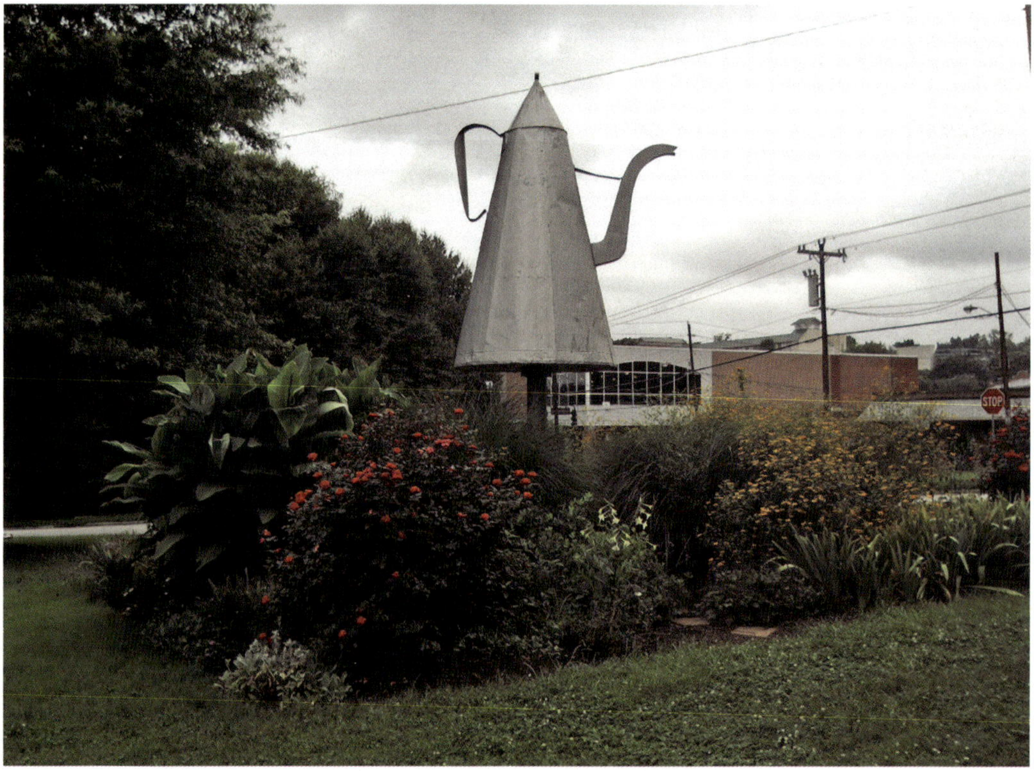

WEST OF EAST SALEM AT ACADEMY STREET:

Salem Town's western side was dubbed in 1770, 'West Salem our western neighborhood' by the Congregational East Salem Moravians. The Moravians' lush gardens are shown with the first industrial area in Old West Salem. The complex of buildings housed the Salem Slaughter House, Salem Brewery and Tannery. In the distance at the top of photograph is the Krueser-Brietz farmhouse and plantation photograph *c.* 1863. The restored gardens of Old Salem Incorporated are shown today.

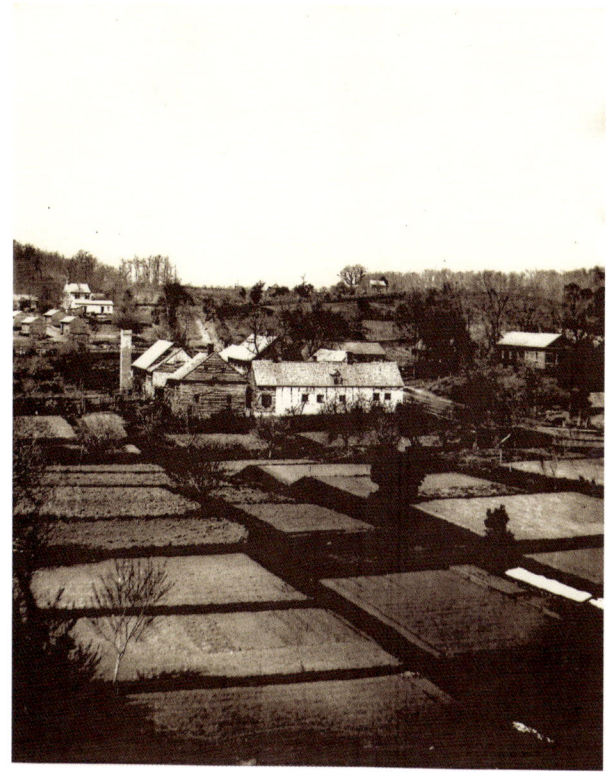

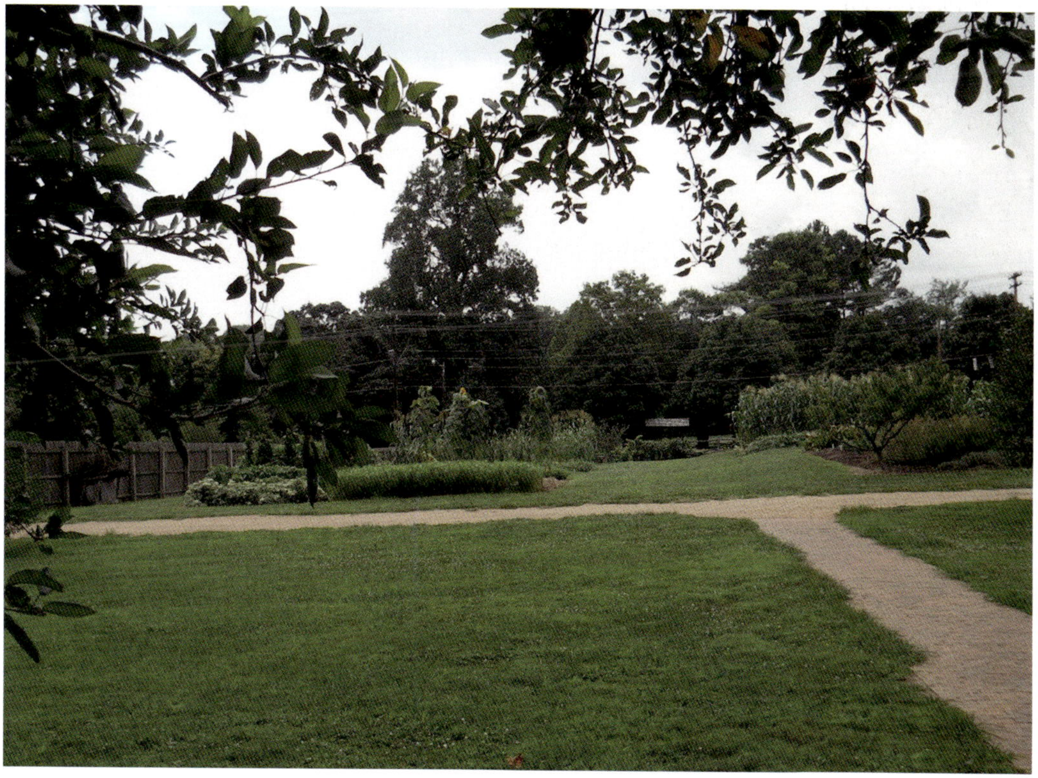

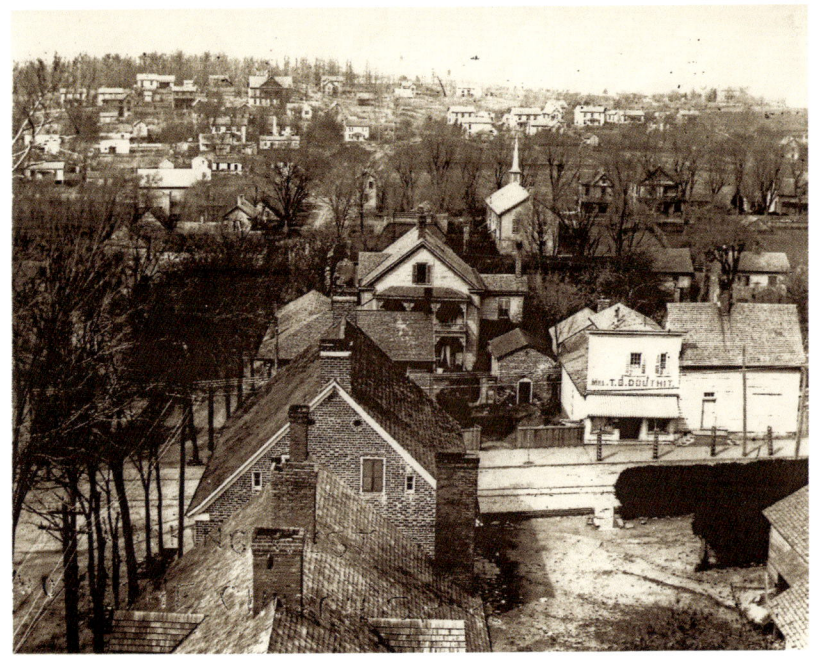

ACADEMY STREET AT CHURCH STREET LOOKING WEST: A large part of the Salem Town lot is shown *c.* 1880. The aerial from the steeple of Home Moravian Church shows both East (in foreground) and West Salem (from the White Church and steeple to background). The Tobacco House depicted earlier is the white building to the right on Main Street. The white church with steeple was the first church of West Salem, the Elm Street Moravian Church on Elm Street now known as Factory Row. The West Salem Graded School circa 1890 on Mulberry Street at Academy Street (largest house/building in upper left photograph), and Academy Street at the Single Brothers' House, westward appears in 2013.

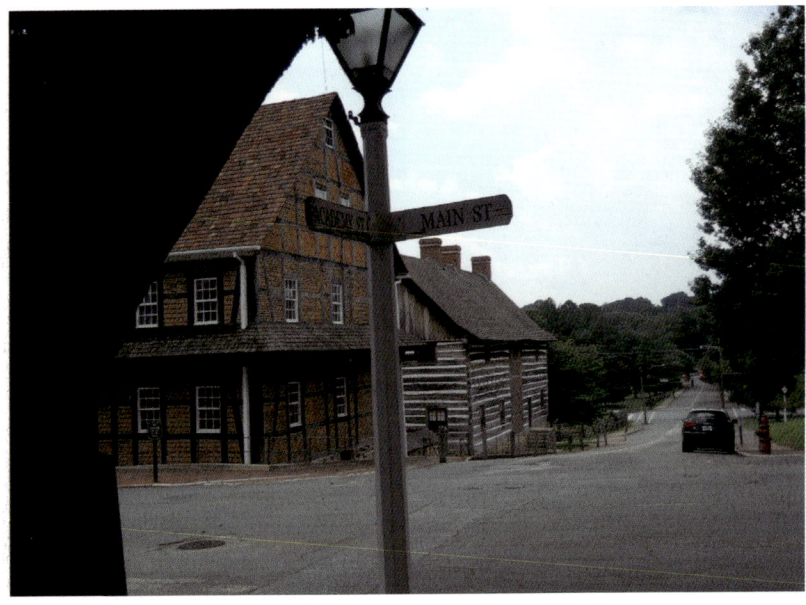

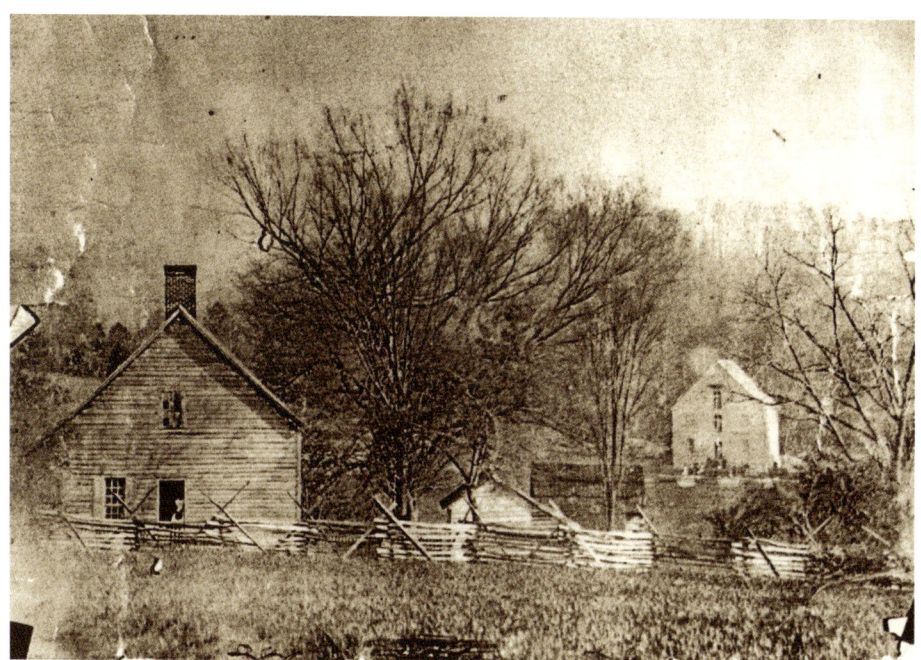

SOUTH OF WALNUT STREET TO SALEM CREEK: The Stockburger Farm House *c.* 1782, left of foreground, reflects West Salem's natural evolution of passage through time. As the first dairy and cattle farm in Salem, forward to 1820 as the millers' homestead the Salem Flour Mill, the mill *c.* 1820 is shown to the right of background, photograph *c.* 1860s. Currently, the Stockburger House is shown in 2013 as a future tourist building of Old Salem, the first tourist building outside the Old Salem Village in Old West Salem.

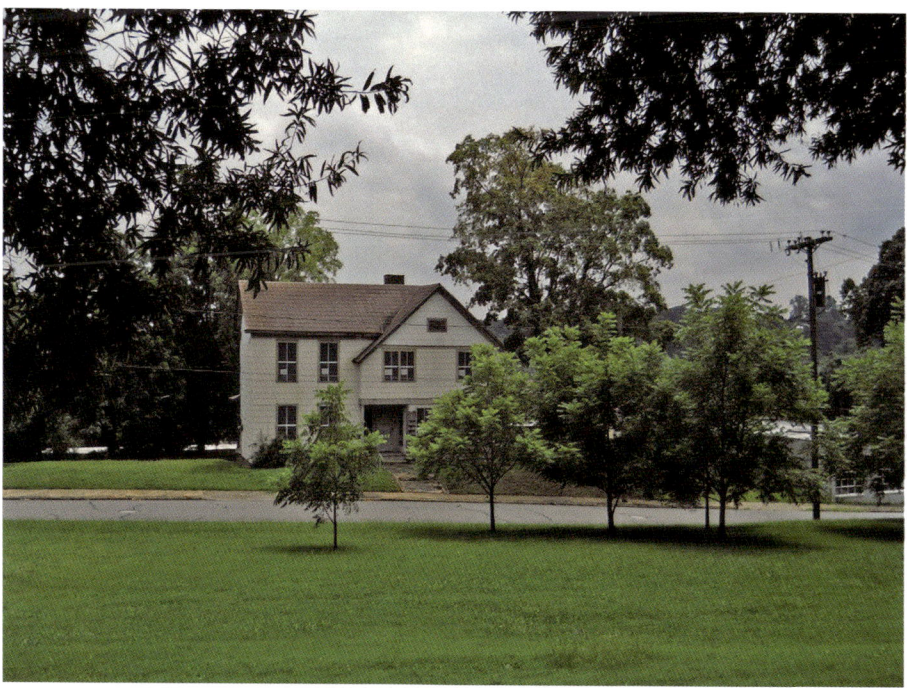

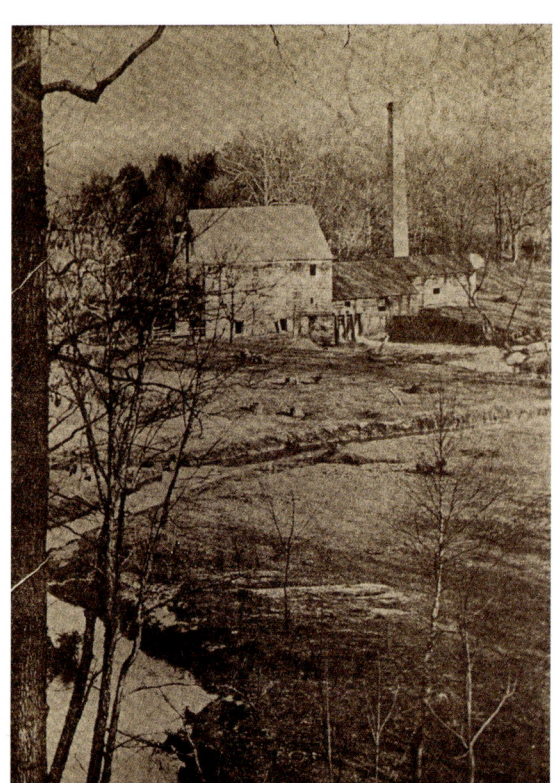

BROAD STREET AT SALEM AVENUE LOOKING NORTH:

The Salem Flour Mill is shown in its grandeur *c.* 1870s. New additions have been made so as the mill functioned as the first commercial flour mill of the area, a very lucrative venture for the Moravians in West Salem's industrial landscape. The Wach (Salem Creek) flows and supplies water for a race and water wheel. Boiler energy had arrived in the nineteenth century and unfortunately the complex was destroyed by a boiler fire in 1901. Currently, a gas station and Novant Health occupy this site today.

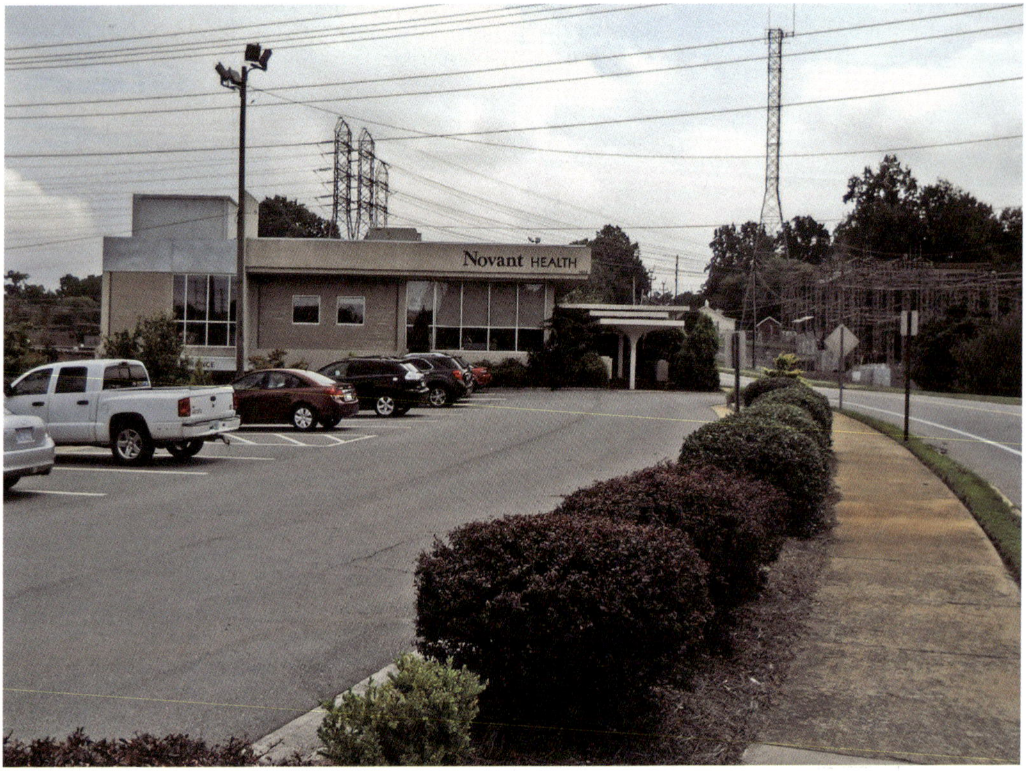

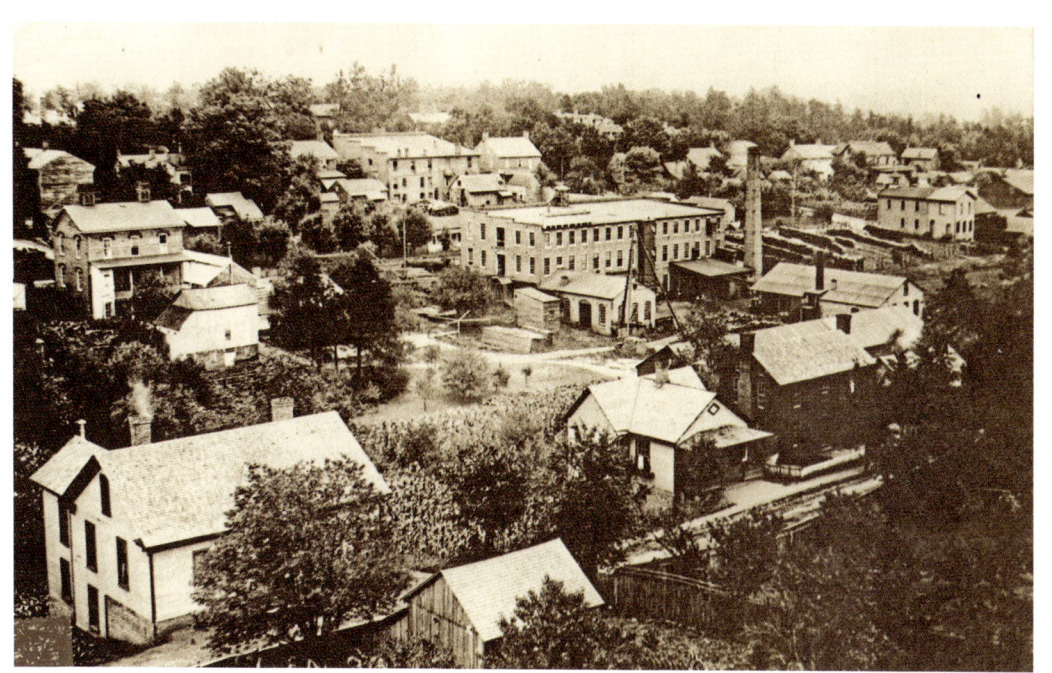

SOUTH CHERRY STREET LOOKING SOUTH TO MARSHAL STREET: The Fries Woolen mill complex after the Civil War evolved into the site of the Salem Iron Works *c.* 1873. The Industrial Revolution advanced the West Salem industrial complex into a producer of woodworking machinery and other mechanical devices, which were shipped across America and abroad. The arrival of the Interstate 40 Highway in the 1950s shows a different landscape at the dividing line between Old Winston and Old West Salem today.

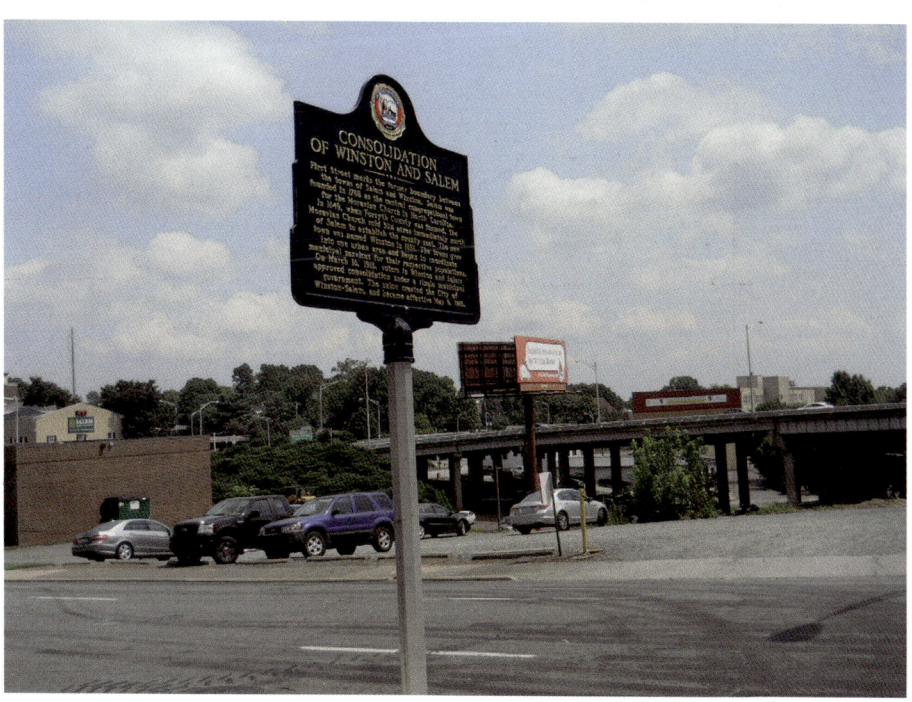

25

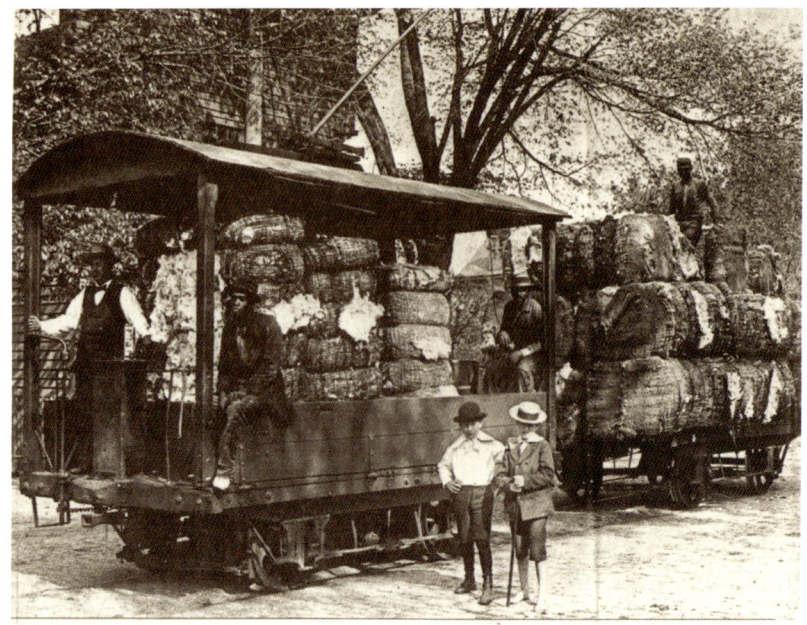

BROOKSTOWN AVENUE AT CHERRY STREET: Textiles, on a commercial scale, arrived in the 1830s. North Carolina had several such textile industries 'cradles'; Cross Creek (now Fayetteville, North Carolina), Lincoln County and Alamance County. West Salem is considered among them. With the advent of the Salem Cotton Mill by Frances Fries in 1836, cotton became 'King'. The streetcar shown is loaded with cotton in this 1890s photograph as it stops in front of the Salem Cotton Mill complex on Brookstown Avenue. As shown in the modern image, the streetcar time period has passed, but the old mill has been converted into a hotel and visitor center.

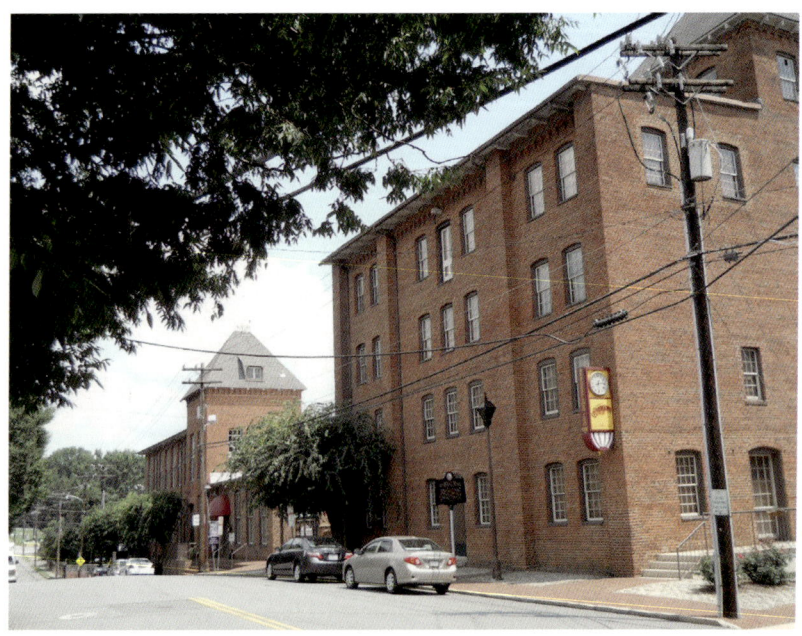

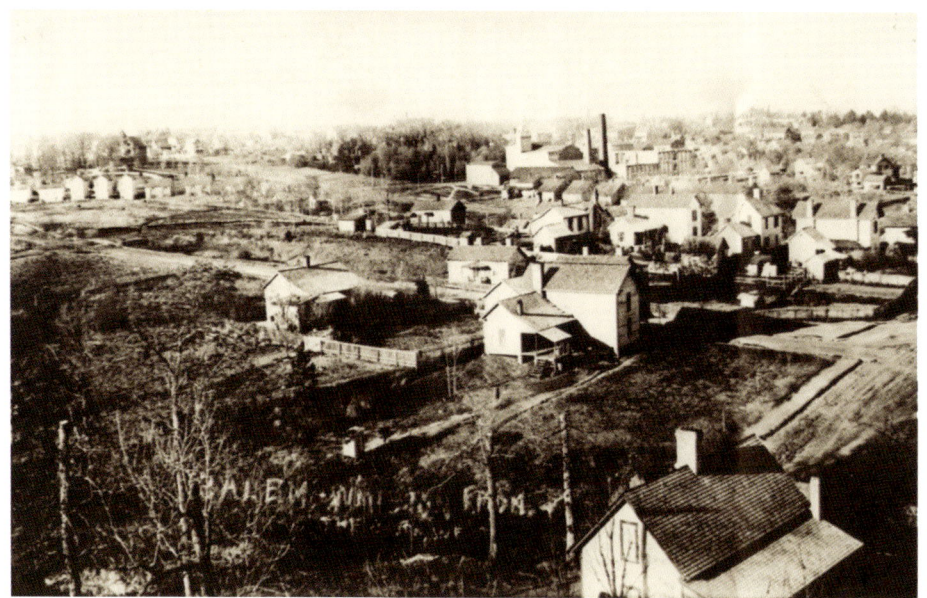

EAST FROM BROAD STREET AT ACADEMY STREET: Life in Salem's first textile mill had grown in this 1880s photograph of the Salem Manufacturing Company. The complex had its own electrical system, the first in the south, and its own mill type village in eastern West Salem. The two houses closest in the photograph are 516 Spring Street (Cook House) and 518 Spring Street (Mosley House). Currently, at Popular Street and Academy Street the area is known as the West Salem Historic District *c.* 1782 with designation as a Preserve America Neighborhood in 2010. The Preserve America Historic District is only one of nineteen Preserve America Neighborhoods in the United States.

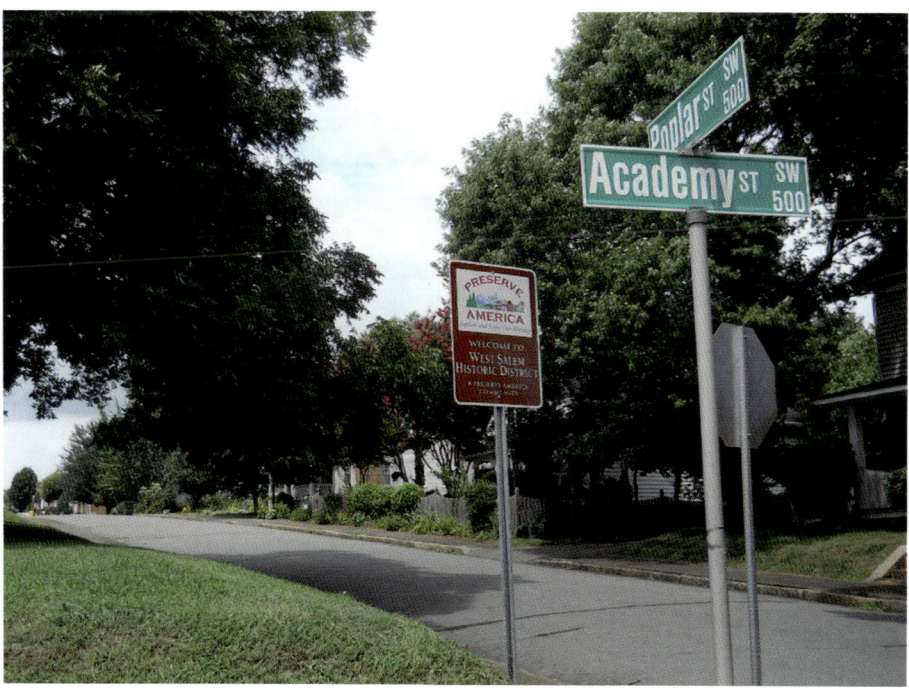

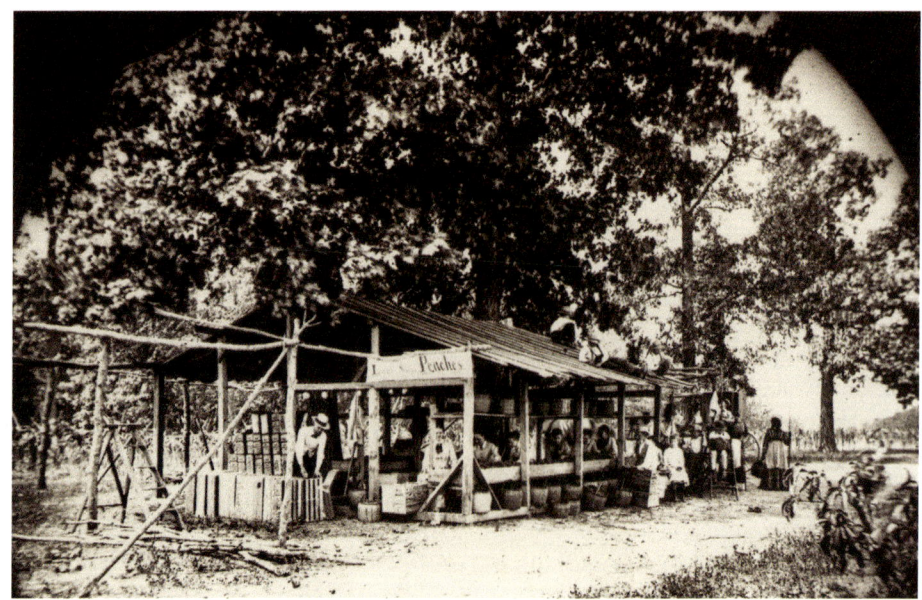

BANK STREET AT GREEN STREET: Before the arrival of the early Moravians to Salem in 1766, the town had previously been planned in the Moravian home state of Pennsylvania. West Salem was to be the home of the farms and industries of the Salem Town lot. A great example of the farms was the Leinbach Farm photograph shown *c.* 1880. The Leinbach family sold fruit, nuts, and vegetables throughout the Piedmont region. The peach stand shown in the photograph resided on the edge of their property at Paper Mill Road (Bank Street) at Peach Lane (Green Street). The Leinbach family worked the land without slave labor throughout the years of 1830-1890. Currently, the site is a residential neighborhood created by the Brietz family in the early 1900s as Wachovia Highlands.

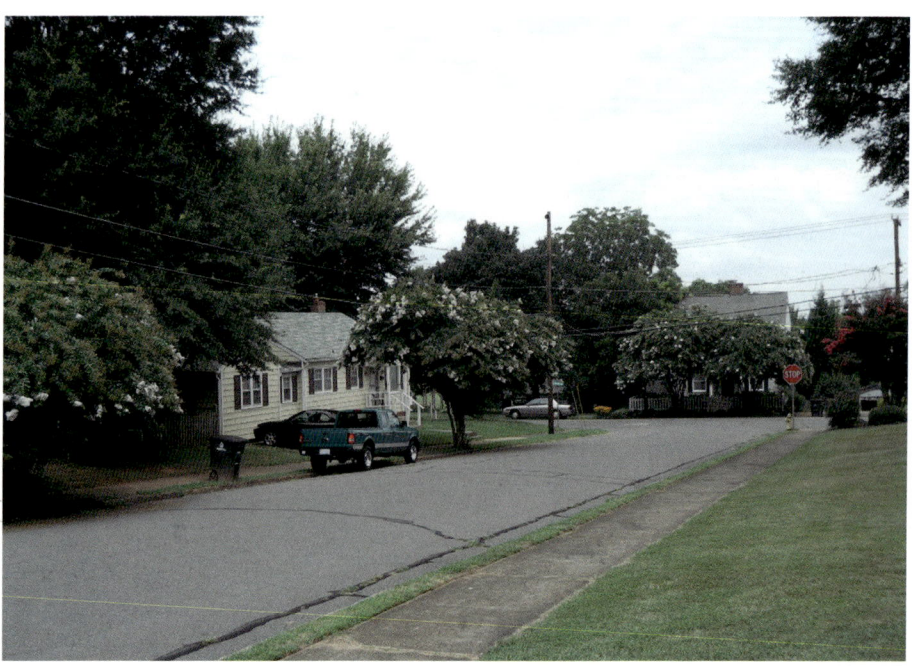

BANK STREET WEST TO BROAD STREET:
The Krueser/Brietz farm *c.* 1816 was one of the largest and earliest of West Salem farms. This Victorian lady of the Brietz family photograph from the 1880s collects flowers in a field below the Brietz farm. The site later was used as the first Baptist Mission Church in Salem. The wooden fences in the background of the photograph ran along the Old Shallowford Road *c.* 1765 (Broad Street), often called 'The Road to Salem'. Tanners Run town homes occupy this site today.

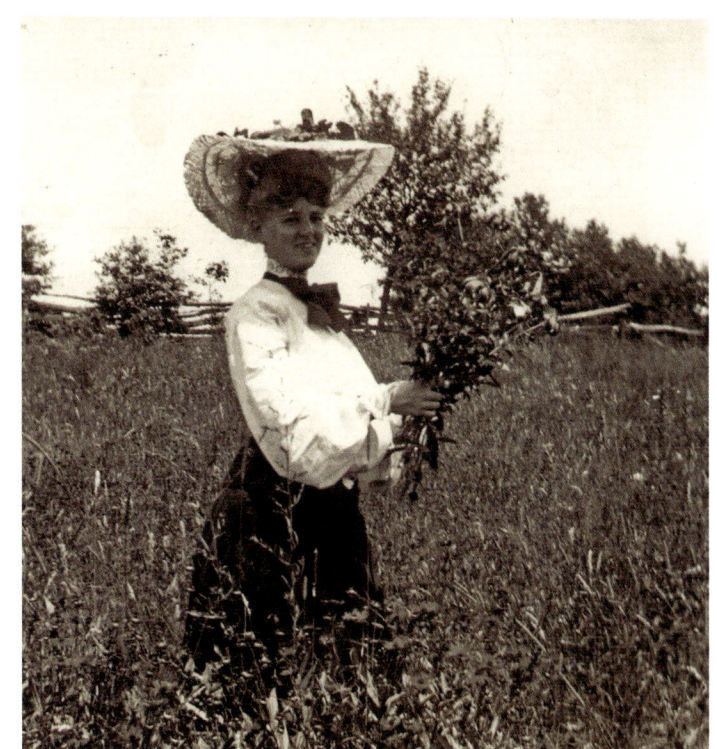

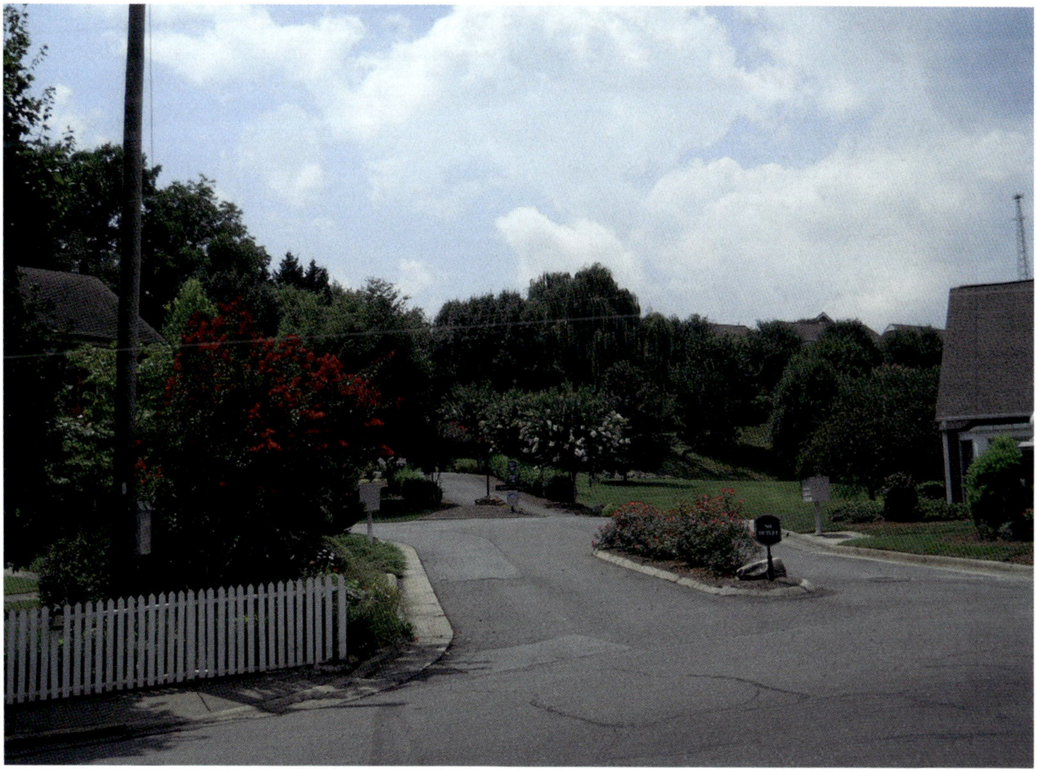

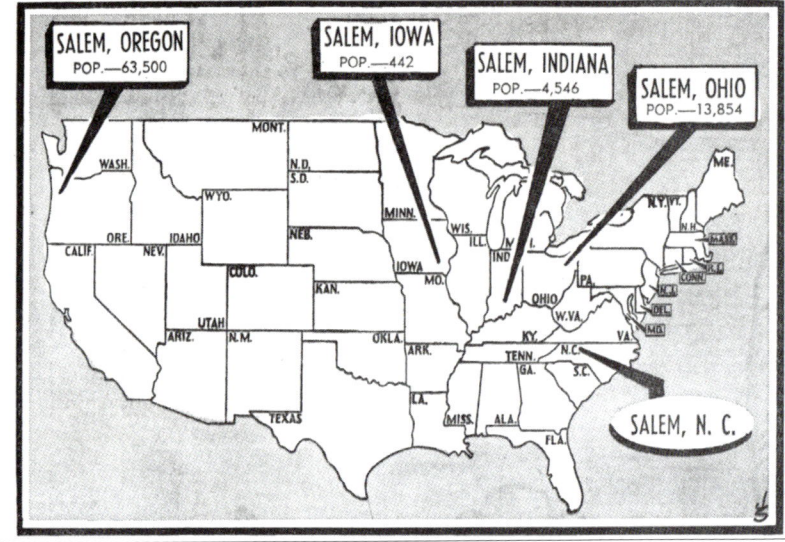

Salem's Own Johnny Appleseed
He Named Towns, Started an Industry

SALEM, OREGON
POP.—63,500

SALEM, IOWA
POP.—442

SALEM, INDIANA
POP.—4,546

SALEM, OHIO
POP.—13,854

SALEM, N. C.

A MAP OF TOWNS CALLED SALEM: Henderson Lewelling was born in Salem in 1809. As an adult with a strong understanding of horticulture, he followed settlers to the new western territory states. He planted fruit orchards throughout this new American territory while creating and naming towns along the way. The towns were all called Salem. The current photograph at Paper Mill Road (Bank Street) at Peach Tree Street (Grandville Drive) existed in the farm and where he perfected his trade. The *c.* 1910 Queen Ann cottage (Robert Miller Home) is an example of West Salem architecture. Often these cottages were built around smaller structures some dating as early as the eighteenth and early nineteenth century.

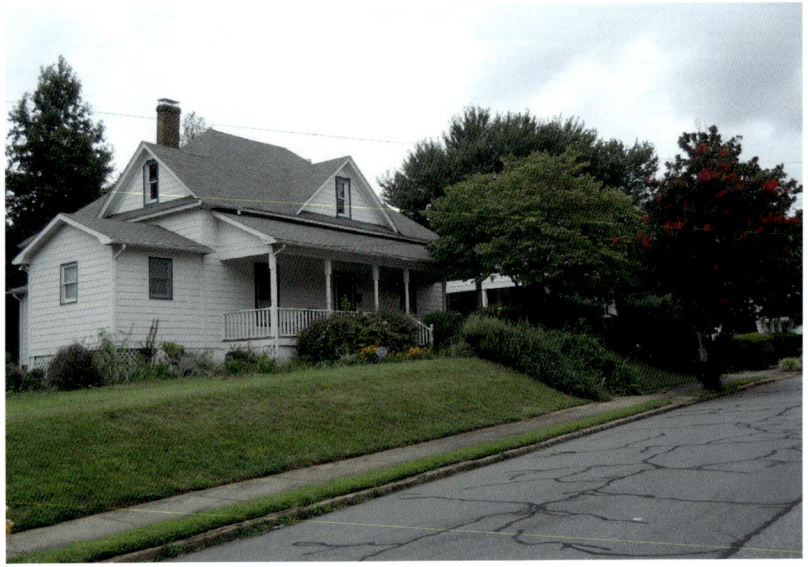

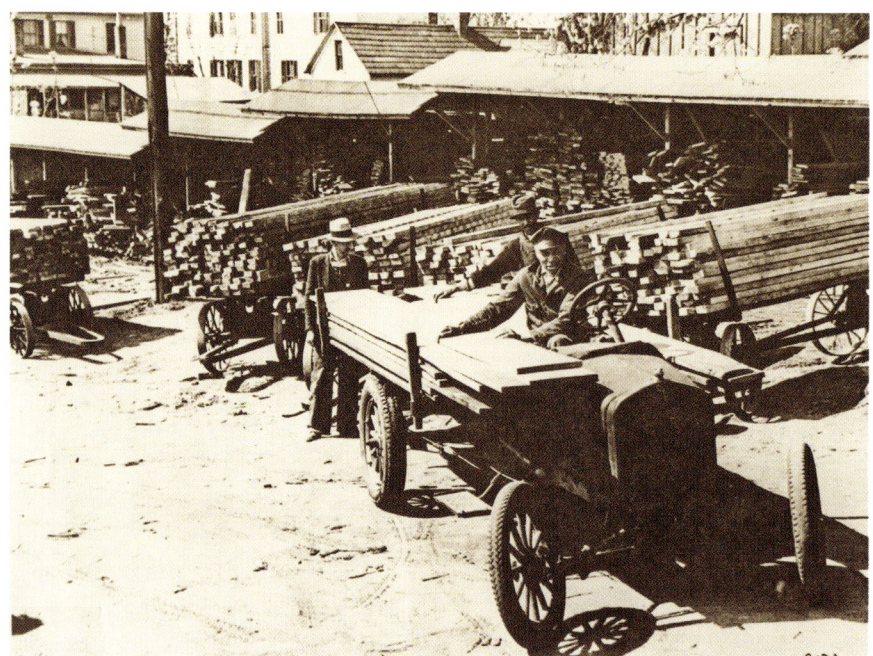

SOUTH AT BELEWS STREET AT CHURCH STREET: Charles and Christian Fogle founded in 1871 the wood working firm of Fogle Brothers Company. The Fogle Brothers' lumberyard shown in around 1900 was responsible along with Piondexter Lumbar Company and Snyder Lumbar Company in building the houses and businesses of a growing Winston-Salem. The site of the lumberyard today is building not structures, but a quality of life mission as a part of the Research Park of the Bowman-Gray Baptist Hospital complex.

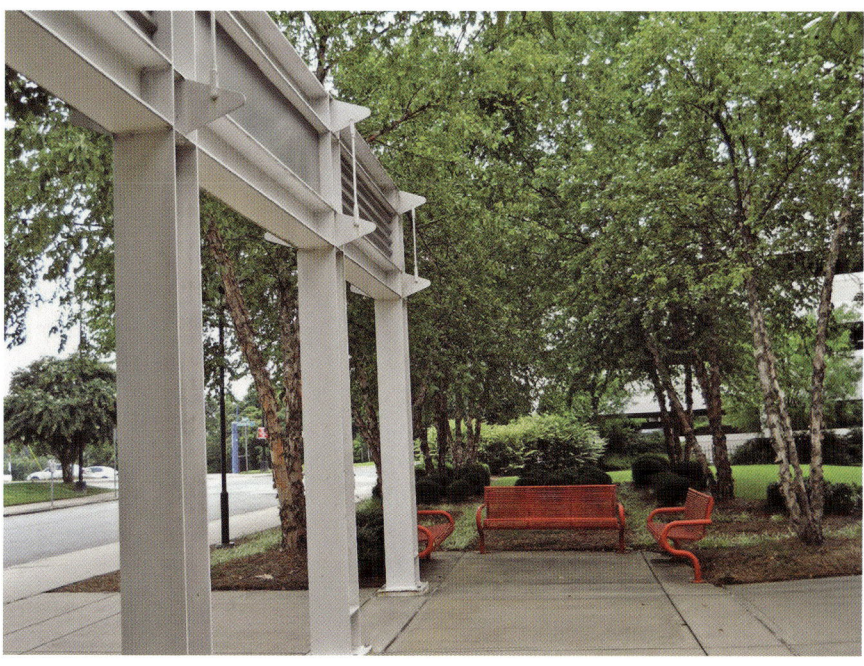

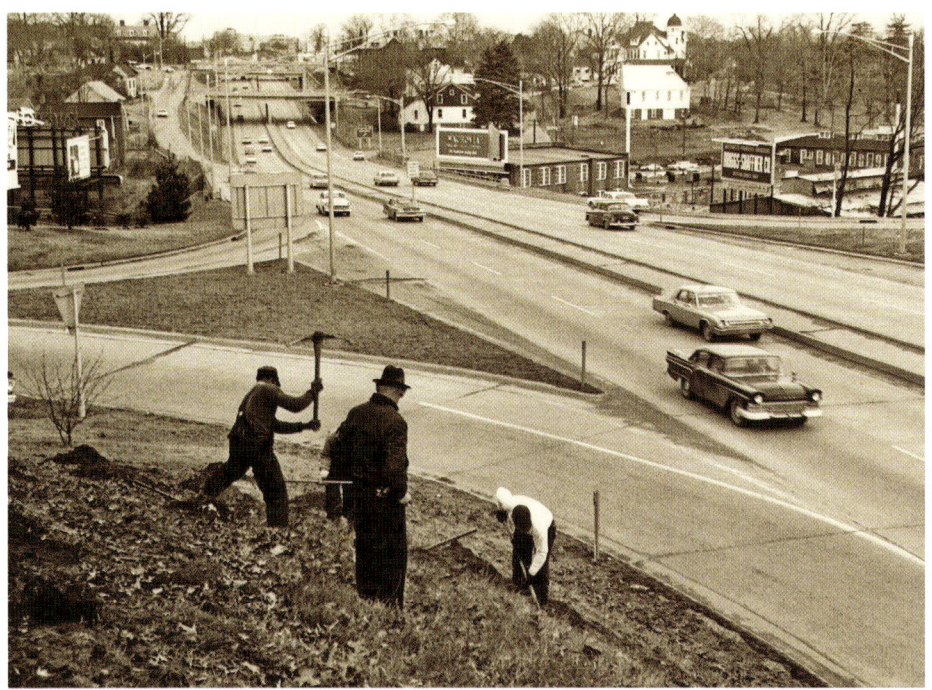

INTERSTATE 40 AT BROAD STREET: An example of two important road systems in Winston-Salem is shown in this photograph from the 1950. From Broad Street, the original road to Salem (Old Shallowford Road) overlooked the modern Interstate Highway, I-40. Interstate 40 was a state-of-the-art roadway much like the Old Shallowford Road. The road runs east from the North Carolina Coast across America to the coast of California.

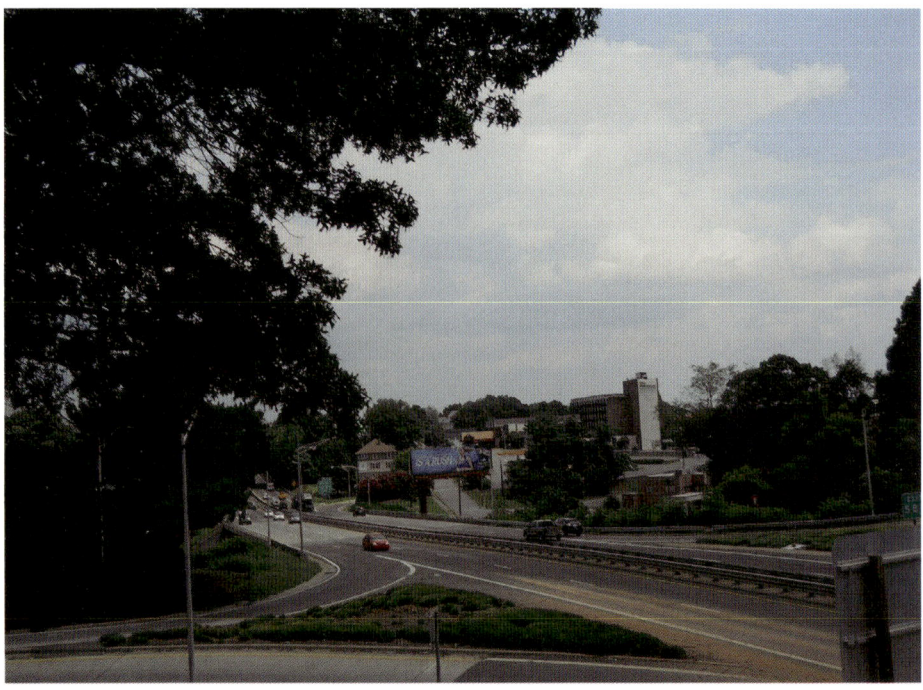

South of Academy Street at Mulberry Street:

The first graded school of West Salem, West Salem Graded School *c.* 1890, appears in a 'Do You Remember?' article in the *Winston-Salem Journal* newspaper photograph *c.* 1915. The graded schools were a product of Mr. Calvin Wiley, the first superintendent of the North Carolina school systems and earlier were born from the Sunday schools of Gottlieb Schober of Salem. The resident home of the Peddycord family *c.* 1880s is seen today next to the site of the graded school.

PAGE 26 —— WEDNESDAY EVENING, MAY 4, 1960

Do You Remember . . .

By BILL EAST
Sentinel City Editor

The West Salem School (above) already was an old institution when a young principal arrived in 1911 to take over. He was W. B. Clinard.

Clinard, now retired after 33 years as a principal and living at 2252 Elizabeth Avenue, recalled yesterday that the school occupied a 200 by 200-foot lot facing Mulberry Street with Laurel Street at the rear. Academy Street ran alongside the building.

The school, which had five classrooms and a large assembly room, was part of the Forsyth County system until Winston and Salem were merged in 1913.

At that time, the Winston-Salem school system was organized. It immediately started hunting for a site for a new school in the West Salem area.

The school system obtained a 300 by 300-foot lot on Granville Drive from the Moravians. Work was started on a new school building.

The picture of the ____ st Salem School shown above was believed to have been taken about 1915—the year that it was abandoned in favor of Granville.

Clinard said the new school was named after the street which ran in front of it, "although Granville Nading, who lived nearby, said he thought it was named for him."

On moving day, Clinard recalled that he had the larger boys in the old school carry the desks four blocks westward to the new Granville School "because we already had new desks and didn't want to get them scratched on a moving wagon."

Later, another 300 by 300-foot lot was obtained from the Moravians to form the present Granville School playgrounds. The city purchased the land later to establish tennis courts a short distance away.

After his arrival from High Point to take over his school job here, Clinard met the principal of the East Salem School on Belews Street—Maude Alspaugh. They were married in 1913. Afterward, she continued teaching for some time in the schools here.

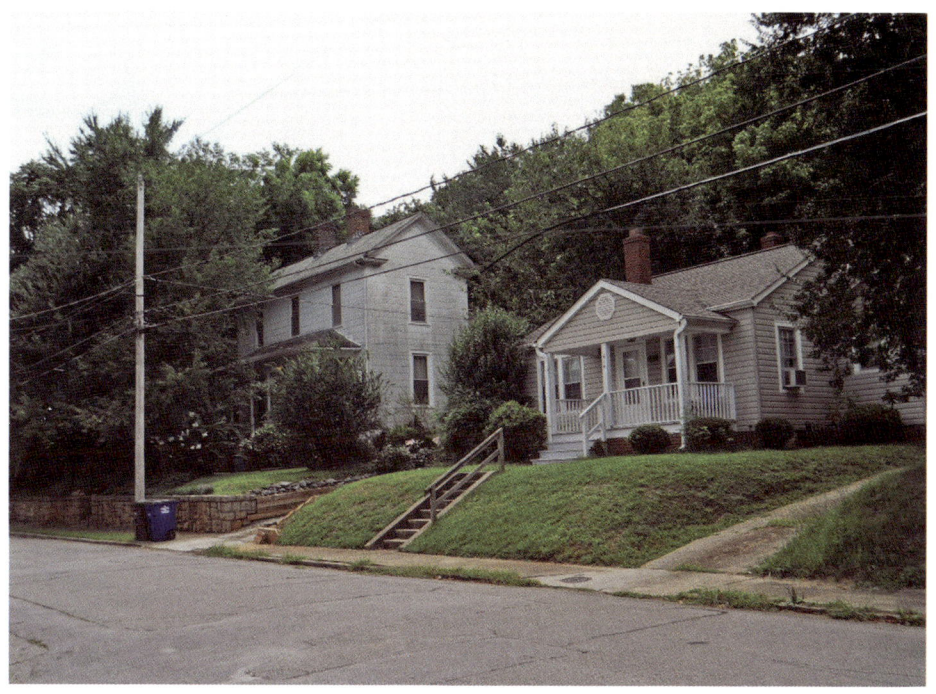

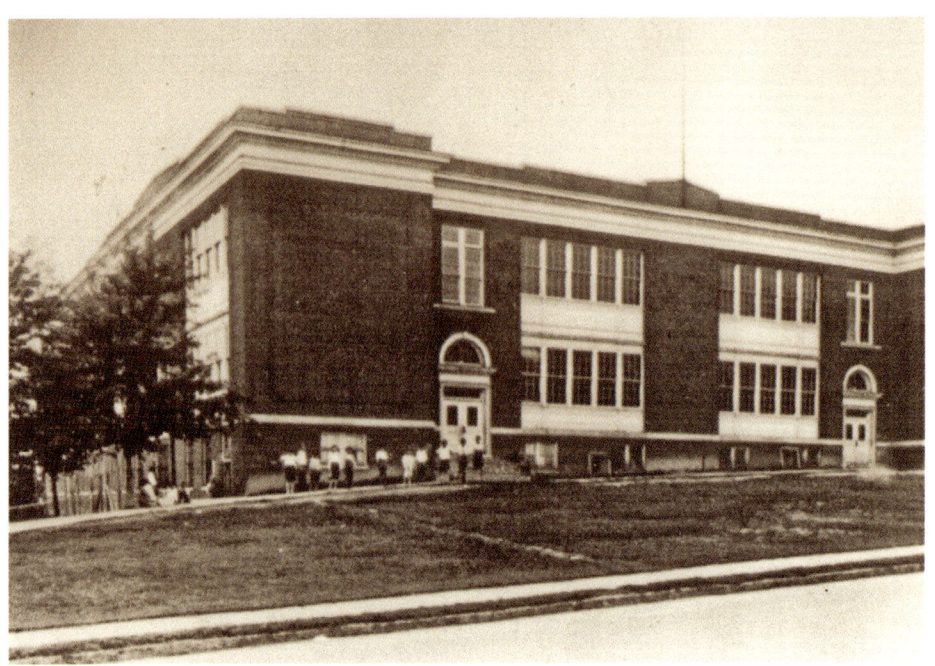

GRANDVILLE DRIVE LOOKING WEST FROM ACADEMY STREET: In 1915 the West Salem Graded School students moved their desks and school equipment up Academy Street hill to the site of the new school. The newly created Grandville Park subdivision of West Salem *c.* 1914 had a new resident, the Grandville Park Grammar School. The school was a state-of-the-art education facility and recognized as one of the best grammar schools in the state. Currently, the site is home to the Grandville Place Senior Apartments for the elderly.

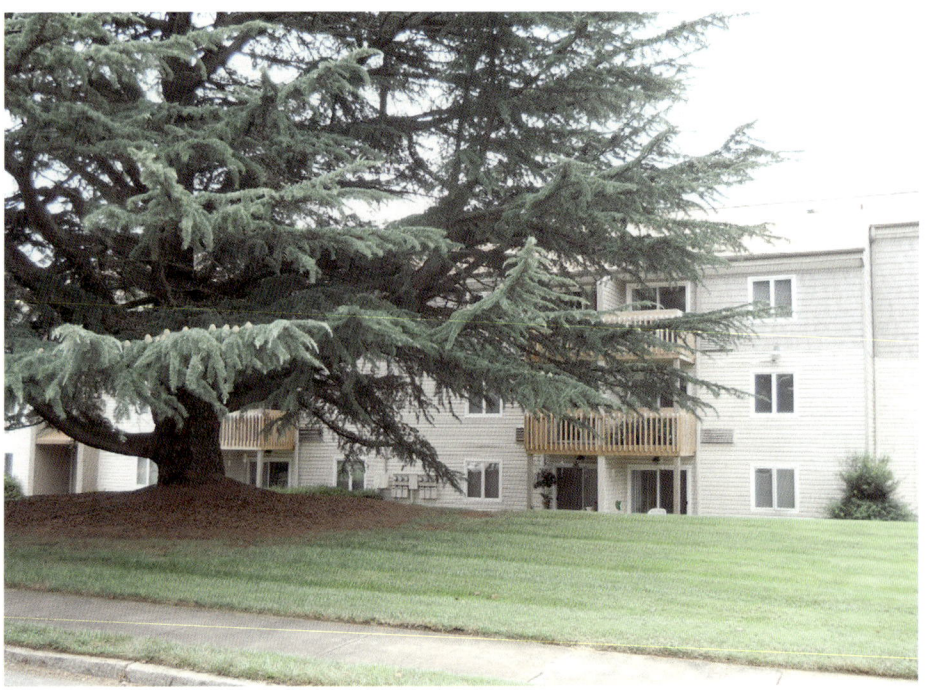

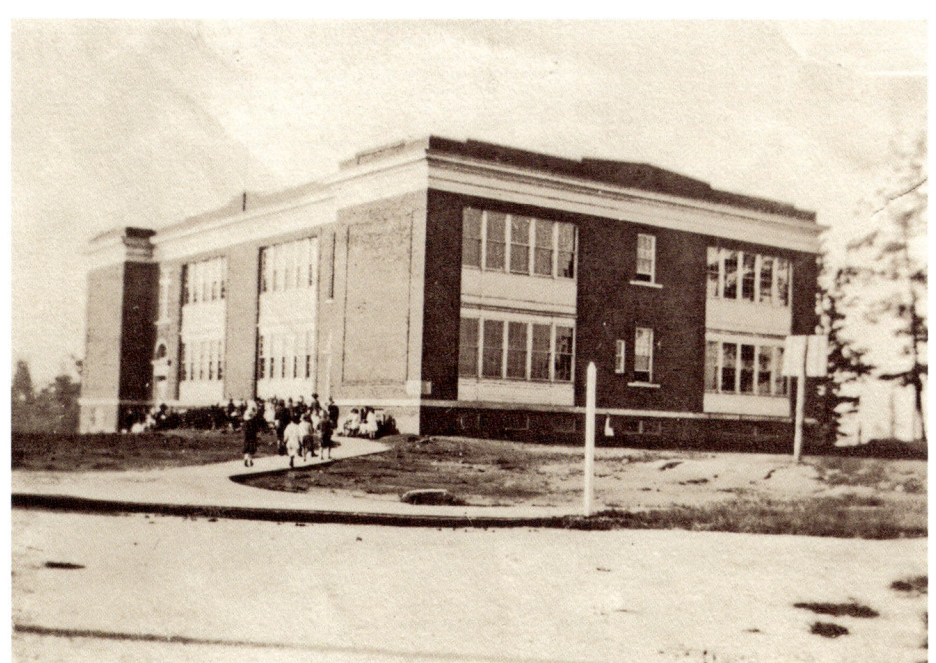

THE GRANDVILLE GRADED SCHOOL INITIATED A NEW ERA FOR THE (FARMS AND INDUSTRIES) OF OLD WEST SALEM HISTORY: The farms and industries had brought to West Salem farmers, mill workers, and factory workers, who produced the lifeblood of Winston and Salem. New professionals such as doctors, ministers and business owners became residents of the Grandville Park neighborhood. The last remnant of the school lies in a placard of its building committee *c.* 1914 in 2013.

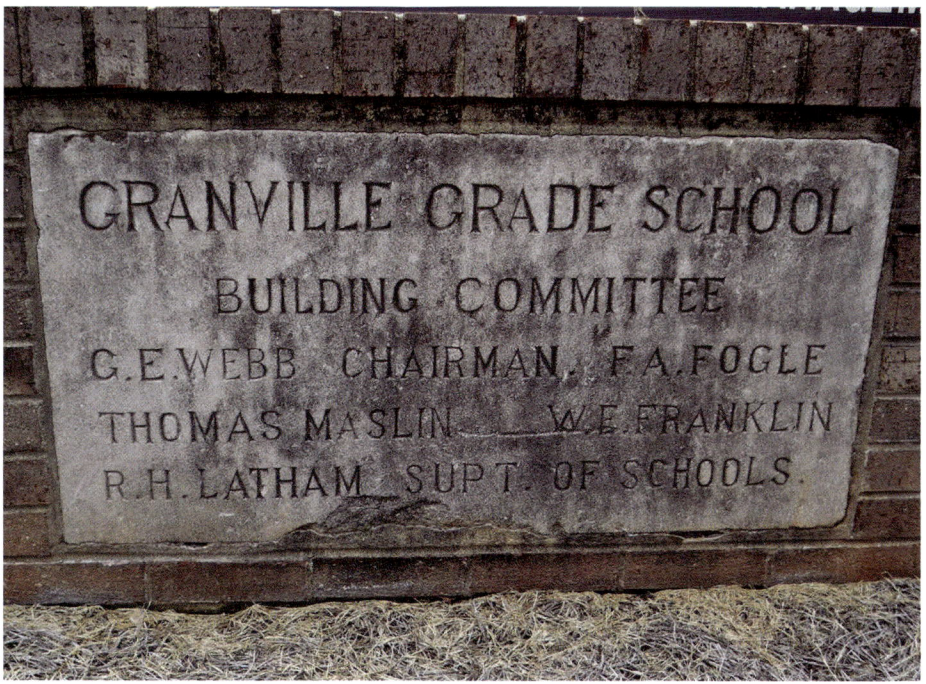

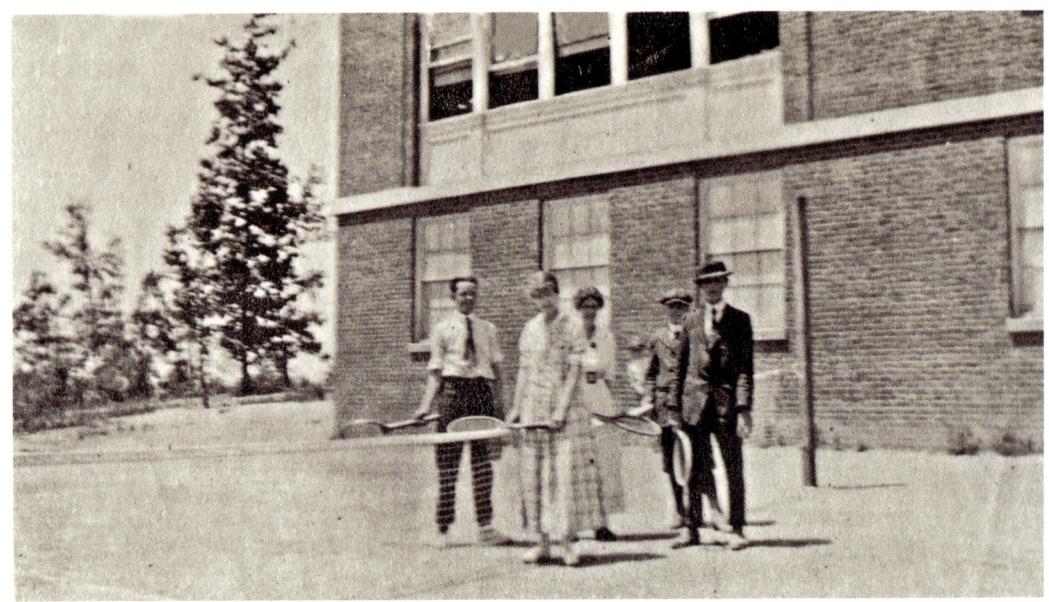

SOUTH ON ACADEMY AT HUTTON STREET: Grandville School brought another needed commodity to Old West Salem, recreation. The school was the first to have its own inside swimming pool, coined by the children as the neighborhood bathtub. A ball field and tennis court as shown in this 1917 photograph was at the rear of the property. Presently, the ball field has been replaced with more building for Grandville Place apartments.

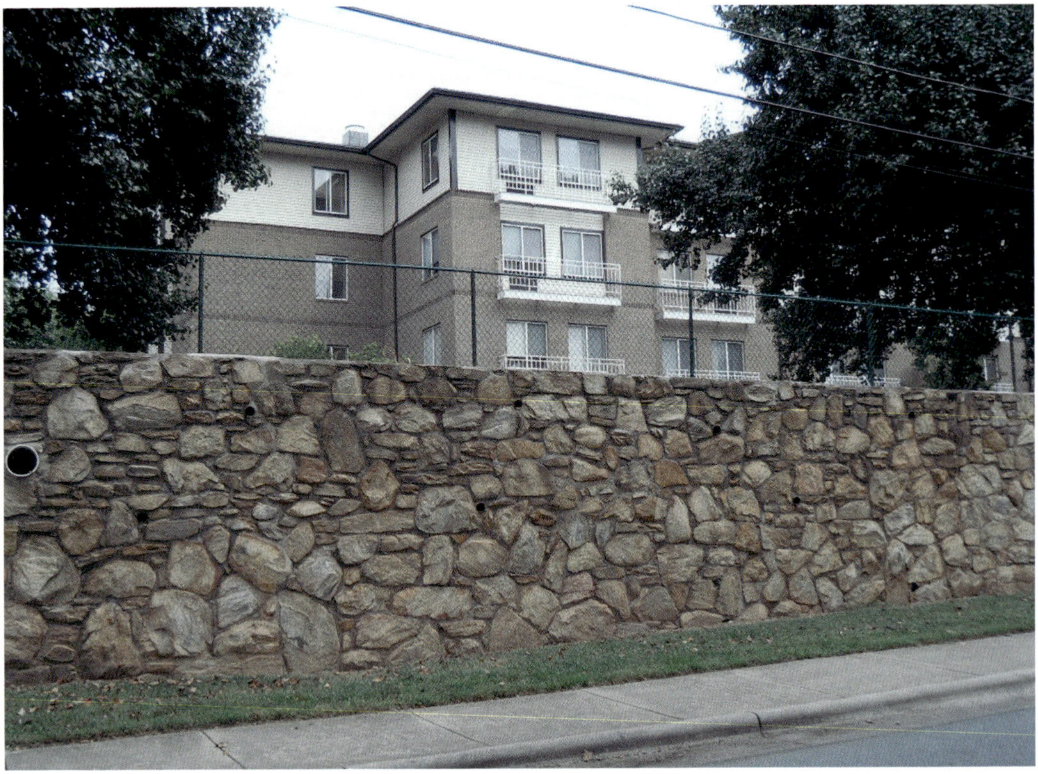

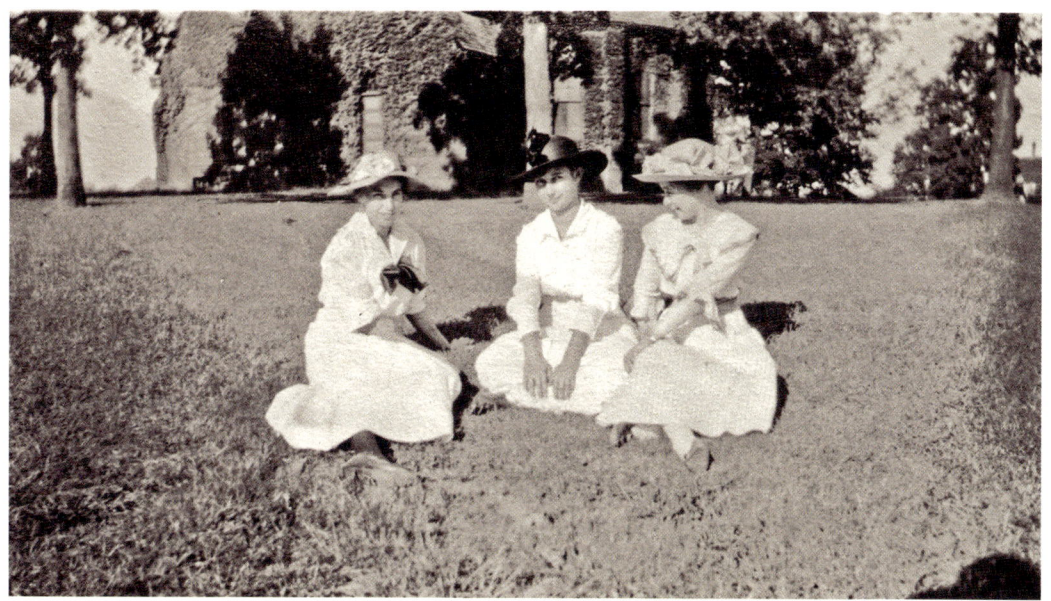

EAST ON ACADEMY STREET NEAR GREEN STREET: The ladies, who were a force behind their husbands in creating the modern day West Salem neighborhood of the 1880s, founded the Christ Moravian Church in 1895. The church began as an experiment by Home Moravian Church of East Salem. The Home Church Moravians never fully believed the neighborhood or church would last. These three sisters pictured in around 1914; Miriam, Marie, and Ethel Brietz along with other lady friends, helped to provide the church success. The modern image shows the church majestically from Academy Street at Green Street.

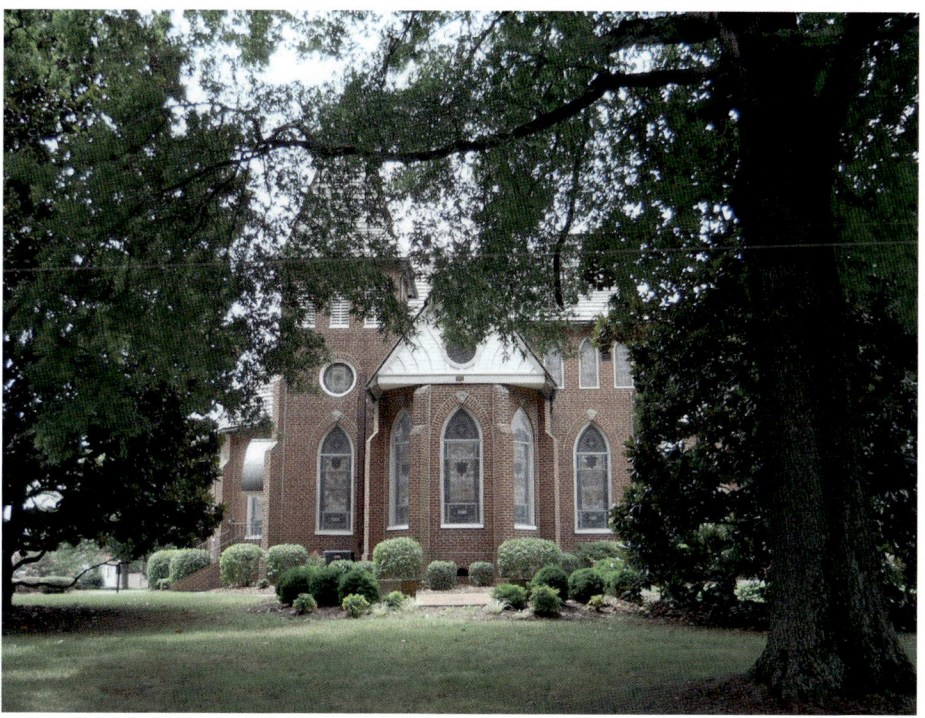

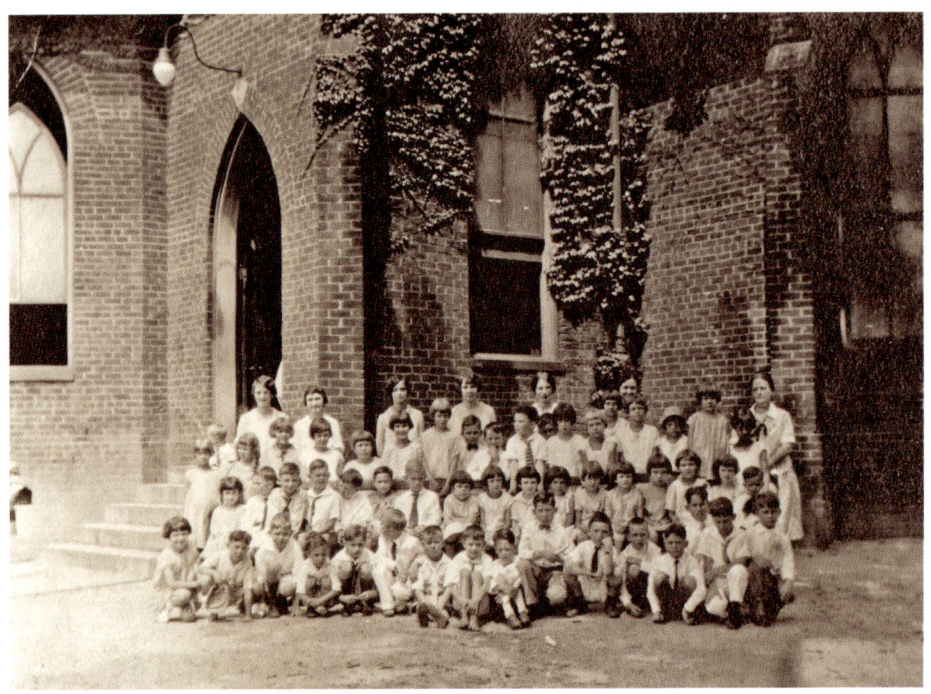

WEST OF ACADEMY STREET AT GREEN STREET: Similar to the Moravian Sunday schools of Home Church *c.* 1800 and Elm Street Chapel *c.* 1867, the Christ Moravian Sunday schools would flourish and teach Christian doctrines while working with the Grandville School toward secular academic excellence. The photograph today shows the site of the earlier photograph taken from the parsonage site across from church.

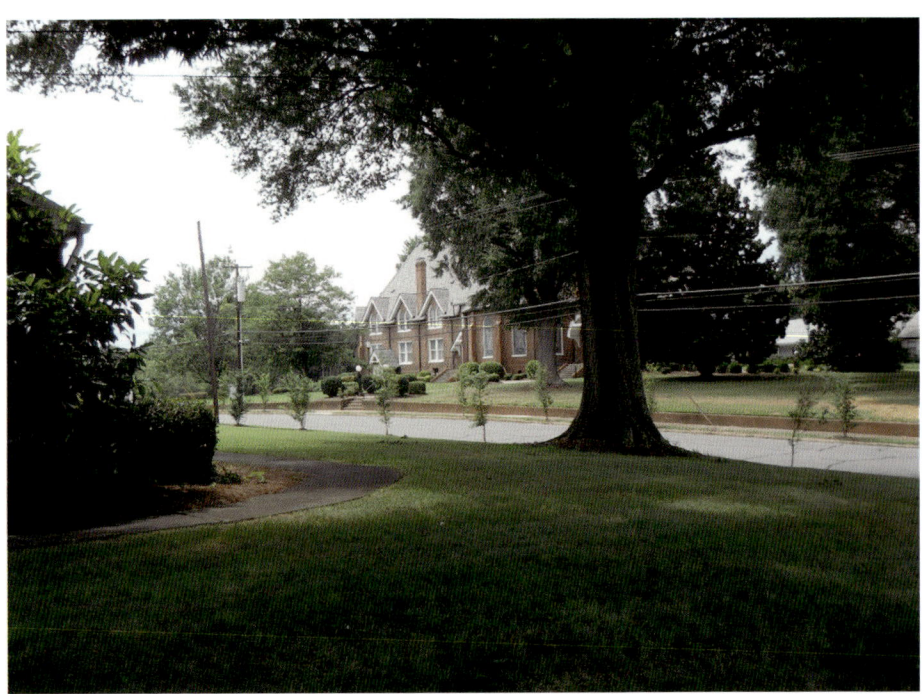

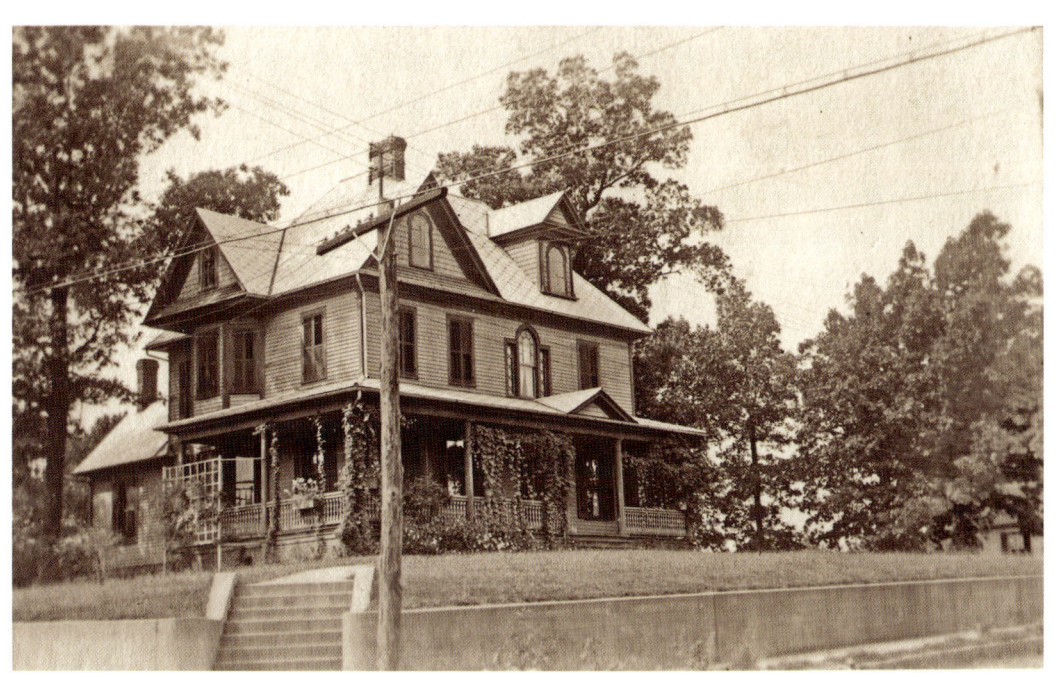

SOUTH OF ACADEMY STREET AT GREEN STREET: In April 1899, the congregation of Christ's Church rose to 200 members. A parsonage was needed. The two-story structure was built on a knoll where the first Christ Moravian Chapel was located across the street from the present church post guard *c.* 1910. Today, the parsonage is a brick ranch structure, which was built in the 1960s reportedly because the new pastor of Christ's Church did not want to live in an old house.

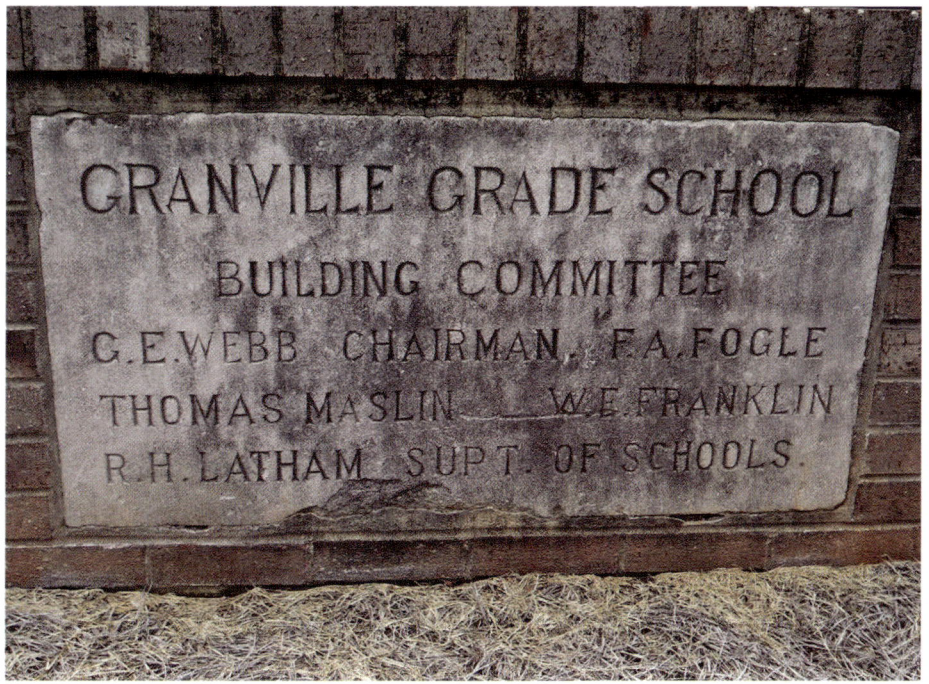

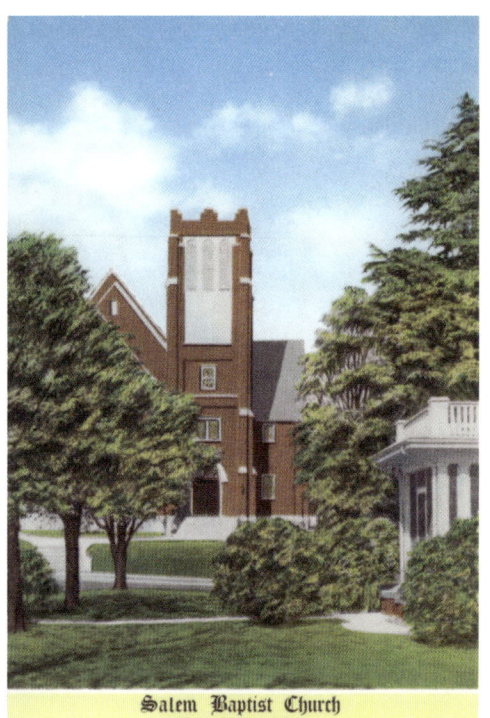

Salem Baptist Church
429 South Broad Street
Winston-Salem, North Carolina

EAST OF BROAD AT PIEDMONT INTERNATIONAL UNIVERSITY:
The Baptist Mission Church arrived to West Salem on Marshal Street in 1900. It began in a mill house near the Arista Mill's complex of the Fries family in 1898. The church was organized by Brother Sam Morton to evangelize the mill workers and their children. The Mission Church grew out of its Marshal Street site and moved due west up Bank Street Hill to Broad Street and built Salem Baptist Church c. 1917. The new church is shown below today as it is in the postcard above from 1920.

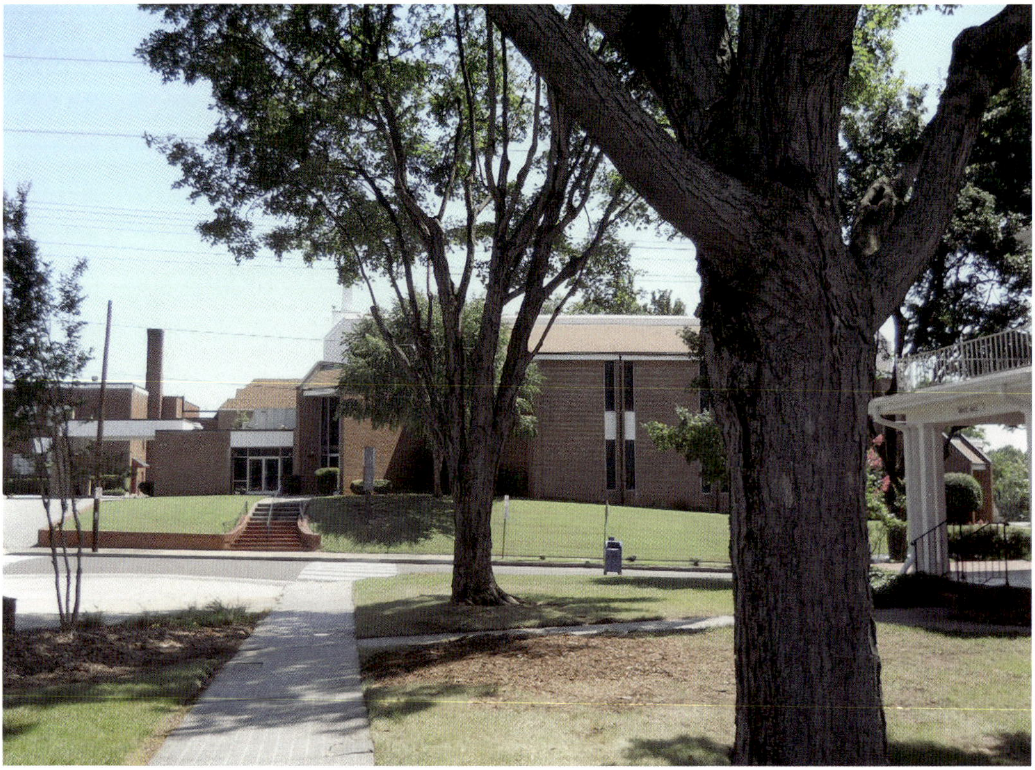

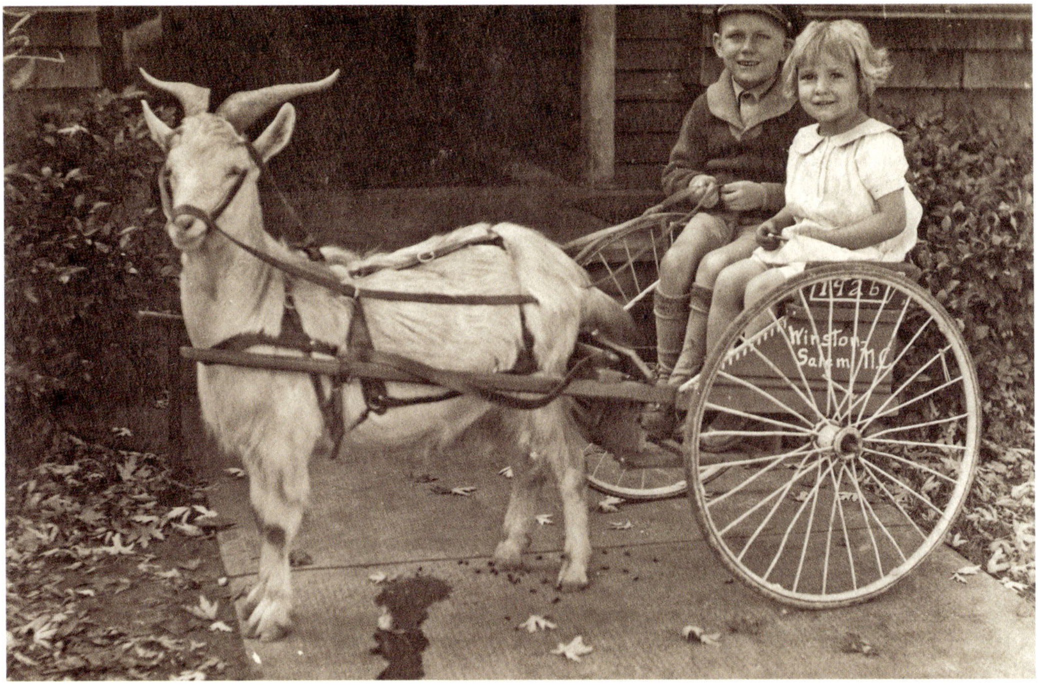

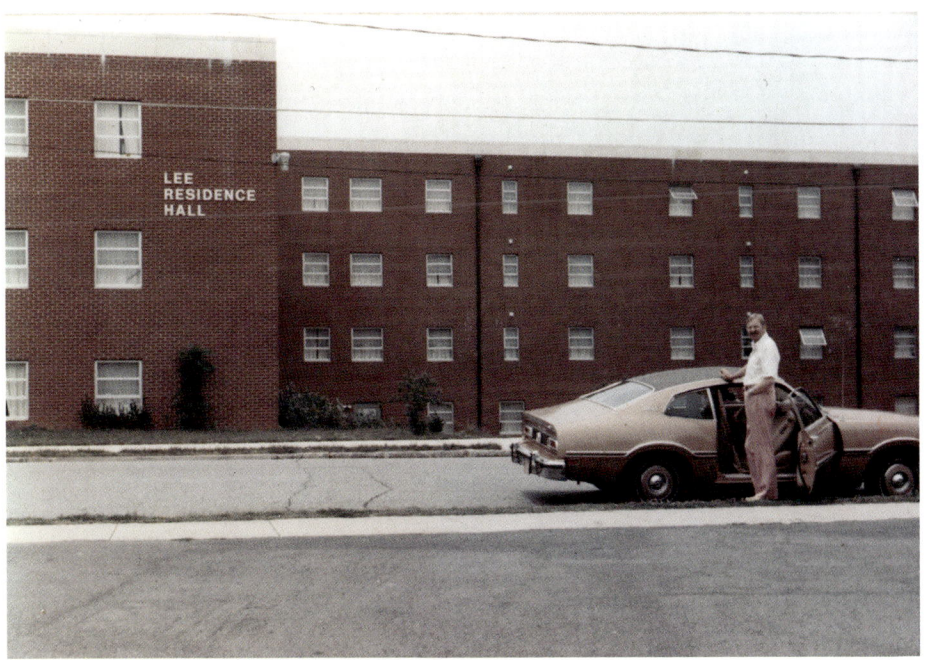

SOUTH GREEN NEAR INTERSTATE 40 BRIDGE: Mr. Bryant Lee and sister Miss Mary Francis Lee are shown with their ride of preference in 'The Goat Cart' photograph *c.* 1930s. The cart was a gimmick for children photographs in Old West Salem since the importance of farms was so prevalent. Bryant Lee and his ride of choice *c.* 1970 are shown in front of the Lee Residence Hall of Piedmont Baptist College. His father, Charles A. Lee and family were members of Salem Baptist Church and contributed greatly to the church and college.

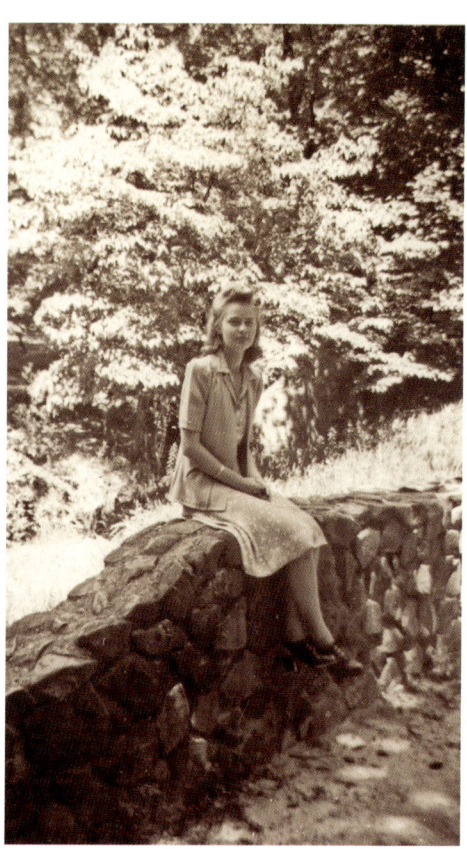

GRANVILLE PARK AT WEST STREET:
Mrs. Lucy Johnson Branscombe is shown in another gem of Old West Salem, Historic Granville Park photograph *c.* 1930s. The park and Granville School were beautiful additions to the subdivision of 1914. The bridge and park have stood the test of time in this 2013 photo.

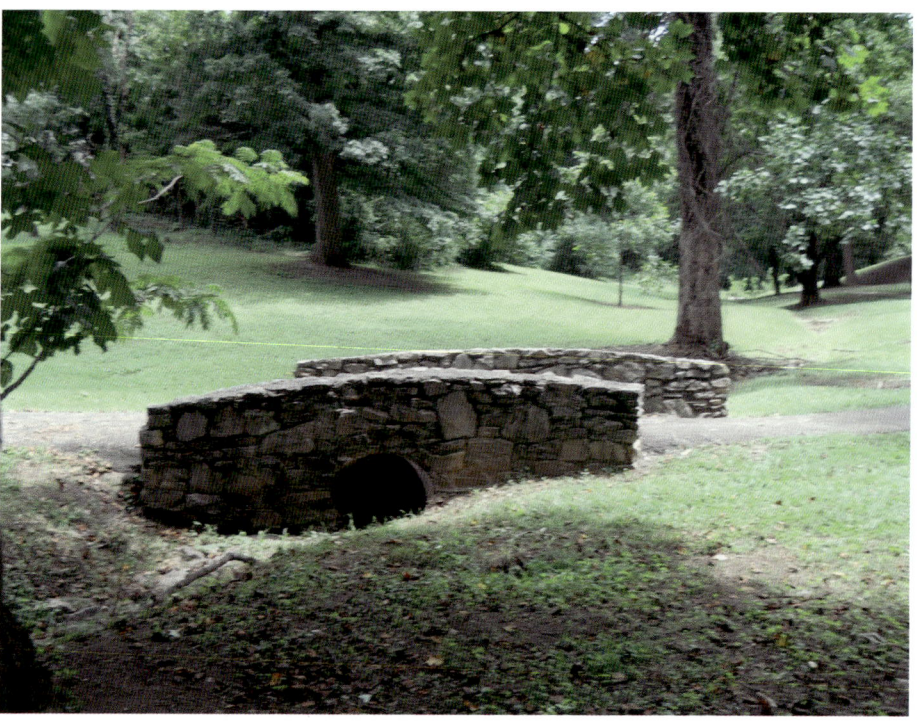

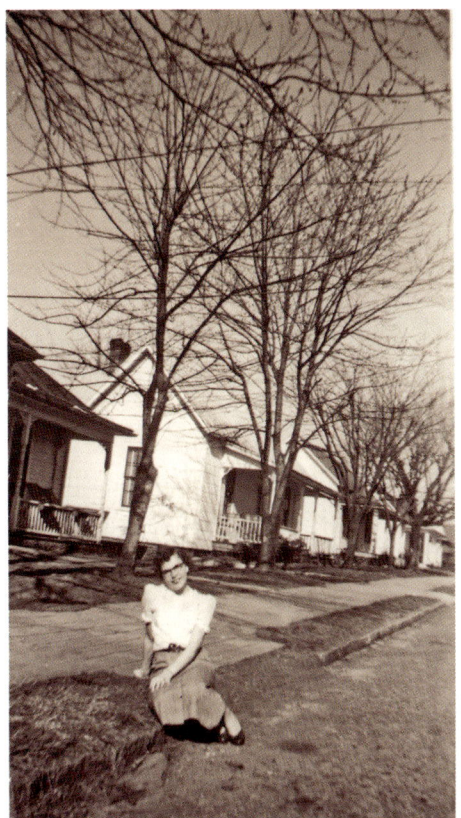

900 Block of Franklin Street looking east toward Green Street:

Franklin Street was created from Farmland of the Brietz and Leinbach family. Mrs. LaNelle Hunter-Church, a resident of West Salem and Franklin Street, is shown with the 'Tinners' houses of West Salem' photograph c. 1940s. An example of the Tinners' houses was 918 Franklin Street, built by Thomas Morgan; owner and operator of Morgan & Blum Tinners in East Salem. Two cottage homes of the block are shown in 2013.

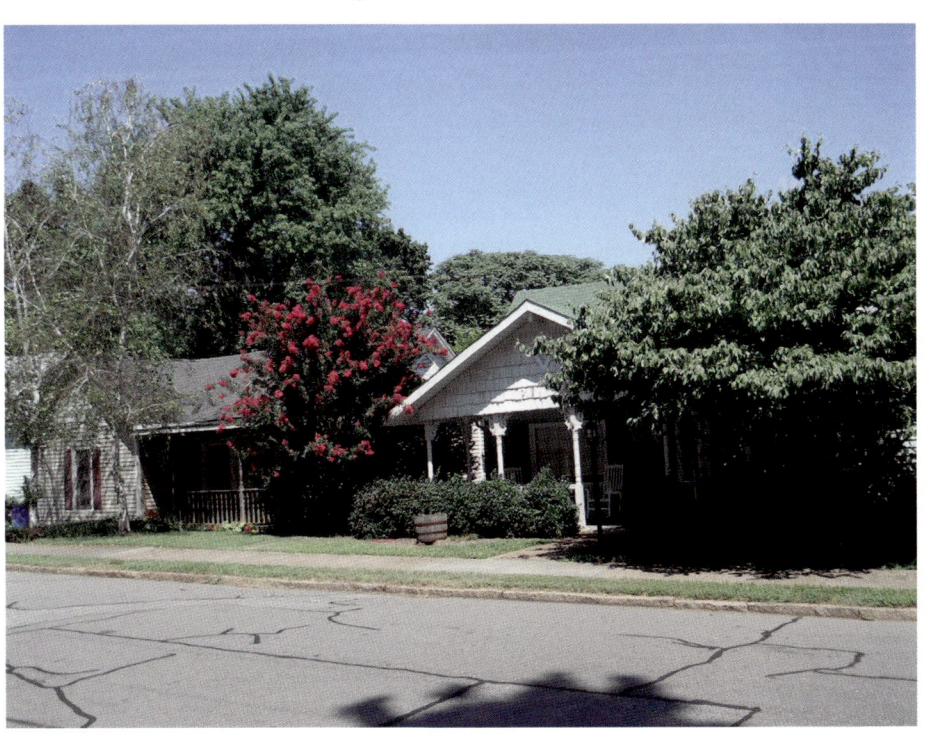

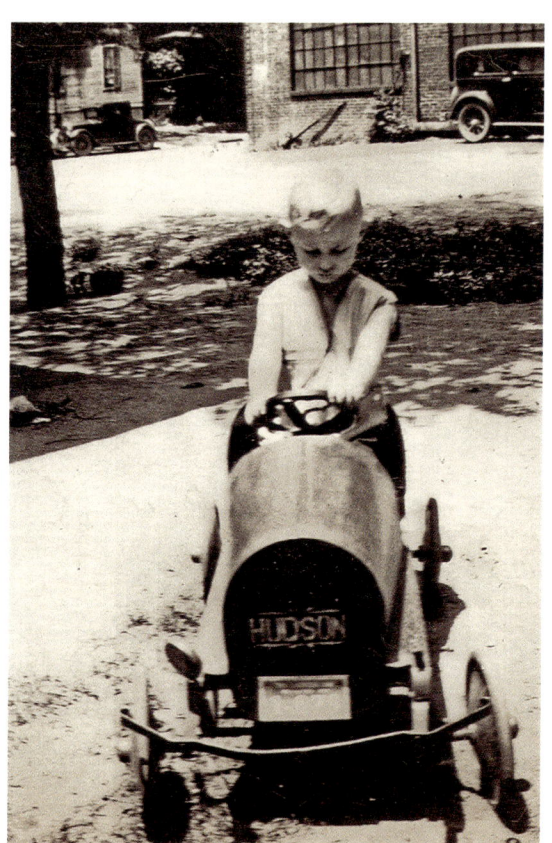

DIVIDING LINE OF SALEM AND WINSTON AT MAIN STREET: Generations of families have called Old West Salem home. A good example is Mr. Roger Willard, often called simply 'Johnny' who is shown in this 1930s photograph. The location of the photograph was the City Hall site *c.* 1925. Across the street and to Johnny's back was the Brown & Williams Tobacco Complex. Mr. Willard would serve in the Second World War, was employed at Westinghouse Corporation, as well as running a 'Ma & Pa' grocery store. One of his greatest accomplishments was his membership as a longstanding member of the West Salem Civic Club. The club was started by returning Second World War veterans in 1945 and is one of the longest running Civic Clubs in Winston-Salem today. The 2013 photograph looking toward the early site shows the statue of R. J. Reynolds, another important member of the city.

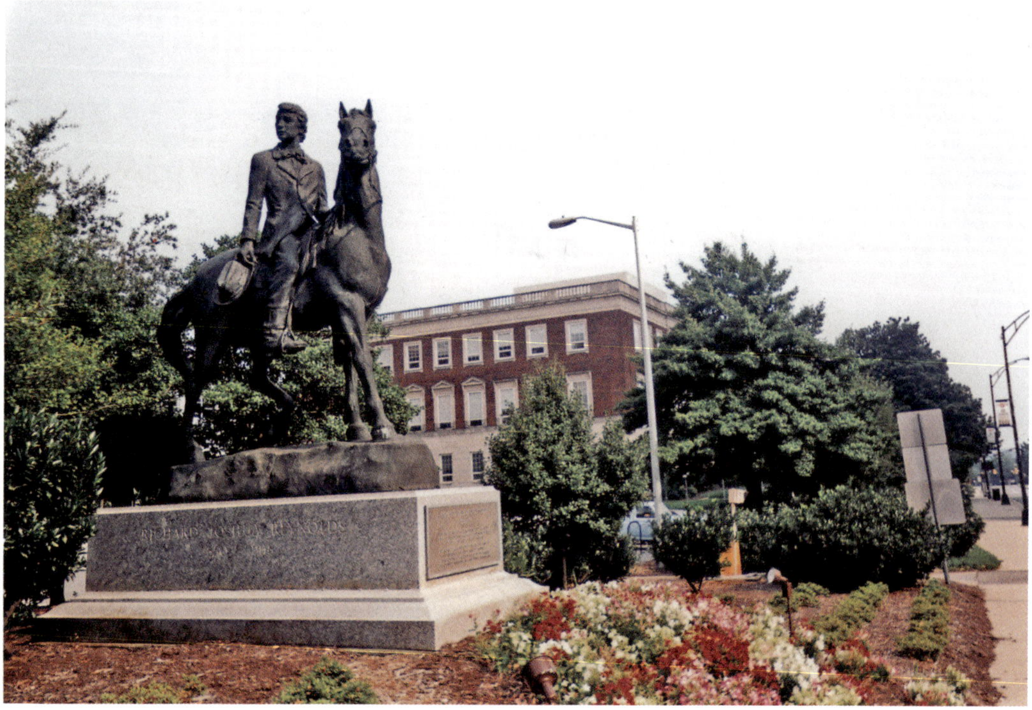

44

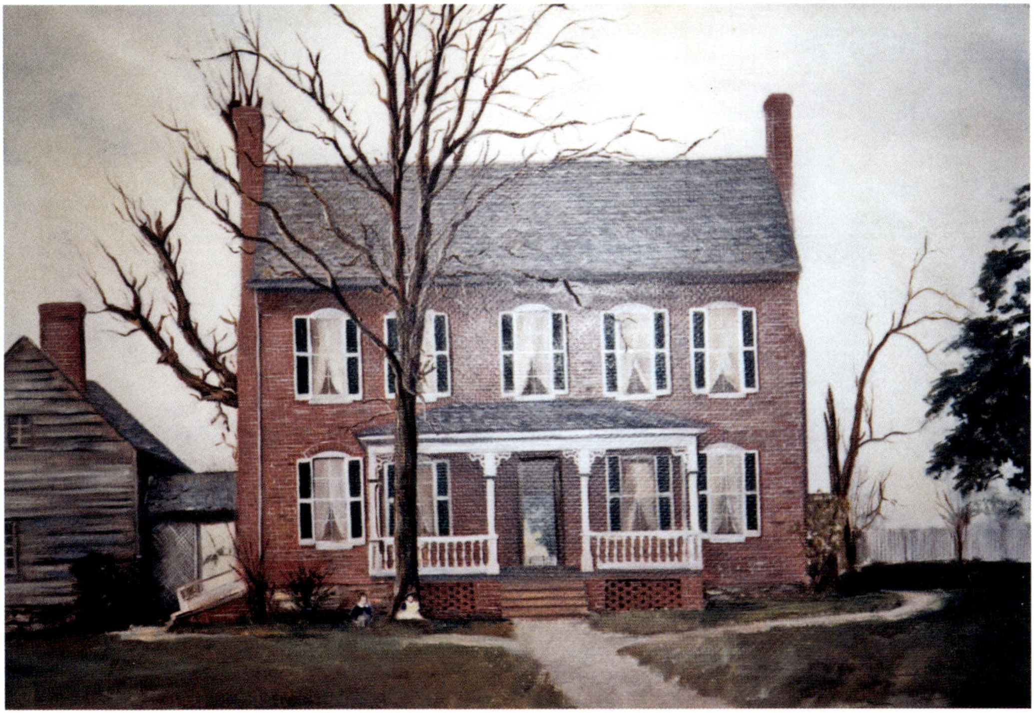

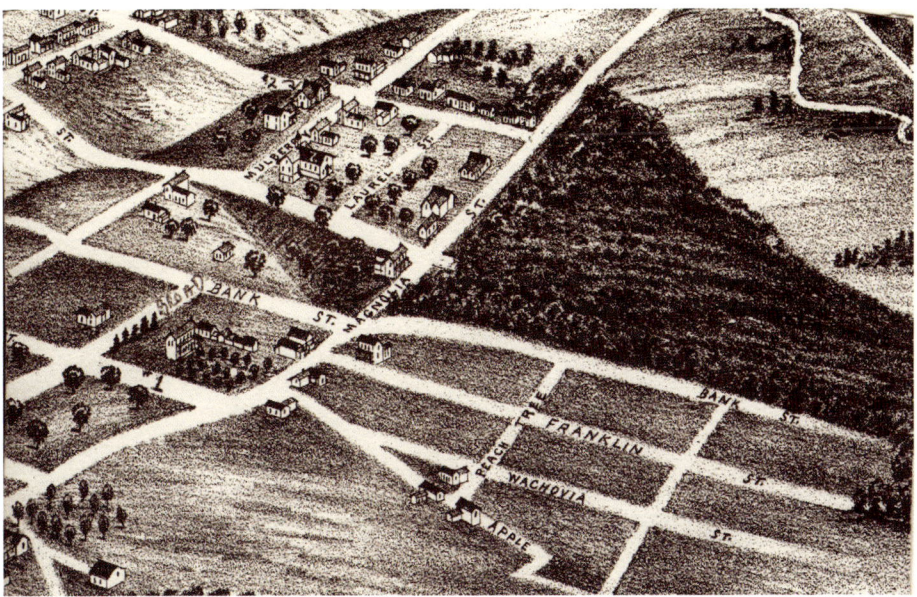

400 BLOCK OF SOUTH BROAD STREET: The Krueser-Levering-Farm began as a 30-acre farm and retirement home for Brother Conrad Krueser *c.* 1816. Brother Charles Levering took over the congregational store on Main Street after Brother Krueser's retirement. Brother Levering moved in 1825 to the farm after Brother Krueser became ill. In 1836, Brother Levering and family moved to Nazareth Pennsylvania and Brother Christian Brietz obtained the farm. Shown is the 1891 bird's eye view of the farm. The Brietz homestead is shown at Broad and Bank and close-up in painted portrait *c.* 1880s.

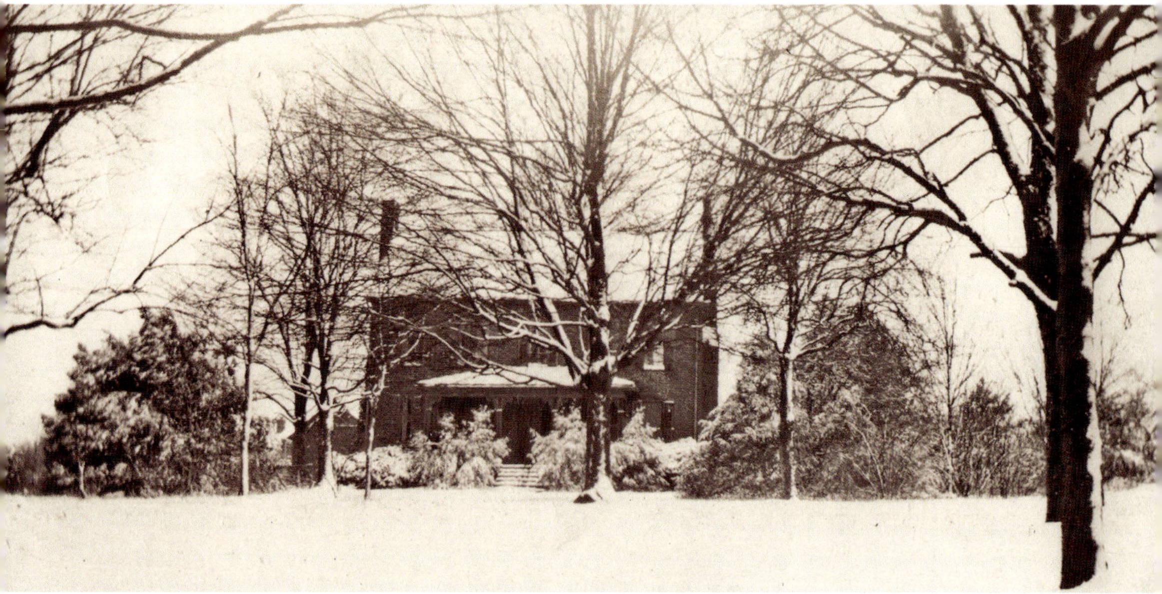

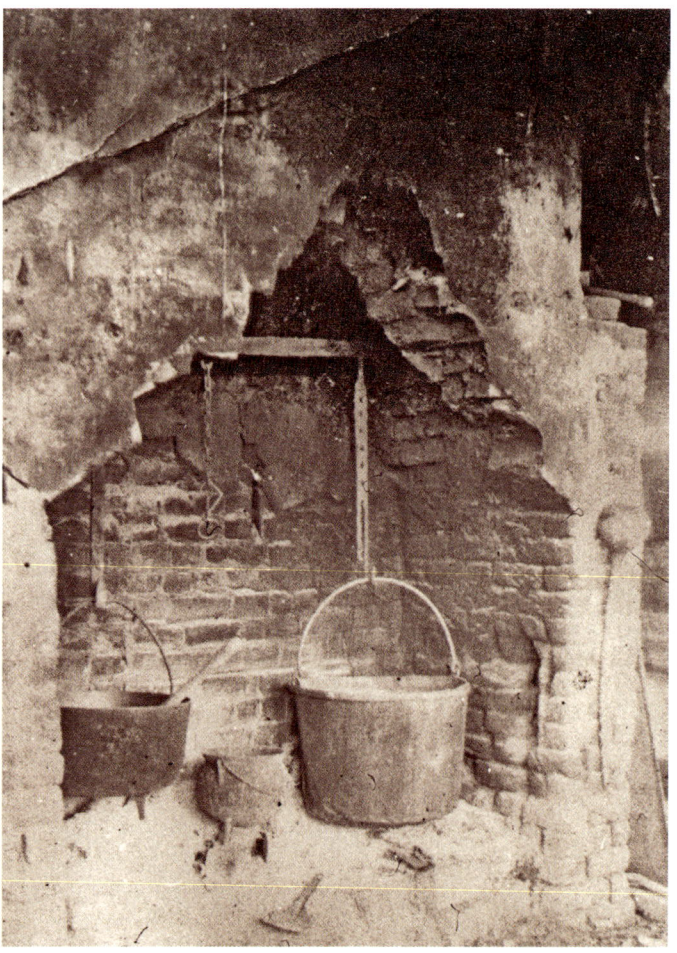

400 Block of Broad Street:

Between 1836 to 1963, eight generations of the Brietz family called the farm and plantation home. Presented in the following pages is the first published documentation of a farm and plantation in the heart of Salem and eventually Winston-Salem. The homestead shown *c.* 1920 was the residence of Miriam Brietz (1897-1997), the first archivist of the family. The early plantation fireplace from the nineteenth century is shown below.

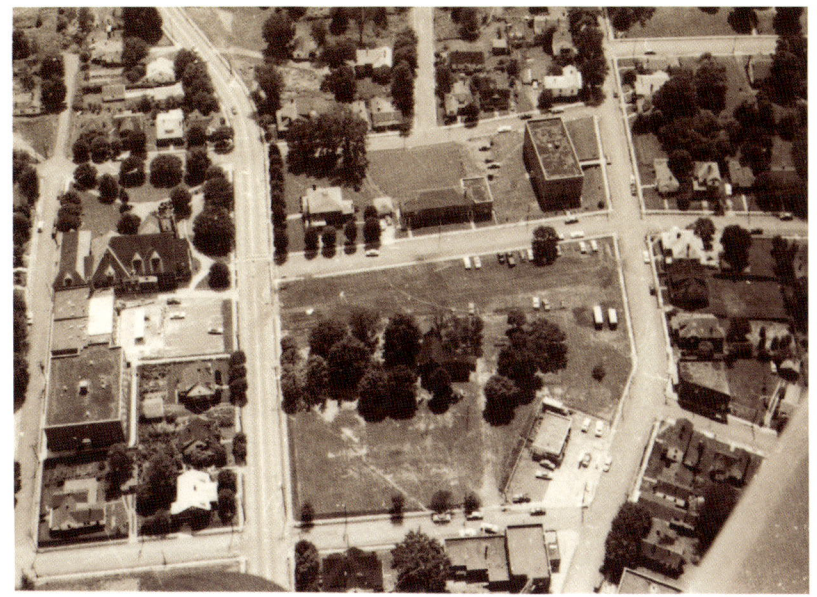

AERIAL PHOTOGRAPHS BROAD AND GREEN STREET: By the 1950s, the 30 acres of Krueser-Levering-Brietz-Farm had changed to showcase the Wachovia Highlands section of Old West Salem. The Brietz farmhouse remains central and is surrounded by the Salem Baptist Church (to the left), Piedmont Bible College began by Salem's longtime pasture, Dr. Charles Stevens (top buildings) and the surrounding neighborhood homes. The 1970 photograph below shows more growth in the area; however, the last of the farm and plantation, the homestead, was raised even though it had been designated a historic Salem landmark by Old Salem Incorporated in 1960.

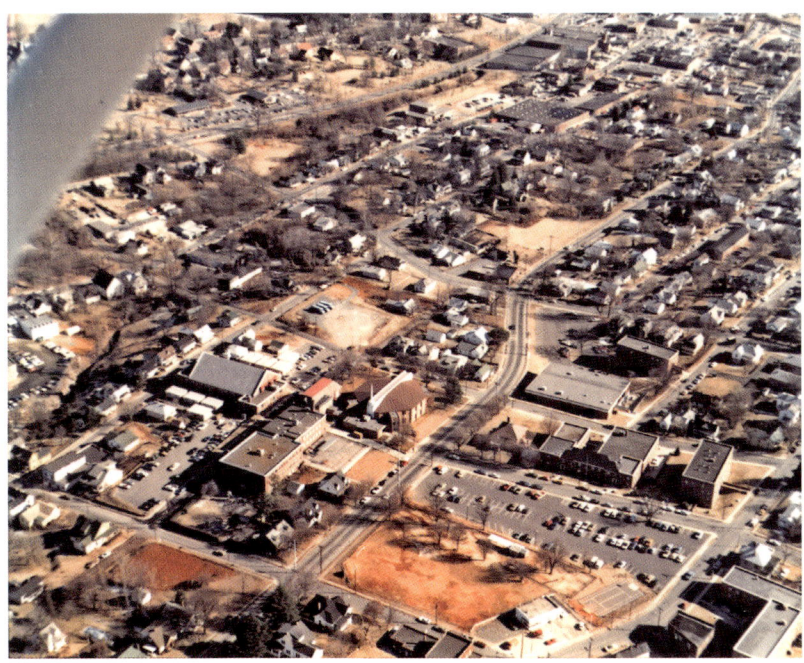

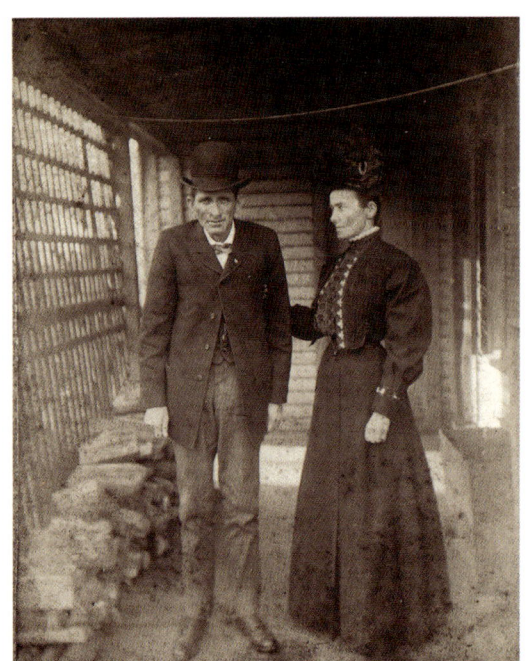

LOOKING BACK EAST AT 400 BROAD STREET:

Returning to the farm and plantation of the 1830s and 1840s, we find Christian Brietz not only the patriarch of the family's plantation, but Supervisor of the Red Tannery of the Salem Moravians and future Mayor of the Salem Town-lot. Shown in the photograph are Christian's son and daughter-in-law, Levin Renatus Brietz and Sophia Blum Brietz, who followed in dad's footstep as landowner and Mayor of Salem. On the same back porch was Levin and Sophia's grandson Raymond *c.* 1915 with the West Salem Firehouse in the background.

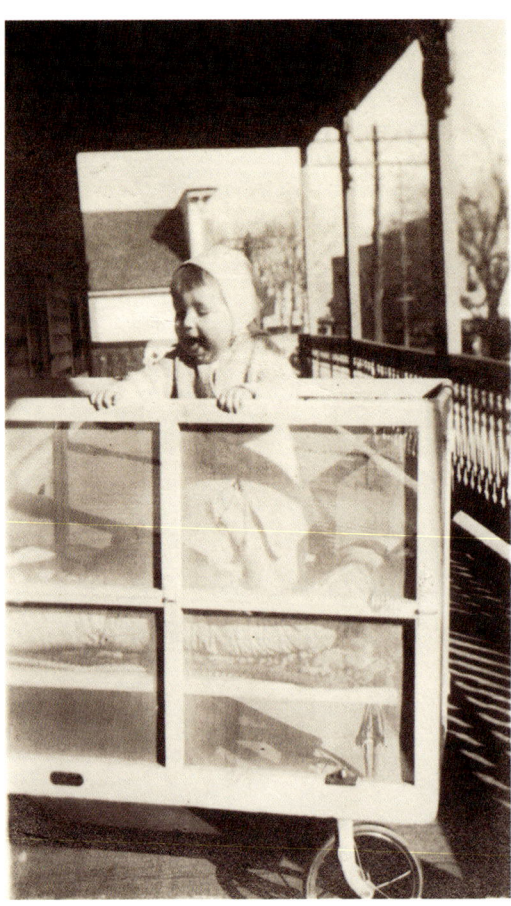

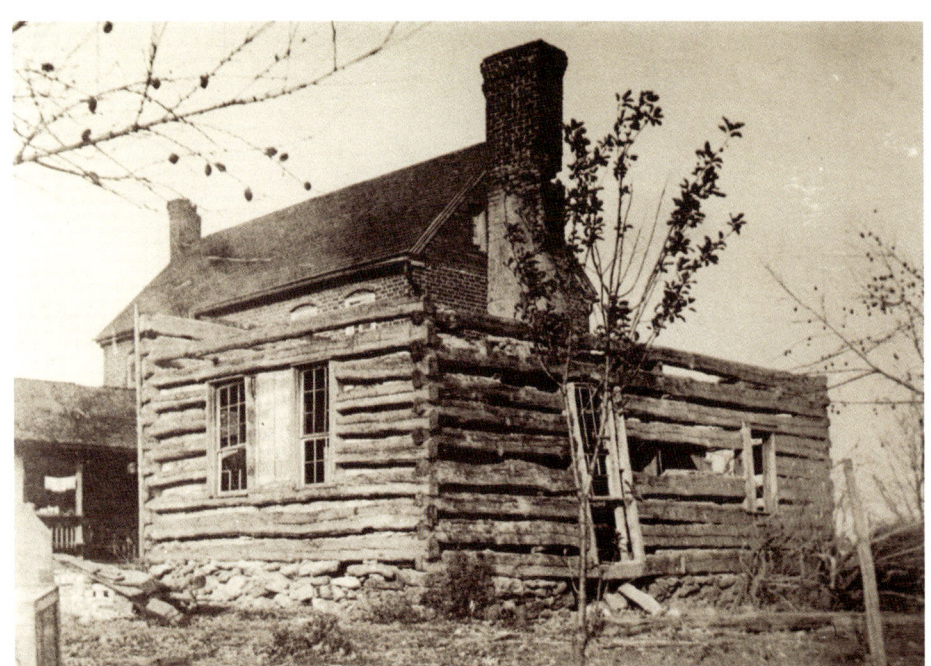

400 Block and 100 Block of Broad Street: Renatus Brietz extended his business dealings by purchasing the Salem Flour Mill in 1847, the largest commercial grist mill in North Carolina which was located four blocks south at Broad Street (Mill Street) and Salem Creek. The kitchen of the plantation was being rebuilt further from the homestead for fire safety reasons in this photograph from the 1860s. Renatus' grandson, John Levin Brietz in the 1926 photograph began another profession of the Brietz family, a 'Ma & Pa' grocery store at 100 Broad Street at First Street. For fifty years, the store was called the Green Front Cash Store.

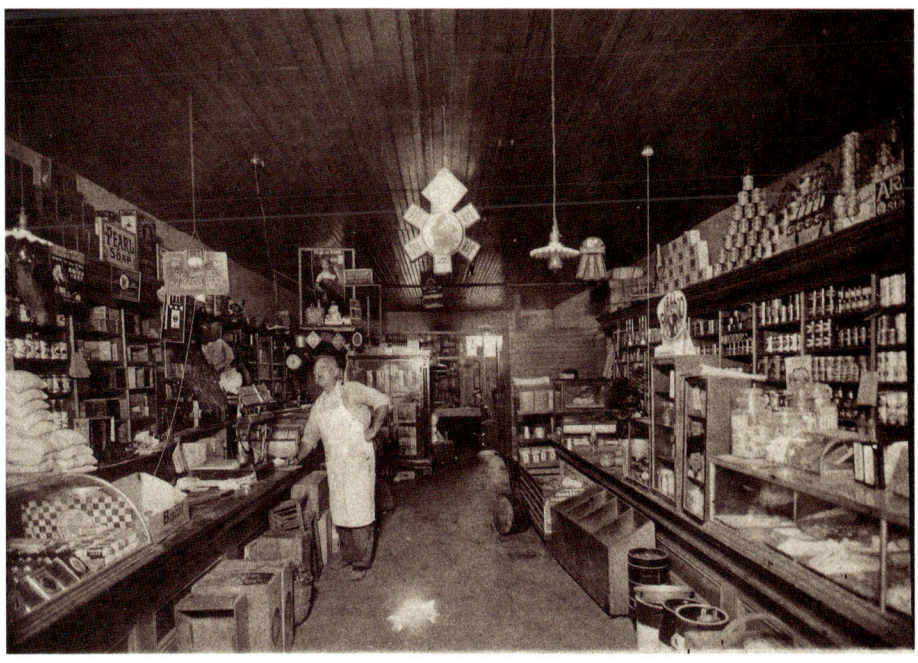

49

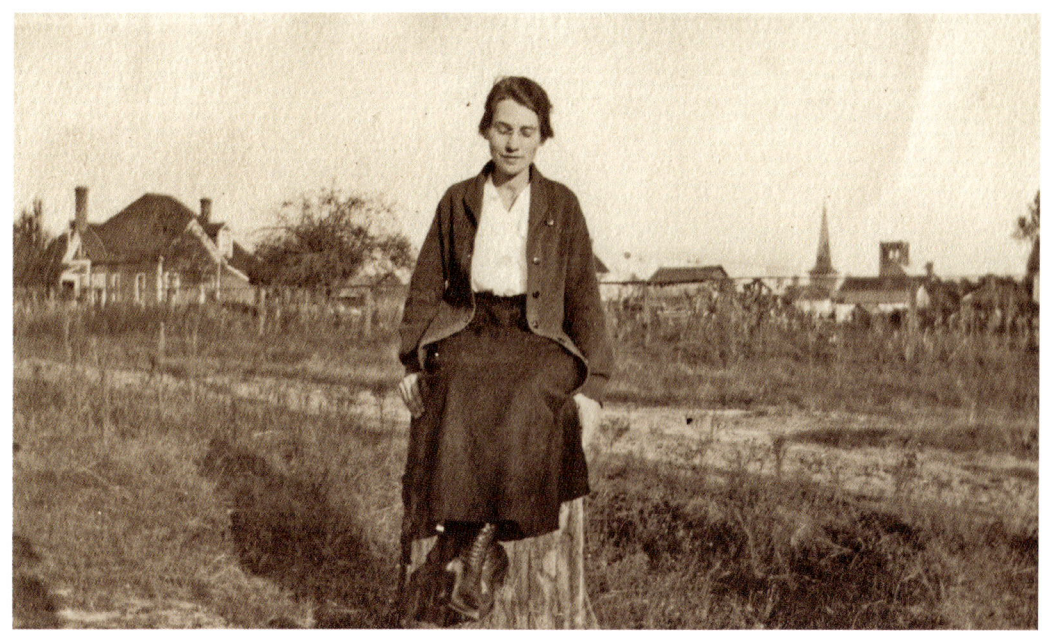

CENTER OF FARM 400 BROAD STREET TO WEST: Ms. Miriam Brietz, the first archivist of the Brietz family, is shown here in 1915. The land is being cleared for the future Wachovia Highlands neighborhood development by her father, Levin A. Brietz. The background shows the remaining barns, out-building, the church steeple of Christ Moravian Church, and the West Salem Firehouse with homestead to the right. The 2013 photograph shows the original steps leading to the Brietz homestead site. A green space of Piedmont International University and Lee Residence Hall can be seen.

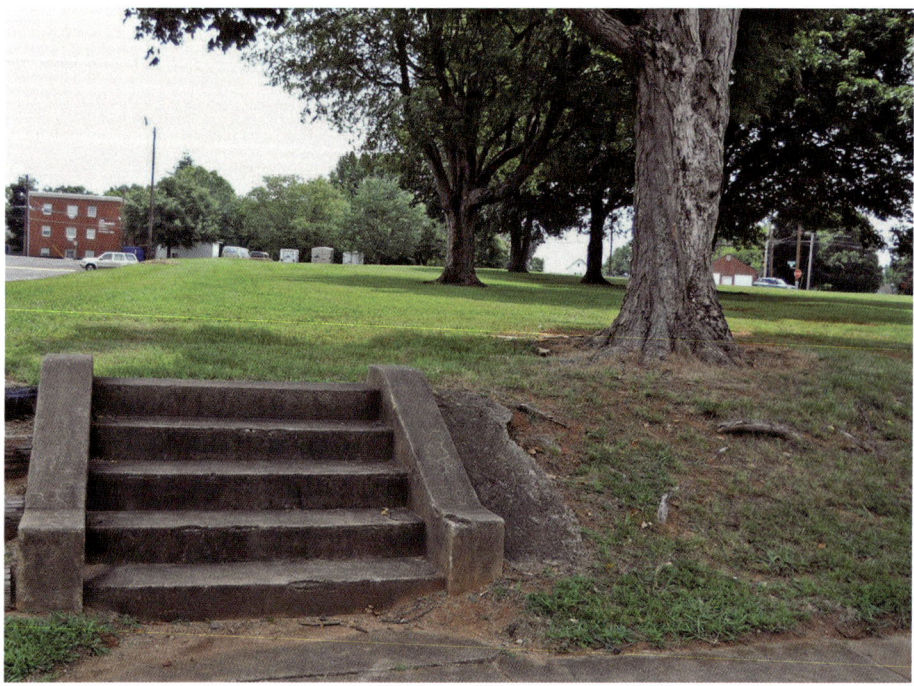

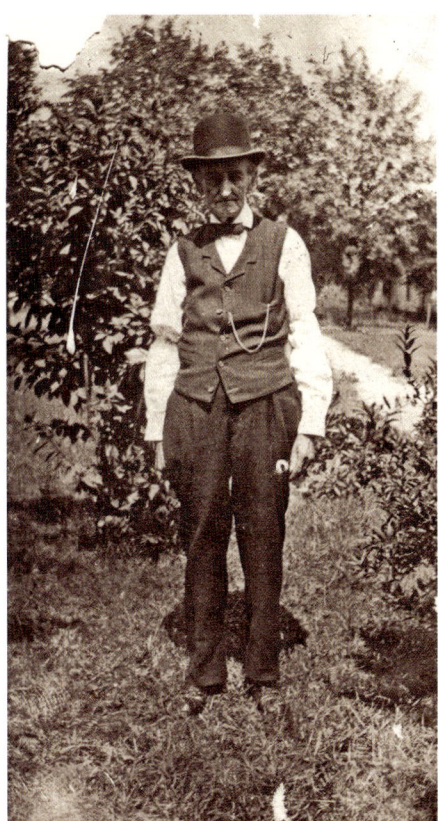

BRIETZ HOMESTEAD LOOKING EAST TO BROAD STREET:

Samuel and Edwin Butner can be seen here in 1915. Edwin was the son-in-law of Renatus Brietz. He was the supervisor of the Salem Textile Mill and also Mayor of the Salem Town-lot. He and his family resided on Poplar Street. Poplar Street became known, in 1850, as the first suburb of Salem's congregational town of East Salem. The 2013 photograph looks east toward East Salem.

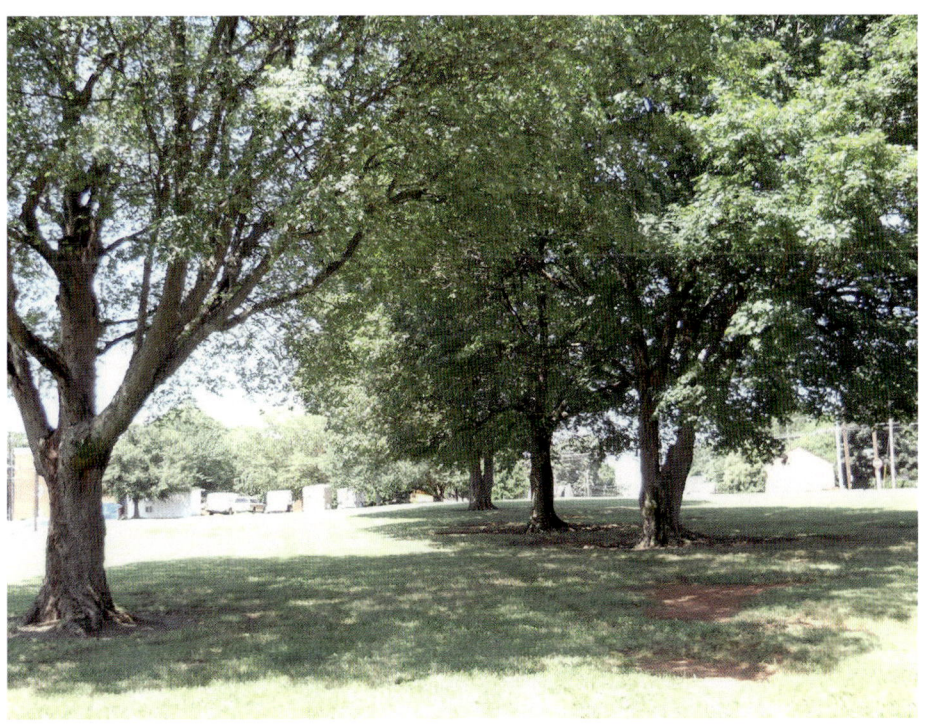

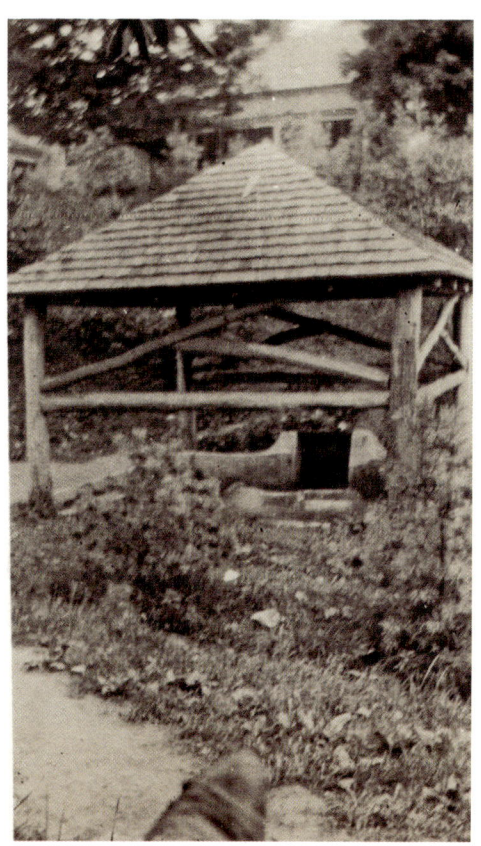

LOOKING EAST FROM 400 BROAD STREET HOMESTEAD:

This late nineteenth-century photograph shows the Brietz's plantation well house. Near the well house was located another business venture of Renatus and son, Levin A. Brietz. In the mid-late nineteenth century, the Brietz began a large commercial hog trade on the plantation farm. He and his son are known today as one of the first commercial meat packers in North Carolina. The modern view shows the green area of the homestead farm with surrounding development of the Wachovia Highland project. Some early twentieth century buildings included Chitty's Barber Shop, Welborn's Radio Shop, and Wachovia Grill.

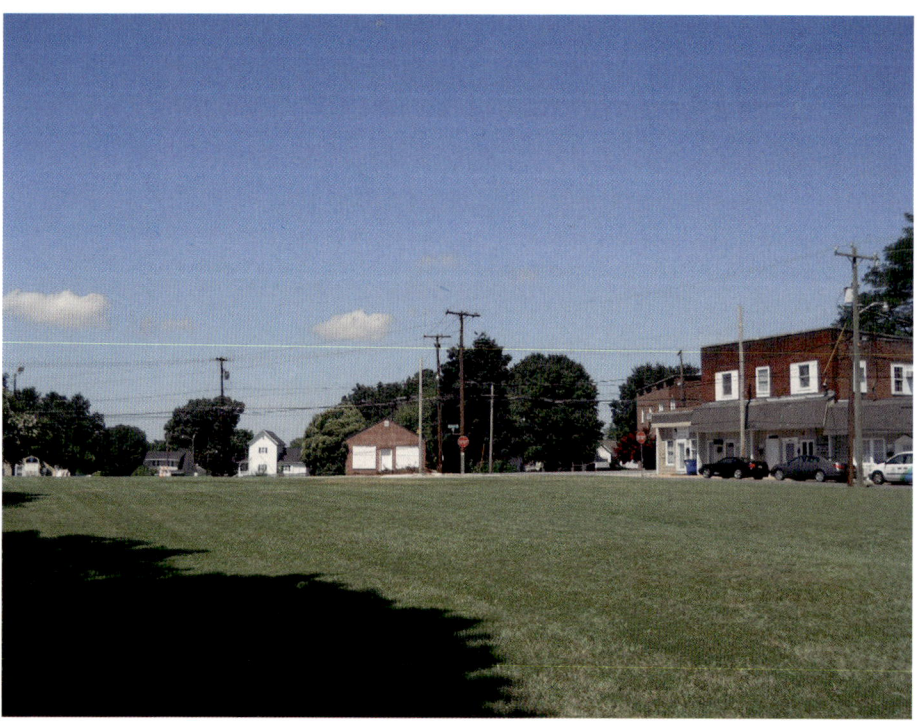

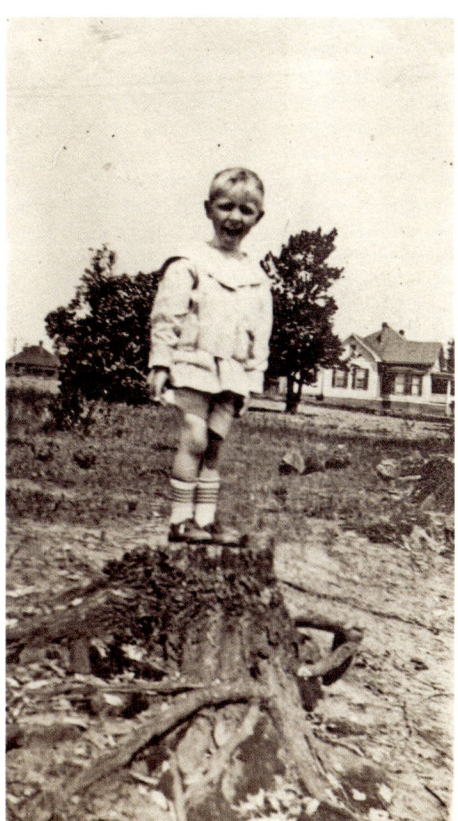

Looking North from Broad Street and Wachovia Street:

Little Raymond Brietz enjoyed his visits to the family farm as shown in 1915. The clearing of another tree made way for the future Wachovia Highland neighborhood. As shown, a Queen Anne cottage, *c.* 1910, was the John King House at 328 South Broad Street. Mr. King was a machinist at Carolina Foundry Company in Winston. The house to the left was 326 South Green Street owned by E. M. Dellinger, cattle driver. In this 2013 photograph, a commercial building has replaced the Dellinger home.

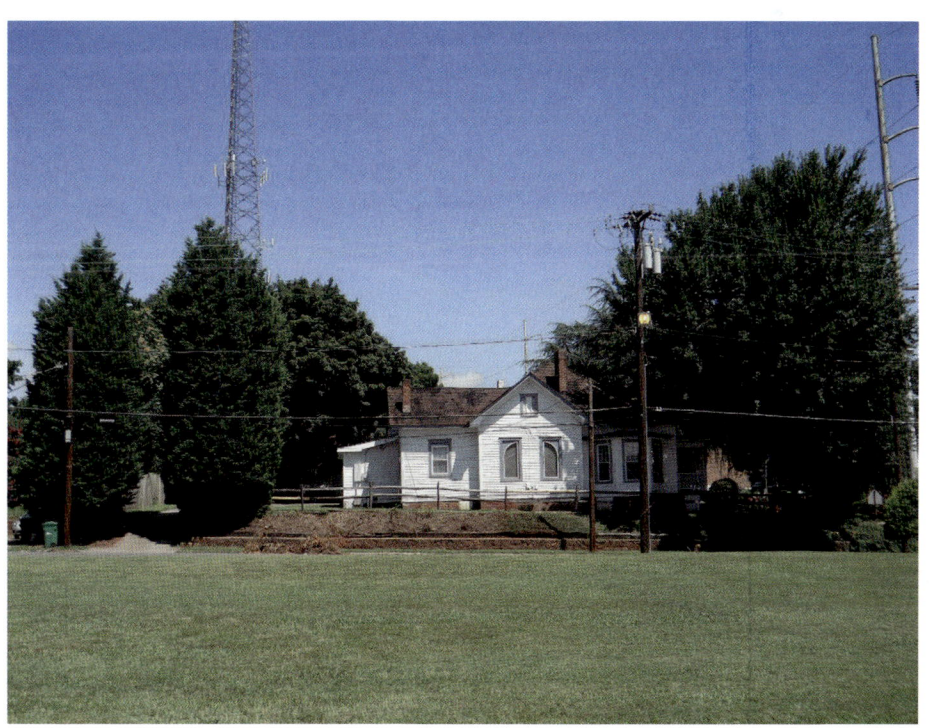

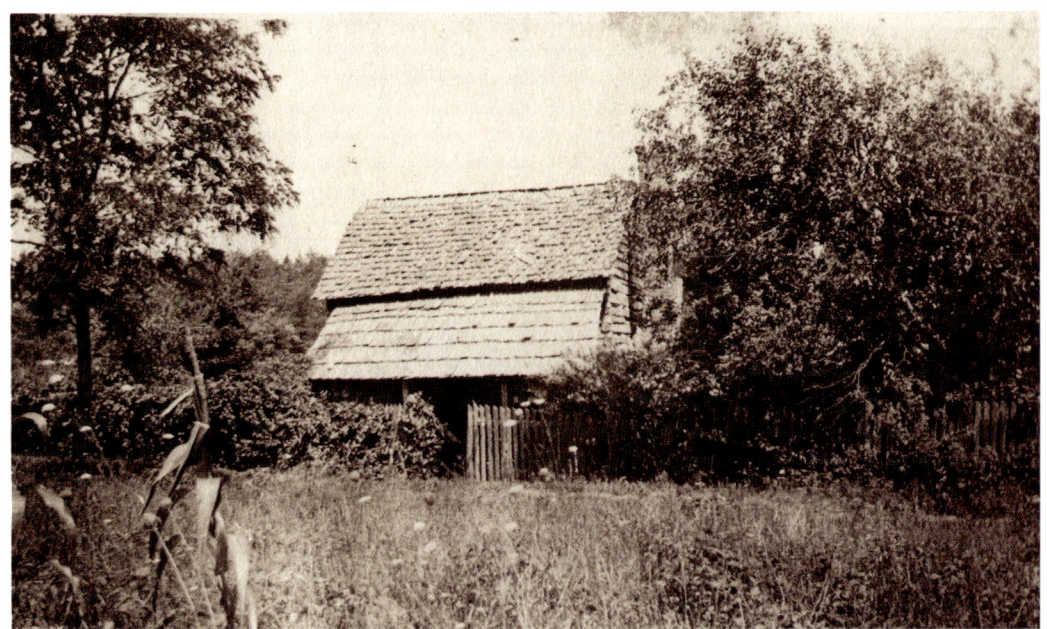

WEST ON GREEN STREET AT APPLE STREET: This farm/out lot building dated to the time period of the 1816 Krueser farm. The Brietz family's earliest fruit orchards including nut trees of all varieties: hickory, pecan, walnut, and chestnut extended west along present day Apple Street, backing the Paper Mill Settlement near present Peter's Creek Parkway. In the 2013 photograph a green space owned by Piedmont International University is a buffer for the school on Apple Street. Distant home is 927 Apple Street *c.* 1899, Victorian I-House, 'The Hanes Home' a builder.

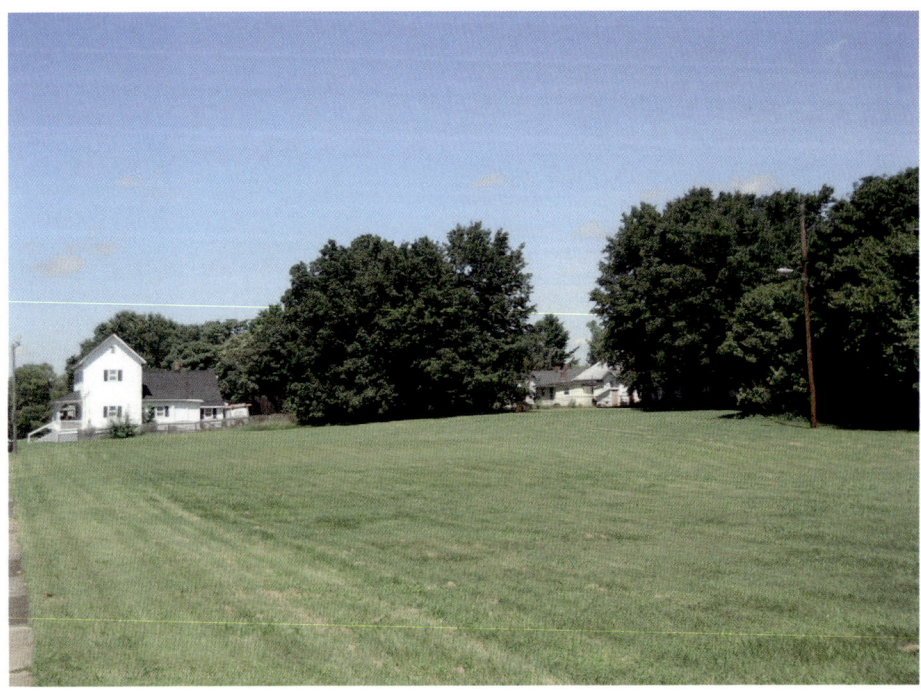

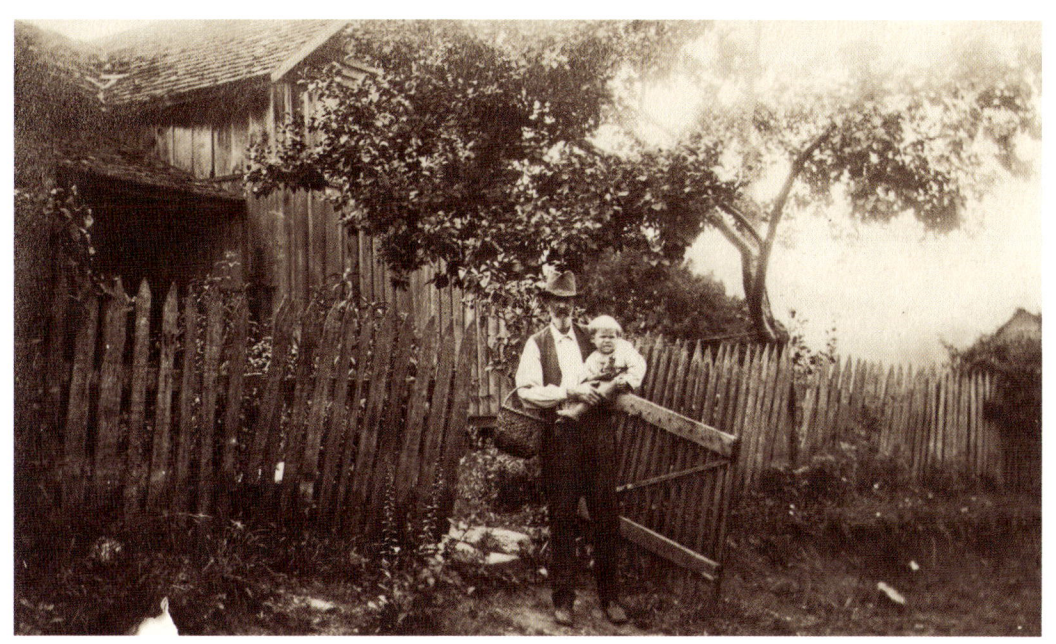

WEST ON GRANVILLE DRIVE BETWEEN WACHOVIA AND APPLE STREETS: Levin A. Brietz is shown with grandson Raymond in around 1915 collecting blackberries. The outbuilding and fence was a remnant of the Krueser farm *c.* 1816. The Brietz had a blackberry and mulberry fruit business in this section of the plantation dating to the 1830s. The dried berry industry during the Civil War period and reconstructive period was the only food and business venture which survived the war period. The early street was called Peach Tree Street, but today survives as 406 and 408 Granville Drive, Gable Ell and Hip Roof cottages.

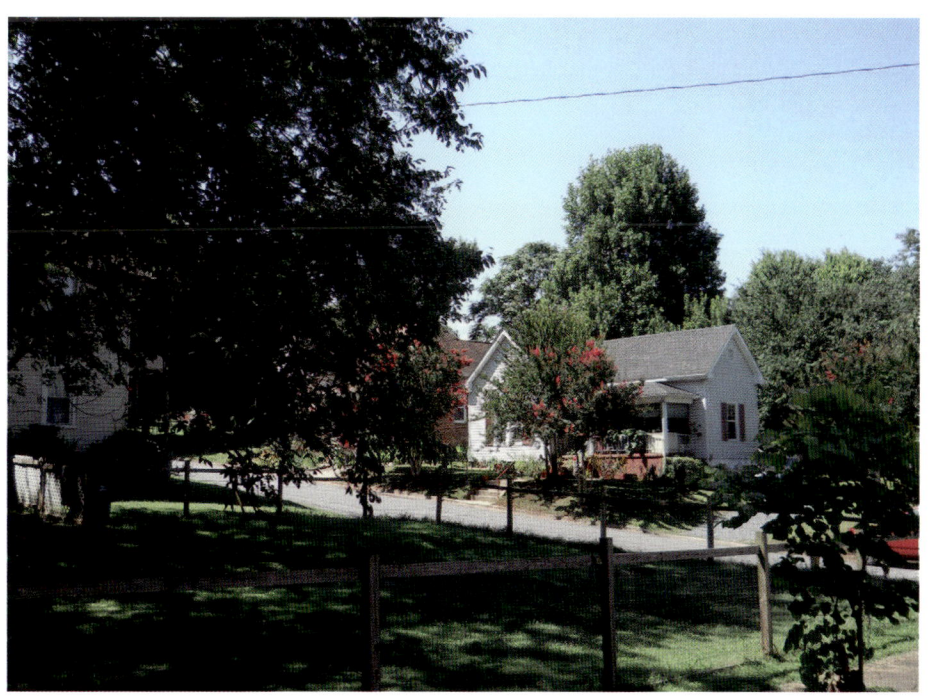

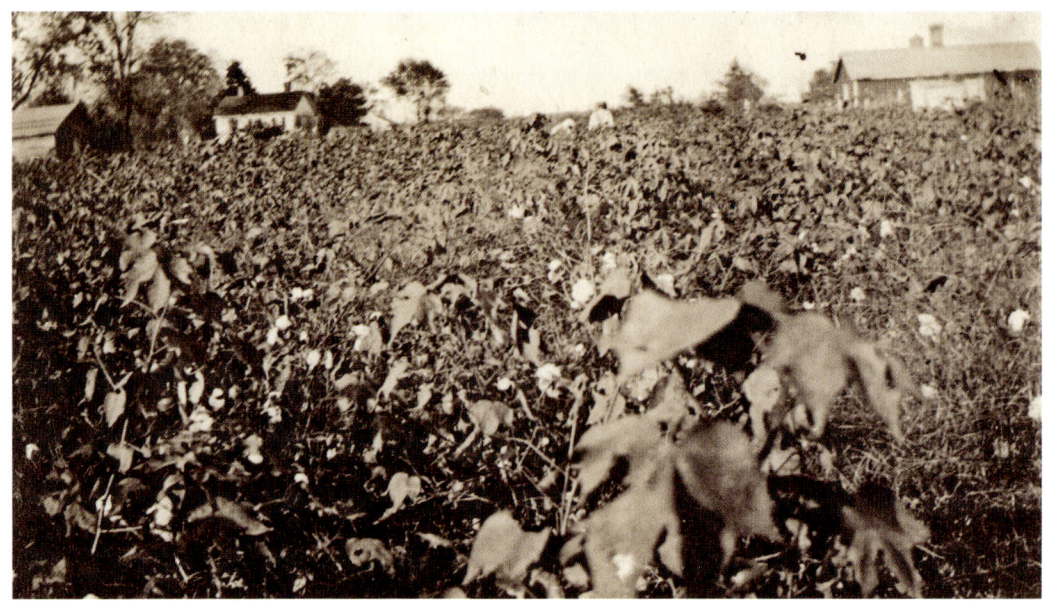

WEST END OF FRANKLIN TO THE WEST SIDE OF APPLE STREET: This 1913 photograph of 'Grandma Brietz's cotton field' is no longer a cotton plantation of the Brietz. However, Sophia Blum Brietz (Grandma) remembers when it was a small cotton plantation worked by her family in the 1830s through the 1860s. The Brietz and Leinbach family had the next-door plantation before the Civil War. Neither family worked slaves in their fields. In 1913, the houses and barns of Moravian out lots were on a ridge near Spaugh Street. Currently revitalization is being planned for the Peter's Creek Parkway corridor.

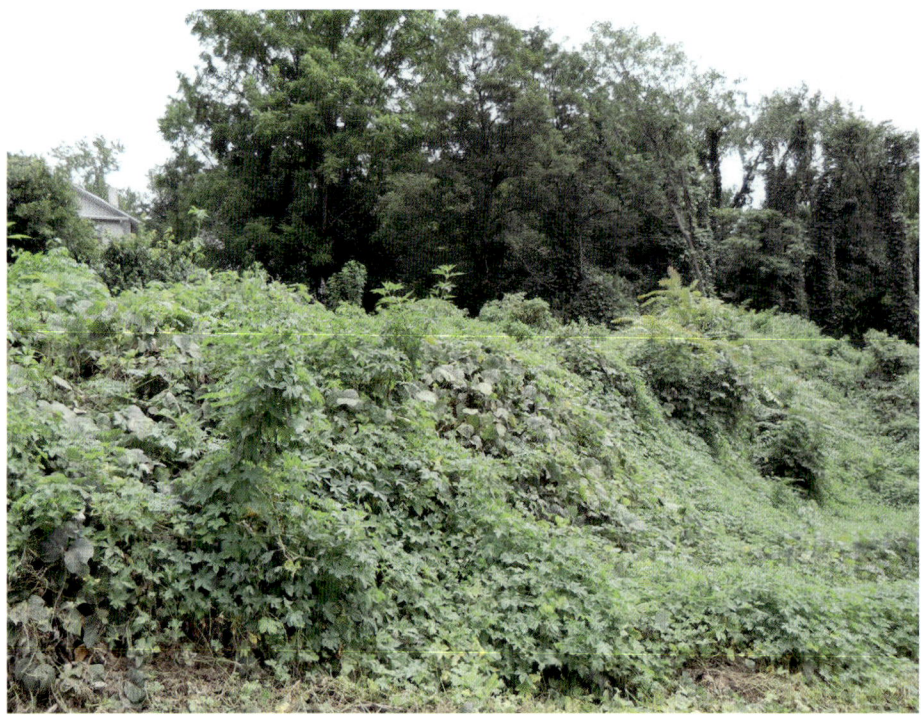

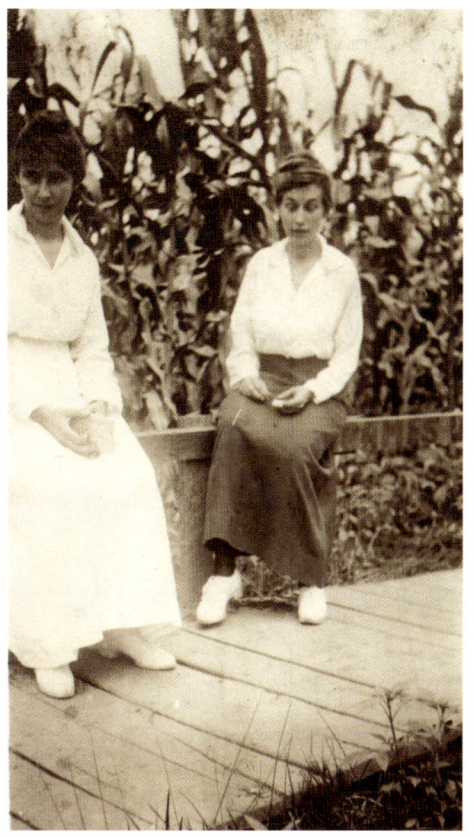

EAST OF BROAD STREET AT THE 300 BLOCK:

Ethel and Miriam Brietz contemplate their years at Salem College after graduating in around 1914 while literally watching the corn grow. The plank sidewalk along Broad Street preceded the massive paving of Salem and Winston beginning in 1919 and throughout the roaring twenties. Charles S. Lee of 224 South Green Street received the contract to do all paving in Salem by R. J. Reynolds himself in 1914 after Mr. Lee's paving work on the Reynolda estates of the Reynolds family. Currently, the farm site of the Brietz's corn field is owned by Dr. Bowman, Professor at Piedmont International University. He farms corn as well.

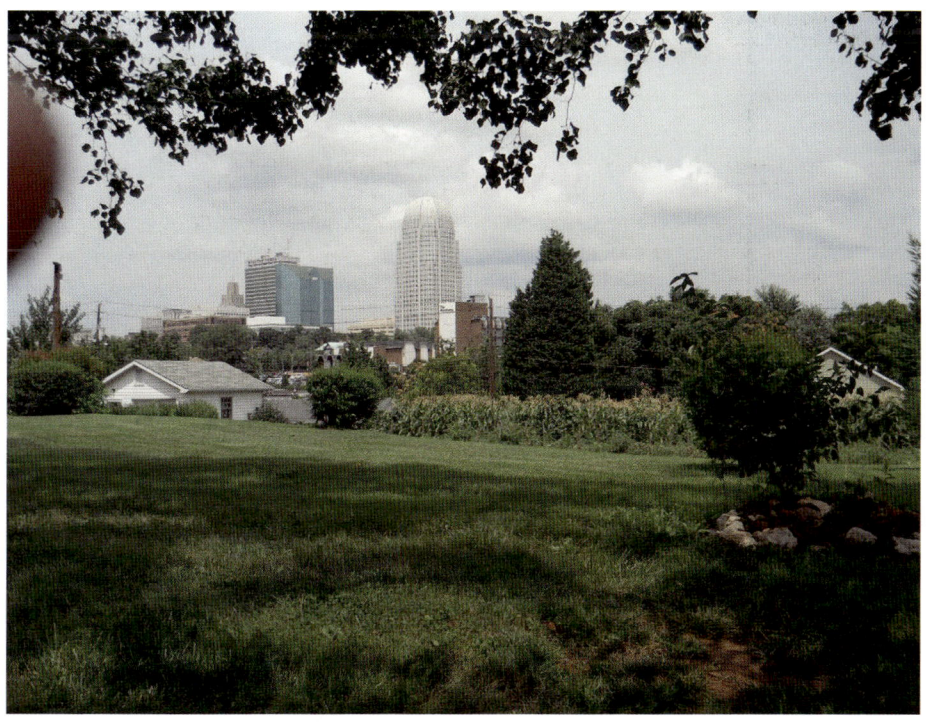

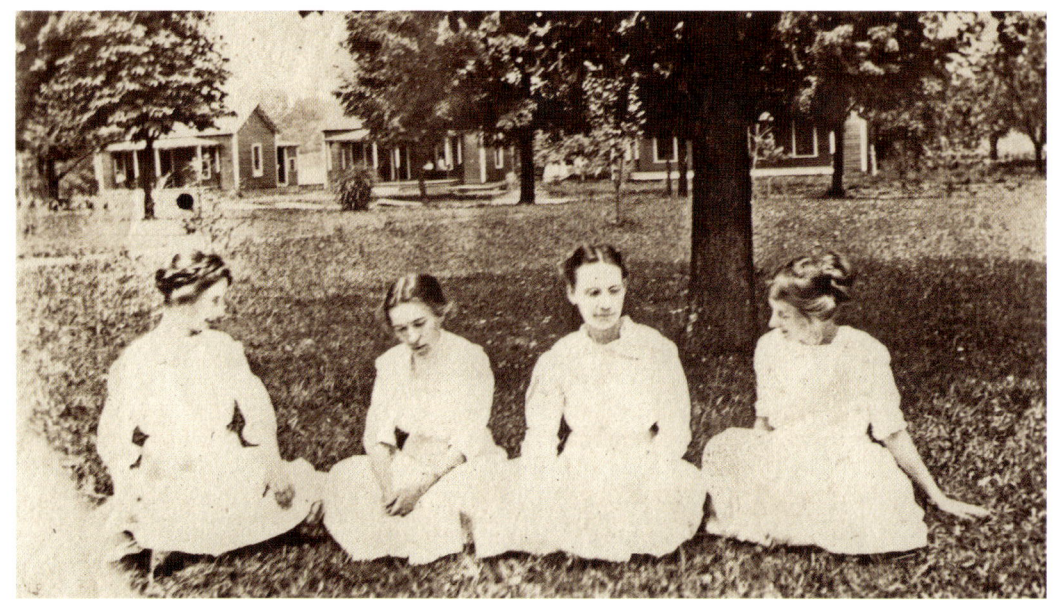

NORTH AT PAPER MILL ROAD (BANK) AND WACHOVIA STREET: Miriam and Ethel Brietz with Salem College classmates enjoy a quiet, shady time in a park area of the Brietz farm before the construction of the Wachovia Highland Project. The peach groves of the Brietz and Leinbach's plantation occupied this space in the early to late nineteenth century. The homes in the background with plank sidewalks and roads housed 'Tinners of West Salem.' Today, these are Victorian cottages and are as just as quaint as the park once was.

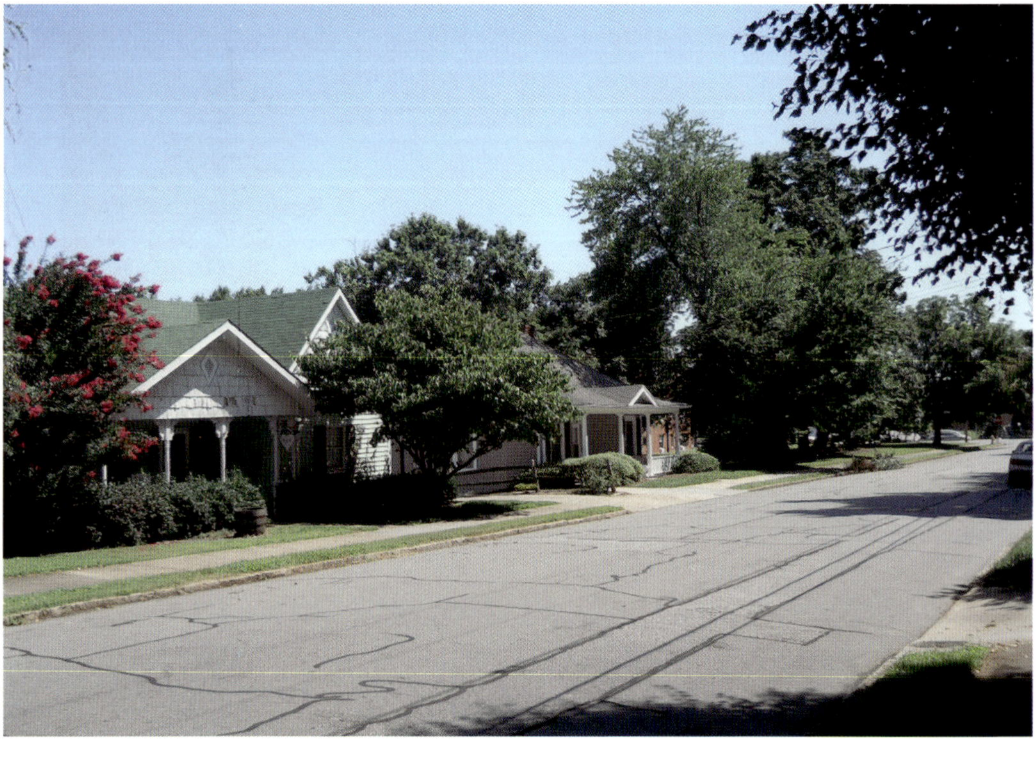

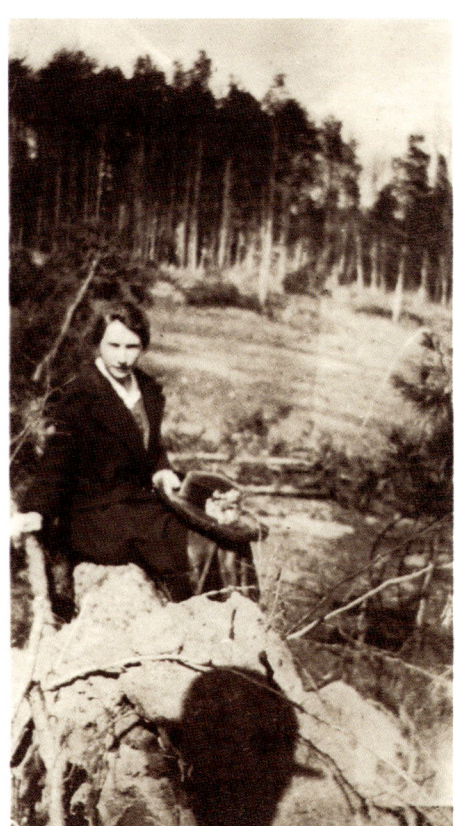

LOOKING SOUTH FROM BEYOND BANK STREET AT PETER'S CREEK PARKWAY: Miriam Brietz surveys the western edge of the Brietz farm in 1913 near the old Granite Quarry site of the eighteenth and nineteenth century Salem Town-lot. The open area to the tree line was the location of the Salem Saw Mill *c.* 1795. The Saw Mill, Paper Mill, and Quarry made up this West Salem industry. In today's landscape the site is the home of the West Salem Shopping Center of Peter's Creek Parkway.

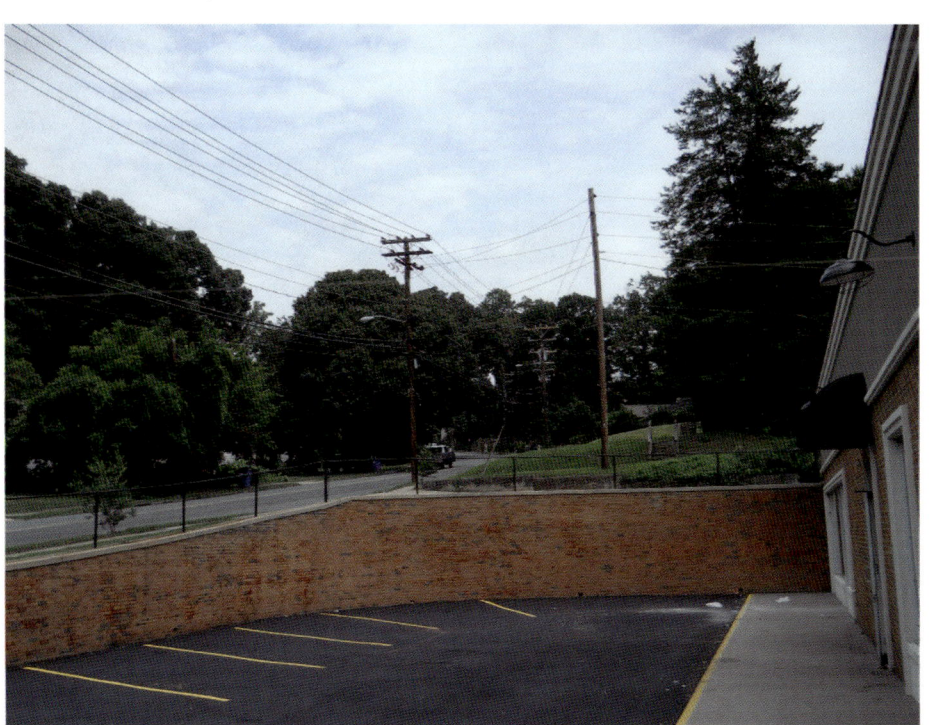

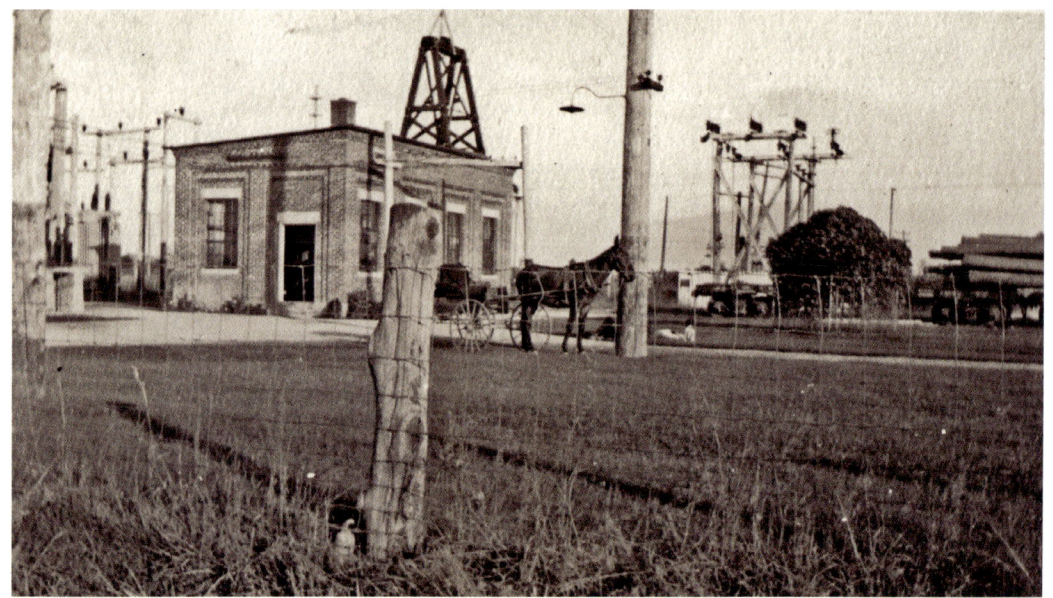

SOUTH ACADEMY STREET AT PETER'S CREEK PARKWAY: The Saw Mill property is seen separated from the Brietz property by the wire fence. The electrical system housed in the small brick building powered the Saw Mill Complex. The electrical system was a substation of the larger Southern Power Company Station located, then and today, on South Broad Street near Salem Creek. Lumber was cut and loaded here as observed by Miriam Brietz and her transportation, Old Buck. The 2013 photograph shows Academy Street and the British Petroleum (BP) Service Station occupying this site.

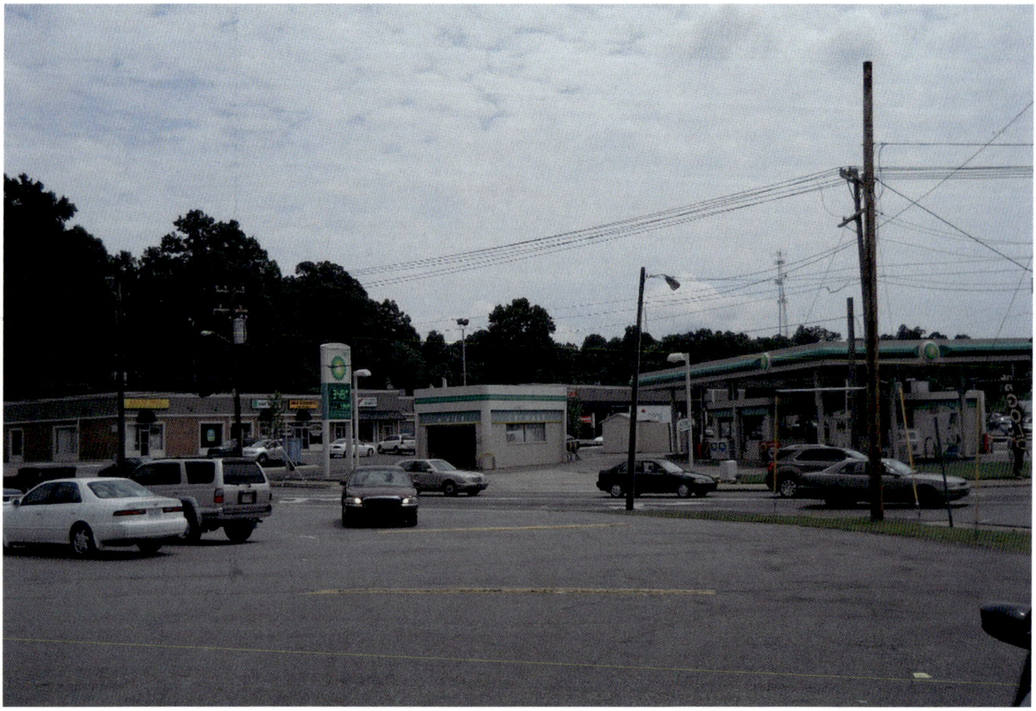

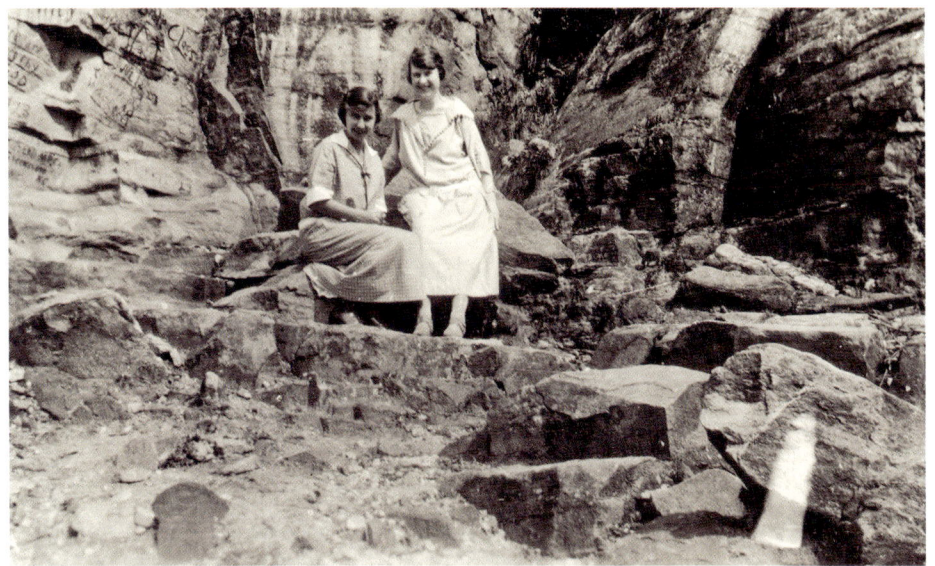

THE OLD GRANITE QUARRY SITE AT APPLE STREET AND PETER'S CREEK PARKWAY: The Paper Mill settlement *c.* 1791 served Old Salem and Old Winston from 1791 to 1878. After the Paper Mill burned in 1878, the site was abandoned. The granite quarry site and Saw Mill site continued until about 1915 when Academy Street was extended for Granville Drive west at the newly constructed Granville Graded School extended to the newly developed Ardmore neighborhood *c.* 1910. In the early years, the quarry supplied the rock for construction projects in the eighteenth and nineteenth centuries in Salem for houses and businesses of Old Salem and Old Winston. Miriam Brietz and friend enjoyed the topography with an occasional caving exploration along the granite ridges of their property. Today, the area is unrecognizable except for houses along Gregory Street.

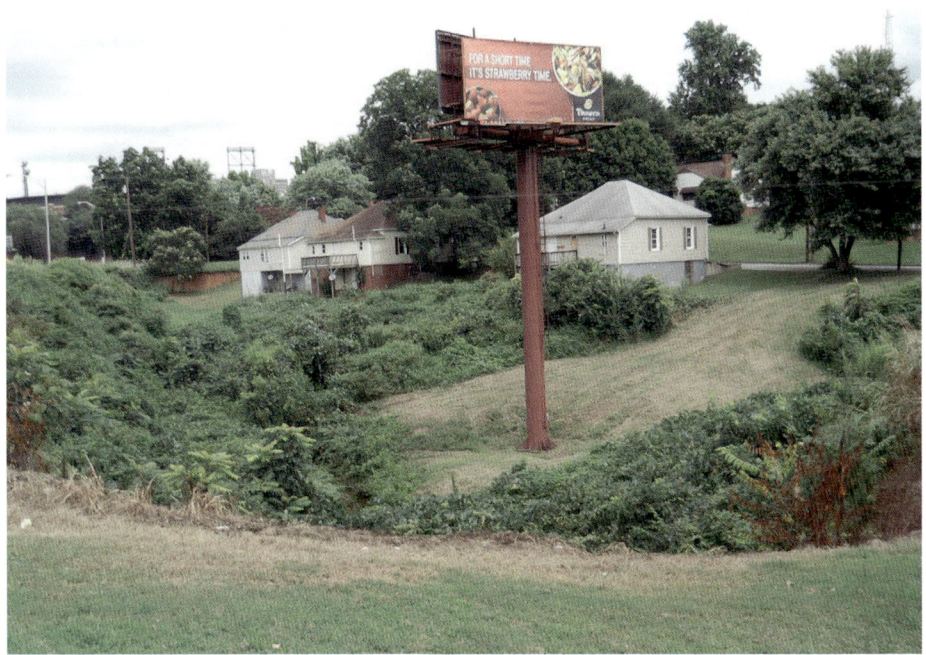

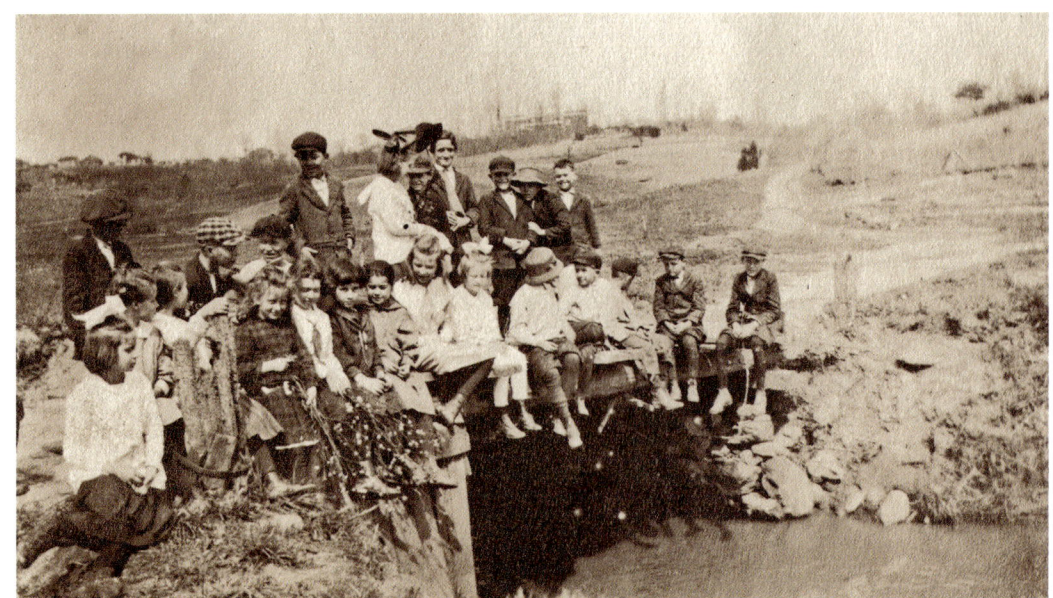

SOUTH ACADEMY AT PETER'S CREEK PARKWAY: The Petersbach (Peter's Creek) had been a recreational area of the Moravians dating back to 1791. The Paper Mill owners built for the pond, a race for powering the waterwheel of the Salem Paper Mill. The pond was used for recreation as a swimming and boating attraction. The colder winters of the past would freeze the surface and provided ice-skating on the pond as well. The first class of Granville School, shown on ridge above *c.* 1915, enjoys their recreation on the old plank bridge over Peter's Creek. The current photograph shows the area as the parking lot of the shopping center and highway system.

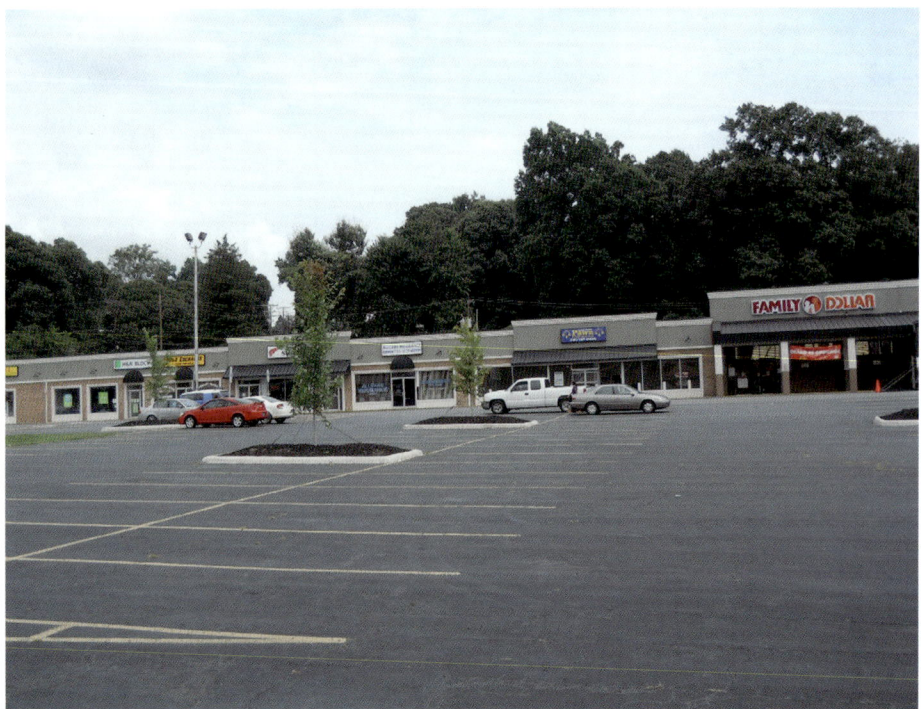

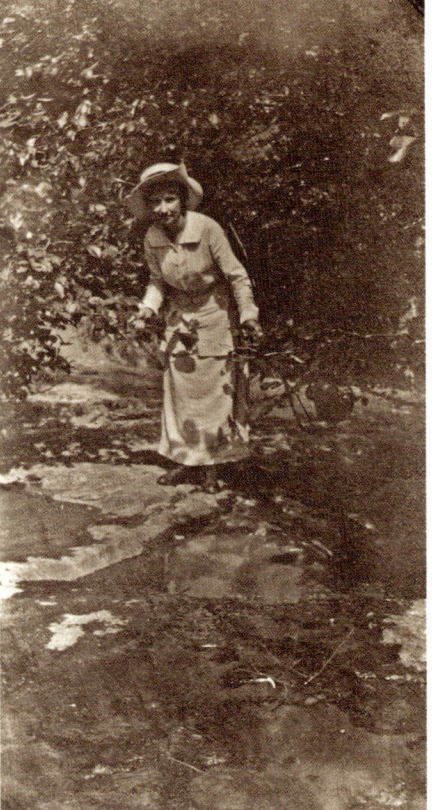

SOUTH APPLE STREET AT PETER'S CREEK PARKWAY:

Miriam Brietz appears as if she has walked out of a prehistoric time period as she enjoyed transverse the creek which fed Peter's Creek. The flat rocks from the quarry and the creek were most excellent for house flooring. If one tours the restored Old Salem village, this type of rock were used and profiled as basement flooring. Many of the mill homes around Old West Salem had this flooring type. Currently in today's landscape, a stream, a billboard sign, and Kudzu occupy this site, which cries for revitalization.

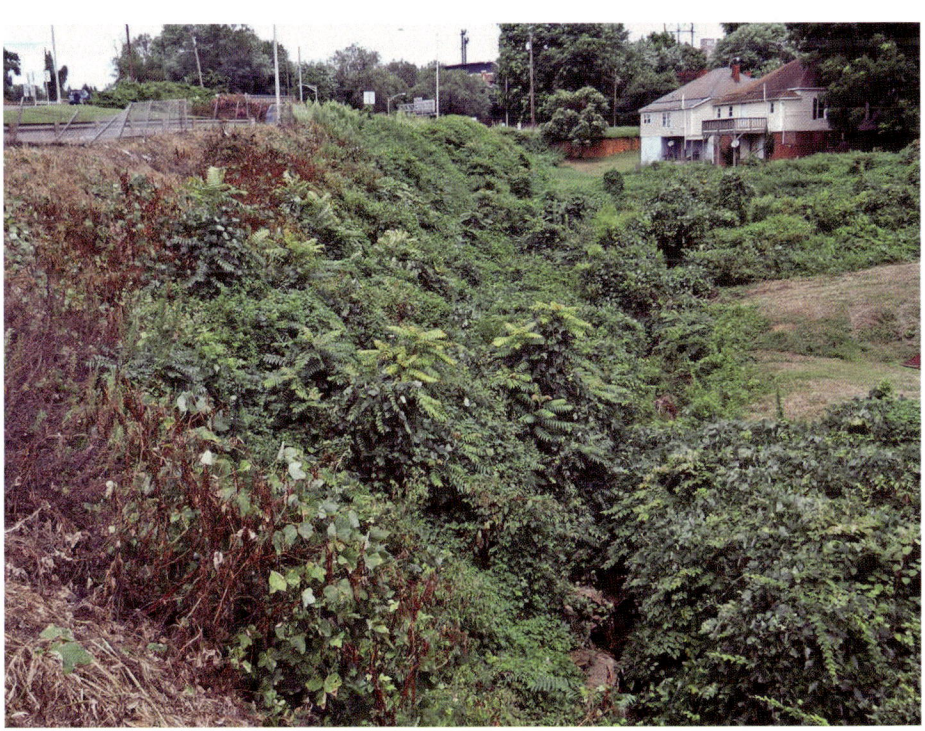

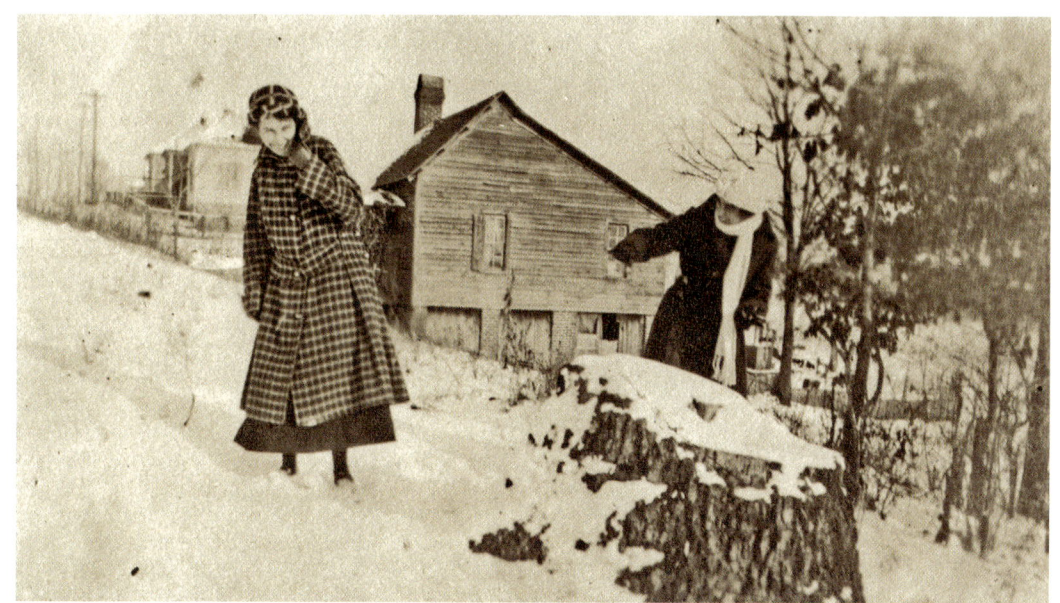

GRANVILLE DRIVE NEAR APPLE STREET: Miriam Brietz and sister, Marie Brietz Chambers enjoyed a Christmas snowfall along Peach Tree Street (Granville Drive). An old plantation barn *c.* mid nineteenth century has been re-worked to a home place in this *c.* 1914 photograph. The home place today appears as 418 Peach Tree Street (Granville Drive). Mr. John Minish was the builder. More remnants of the Brietz Farmhouse and plantation's former grounds hold promise for the historical future of Old West Salem, a Preserve America neighborhood.

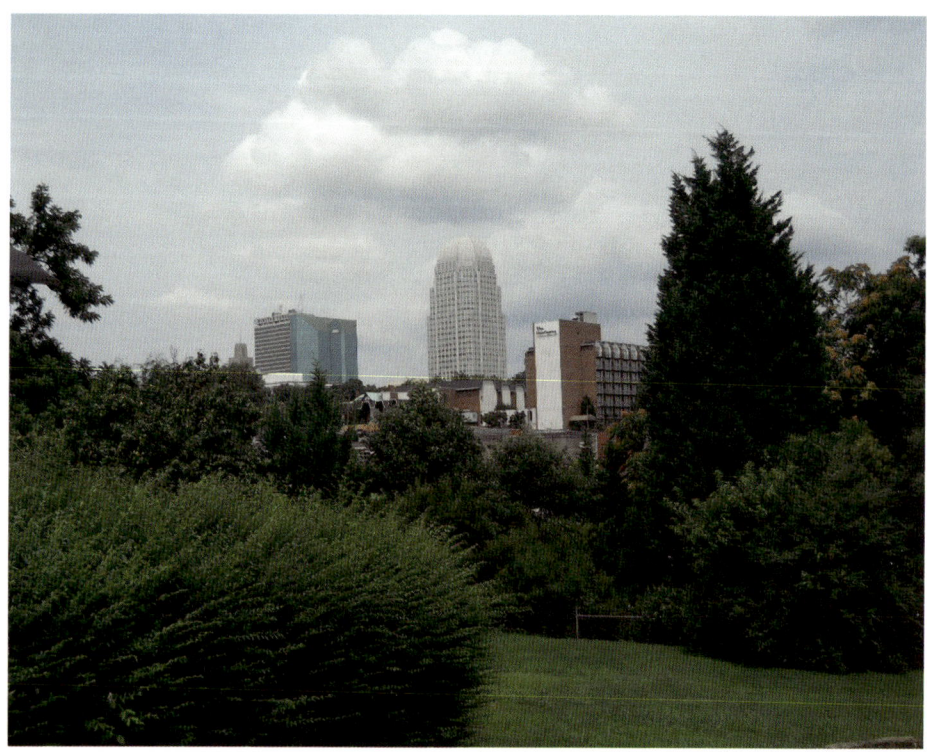

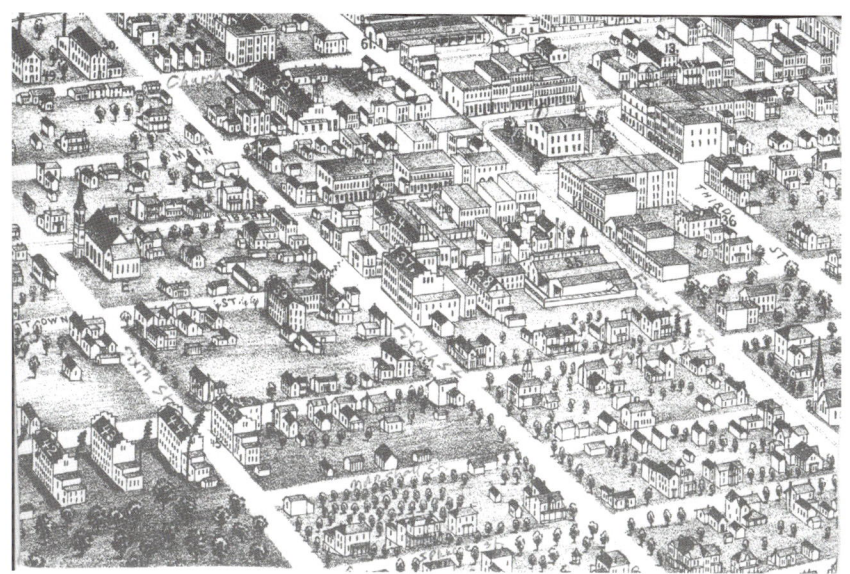

BIRD'S EYE VIEW MAP _C._ 1891 AND PHOTOGRAPH 1940S WINSTON: Old Winston grew out of a need by the Salem Moravians in order to keep outsiders from over running their quiet, peaceful town. In 1849, the General Assembly of North Carolina announced a new county would be drawn and Salem would be its seat of government. Less than half a mile north of Main Street, as shown in above map: 1, the first Winston Court House was erected. The blocks of building directly around the court house represented the town until the Civil War period. By the 1940s photograph, the town was one of the most populated in the state.

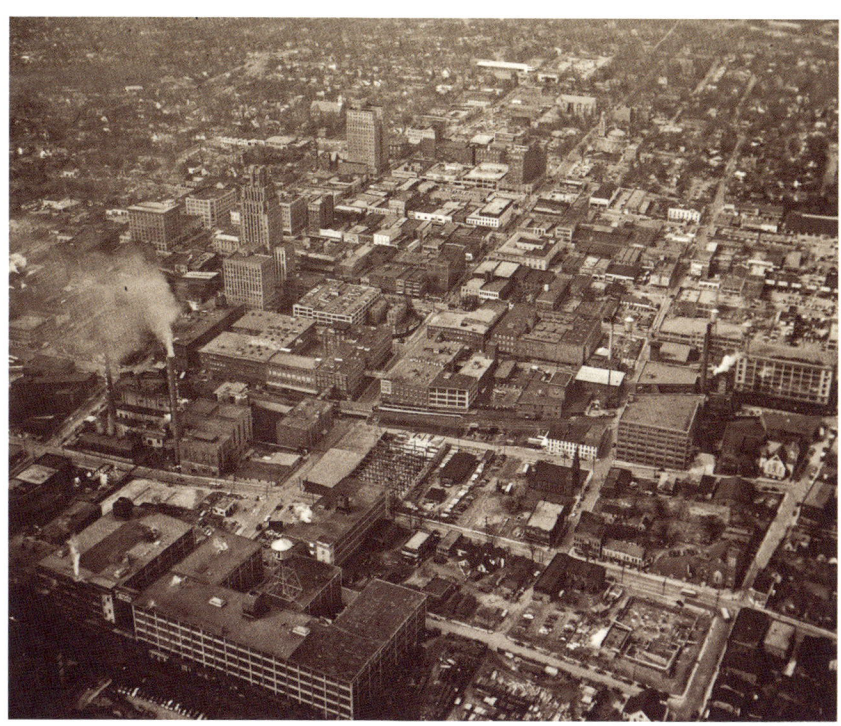

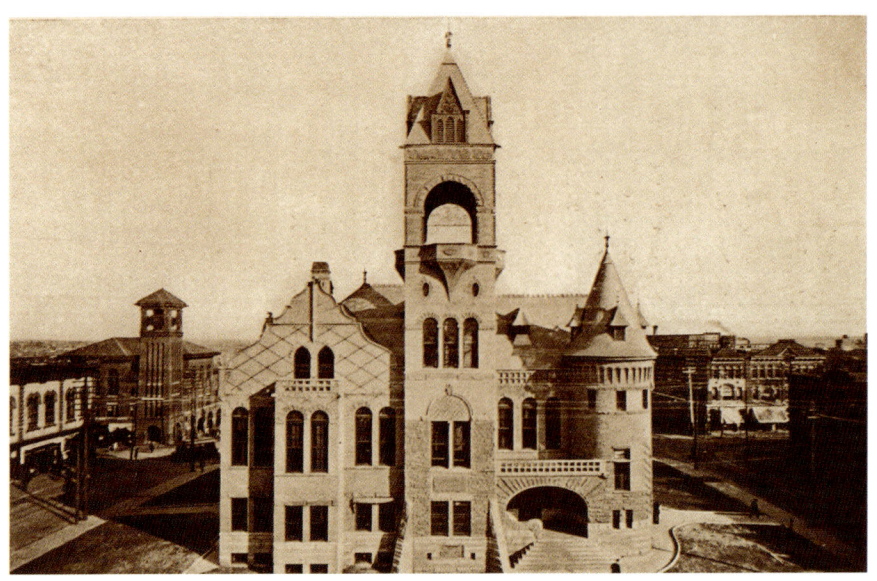

MAIN STREET AT COURT HOUSE SQUARE: In 1896, the Forsyth County Court House was erected. The Romanesque and Gothic architecture became popular in government buildings while ushering the new twentieth-century period. From left of the Court House was F. C. Brown's Dry Goods Store on Fourth; large tower and clock, first Winston Municipal Building housed administrative offices, a jail, an armory, and meat market at Fourth and Main Street. The surrounding structures to the right of the court house were Brown, Rogers, Company (hardware), Robbins Brothers Store (clothing), C. Summerfield (clothing) at Third Street and Main. In 2013 they are the Reynolds Building, Winston Tower (former Wachovia Bank & Trust) One Fourth Street Center and Old Forsyth Court House *c.* 1926.

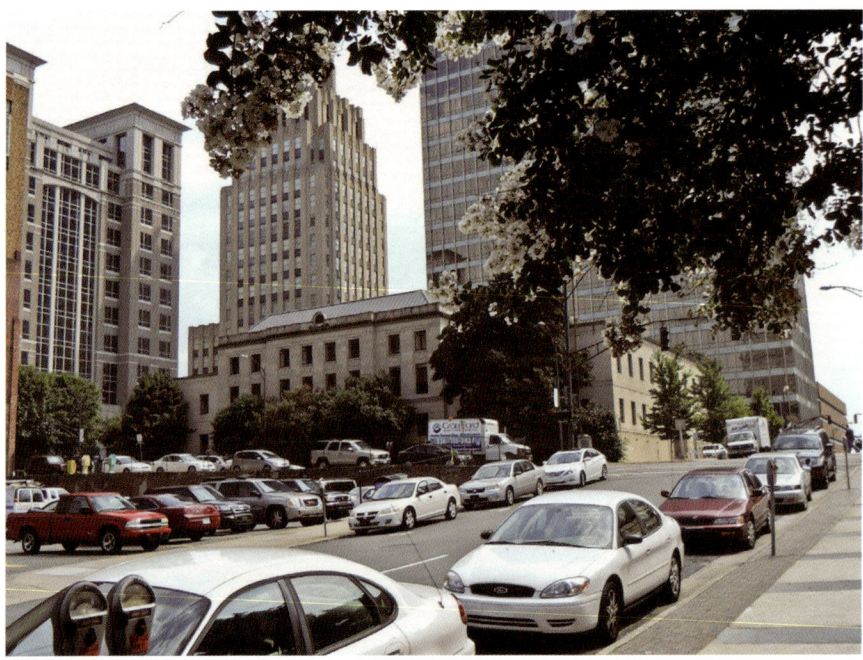

FOURTH STREET AT LIBERTY STREET:

The late nineteenth and early twentieth century brought larger structures to a growing town. The *c.* 1920s photograph above shows the Romanesque Phoenix Hotel built in 1895, and the O'Hanlon Building in 1910 with 1915 additions. Until the mid twentieth century, nineteenth and twentieth century structures existed together. The Phoenix Hotel had seventy-two rooms with steam heat and running water, a real state-of-the-art hotel in the nineteenth century. A cafeteria and W. T. Vogler Jewelry Store (the Vogler family from Salem) shared the building. The O'Hanlon 'skyscraper' was eight stories high with mezzanine on the ground floor. In the current photograph the Phoenix Hotel has been replaced by the Pepper building in 1926. The Pepper building is under renovation currently. The O'Hanlon Building houses businesses and a restaurant.

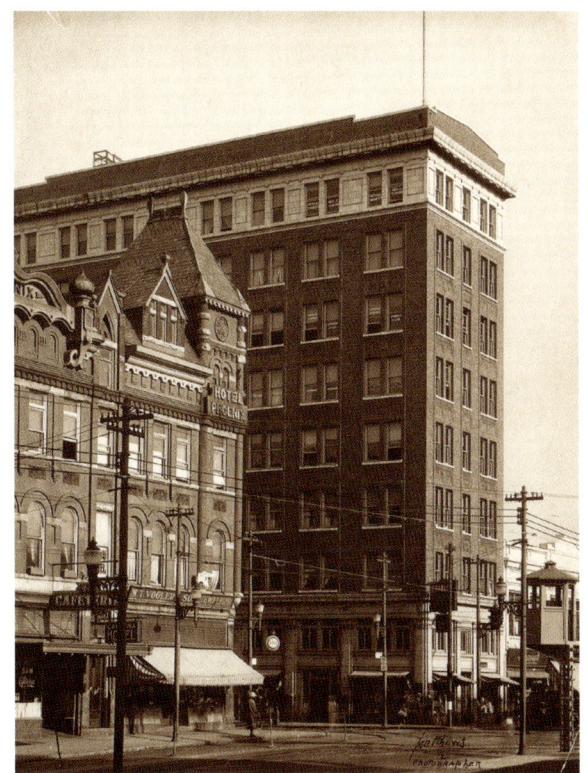

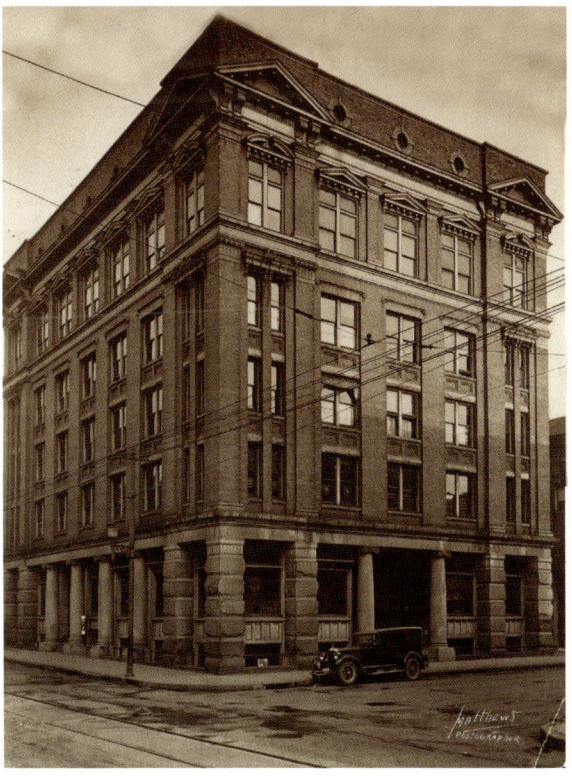

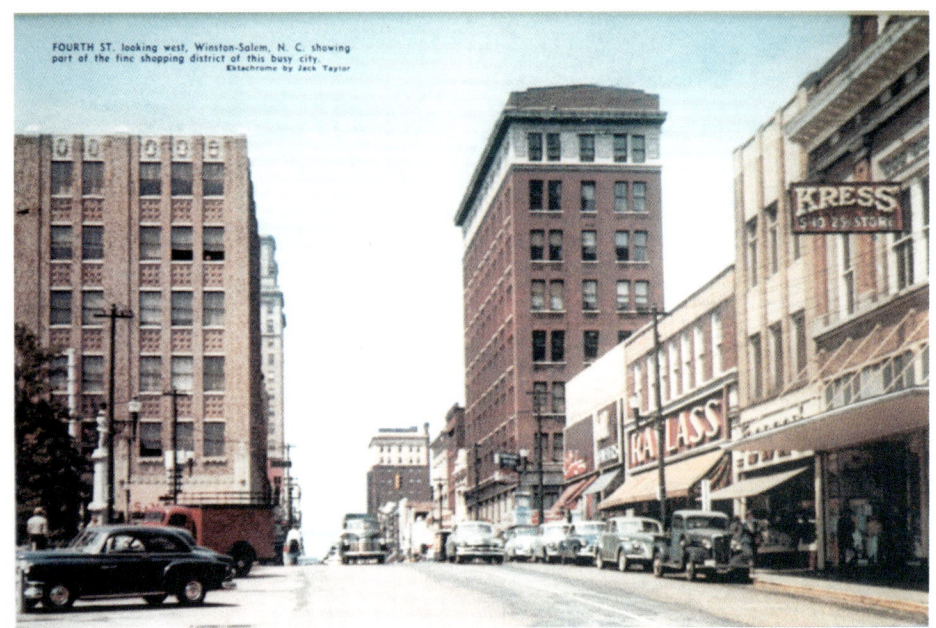

FOURTH STREET AT MAIN STREET LOOKING NORTH: The postcard photograph from the 1940s shows the Pepper Building *c.* 1926 on left and O'Hanlon Building on right. The court house site is just out of view with Confederate Statue, the only visible structure. To the right, the new clothing and dry goods store has been replaced from an earlier time period and replaced by national chain stores: Kress, Raylass, and United Retail Drug Company. Currently, the chain store buildings have been razed and replaced in 2010 by another multistory building, The One Fourth Street Center, a large lawyer firm.

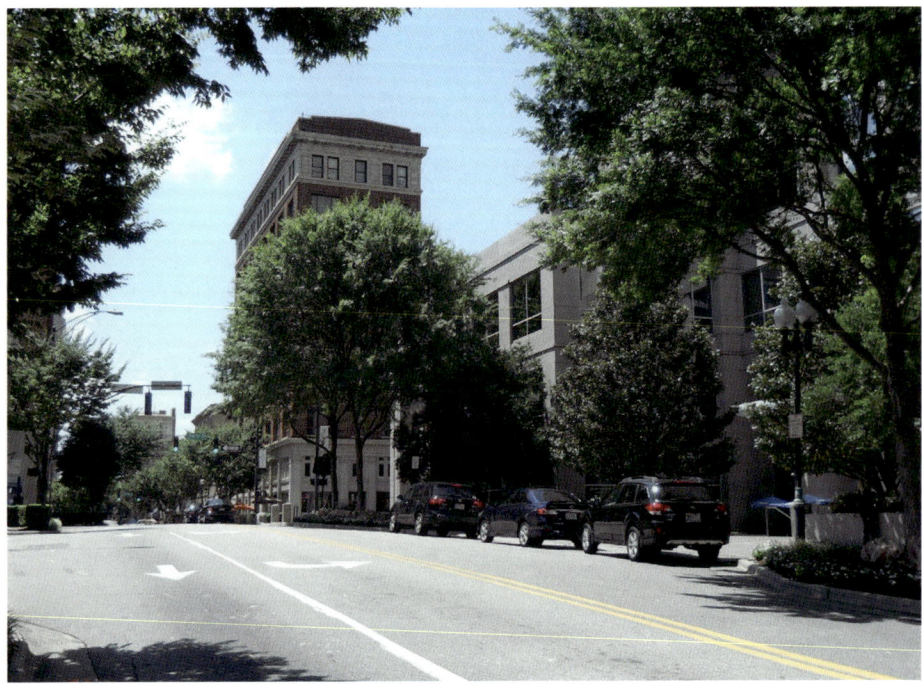

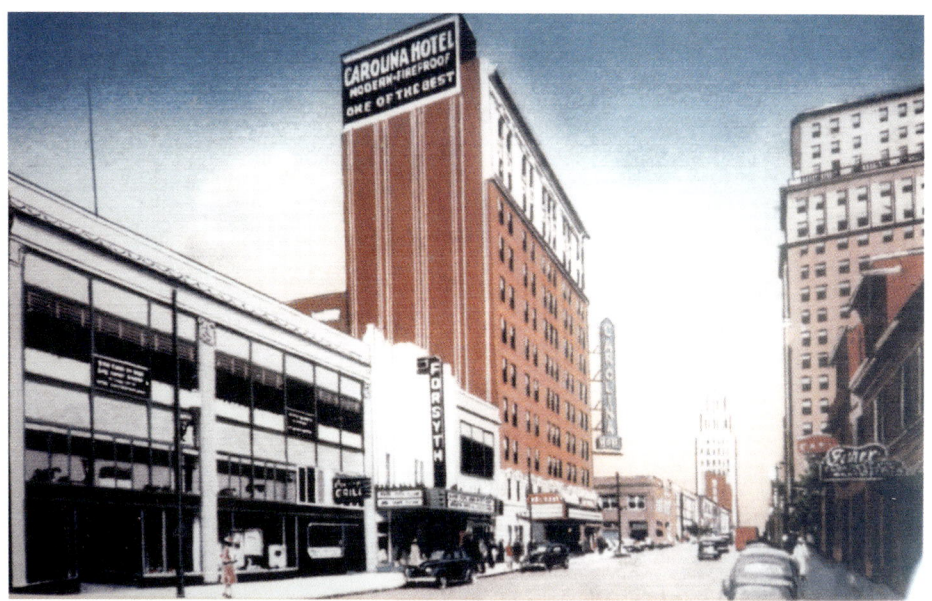

FOURTH STREET AT SPRUCE STREET LOOKING SOUTH: Another postcard photograph looks south from the previous northern postcard *c.* 1940s; left is the Forsyth Theater *c.* 1930s (a 'B' level movie theater), the Carolina Hotel and Theater Complex *c.* 1927; on right the towering Nissen Building. In the distant is the Reynolds Building from 1929. Today, the Carolina Hotel Theater has been revamped and is now the Steven's Center of Performing Arts of the North Carolina School of the Arts. Buildings on left and right are local restaurants and eateries. The Nissen Buildings looms in the background.

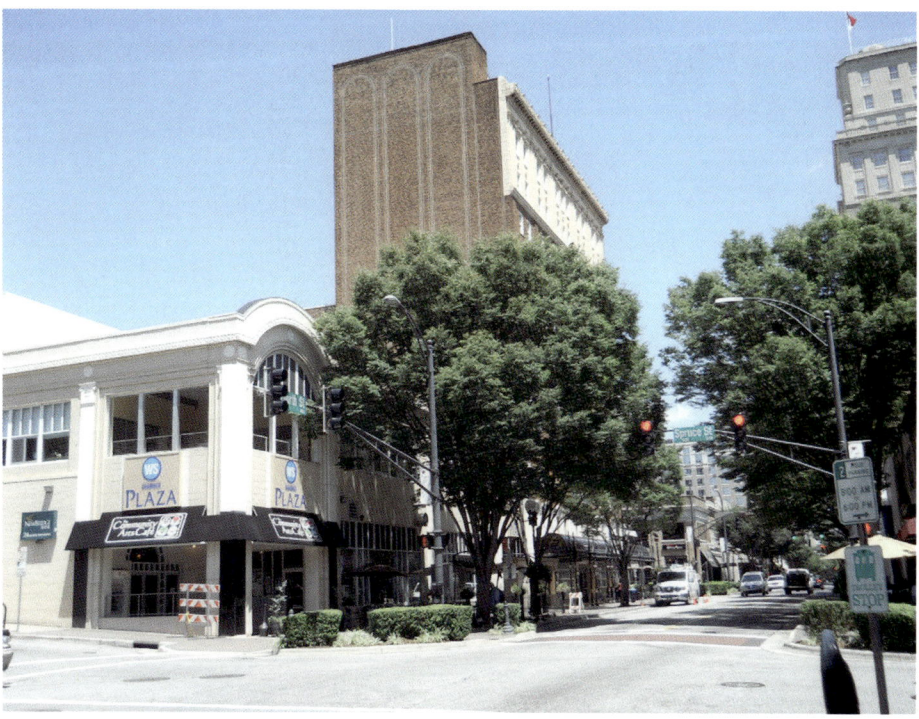

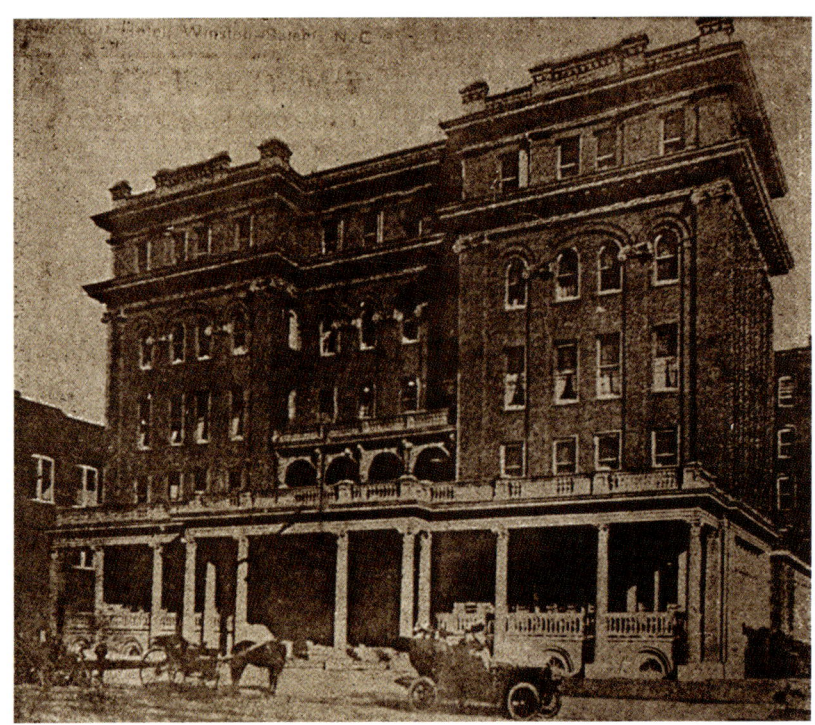

200 BLOCK OF MAIN STREET LOOKING EAST: After the Zinzendorf Resort Hotel burned in 1892, the area became the West End neighborhood. The Zinzendorf name carried on and became the premiere hotel after renovation of the Old Jones Hotel on Main Street in 1910. Today, the Federal Building holding Federal court cases and the International Revenue Service offices (IRS) *c.* 1975 occupies the site.

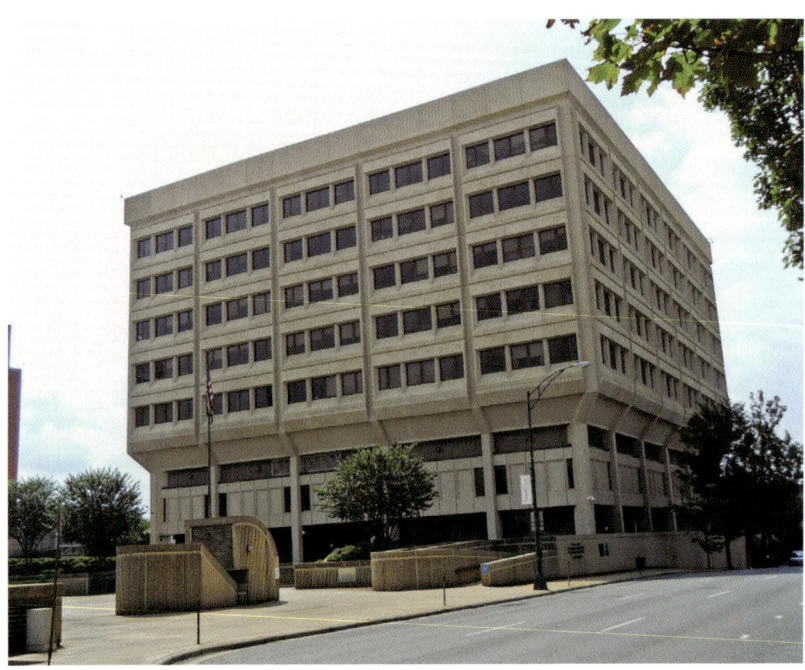

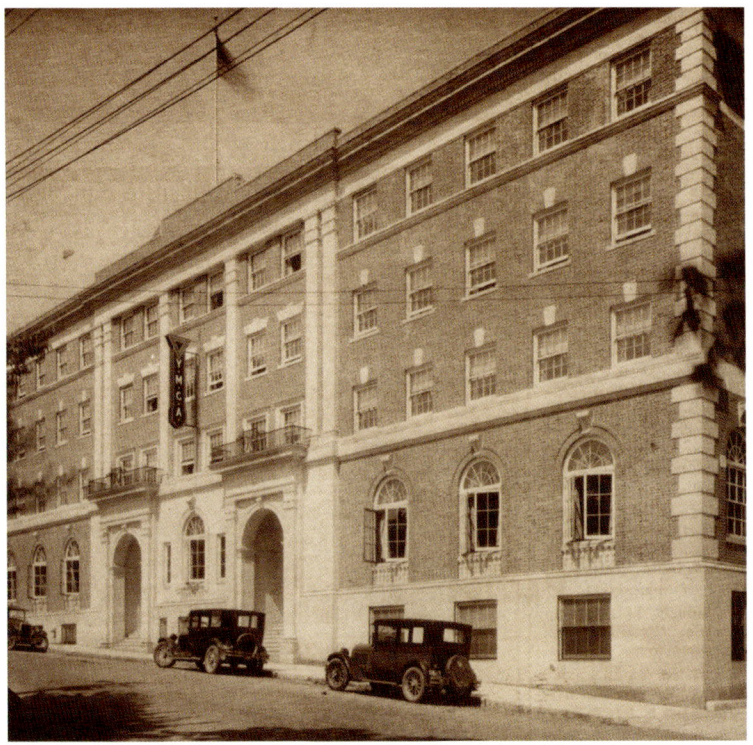

Spruce Street Looking East: The Young Men's Christian Association (YMCA) was brand new in this 1926 photograph. The YMCA in 1907 had relocated from its earlier building at the corner of Fourth Street and Cherry Street, two blocks south. The original YMCA was still in good repair, but the block with the Winston High School next door was scheduled to be razed for the new 'skyscraper,' the Nissen Building. Currently, the YMCA has been renovated for condominiums and offices.

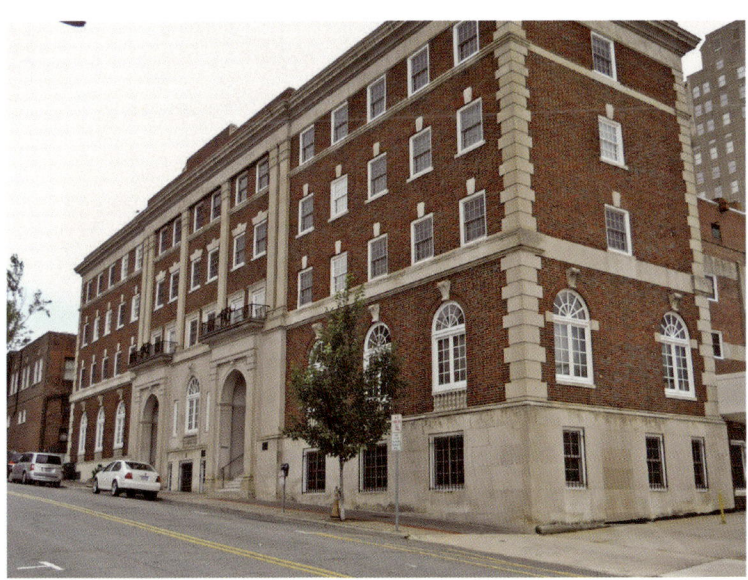

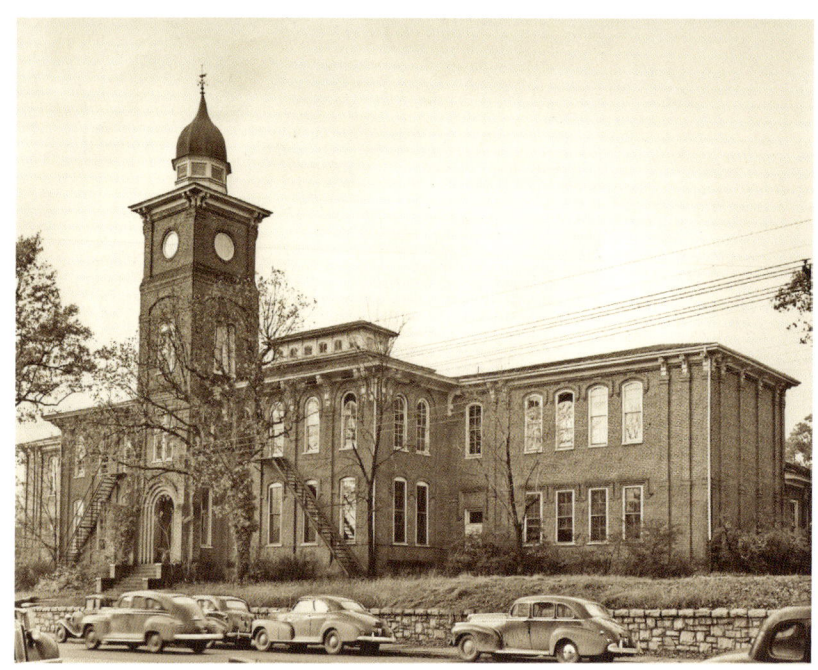

FOURTH STREET AT BROAD AND GREEN STREET LOOKING EAST: The
Winston Graded School *c.* 1882 and photograph 1940 began the exodus of Old
Winston's downtown to move westward. Much like the western expansion into
West Salem by East Salem in 1850, Old Winston's boarders were growing. One of the
first graded schools in North Carolina, Winston Graded School, changed to West
End Graded School to reflect the newly created West End neighborhood. Today the
building shown is the Wells Fargo Bank center formally Wachovia Bank & Trust and
before that the Sears Roebuck & Company.

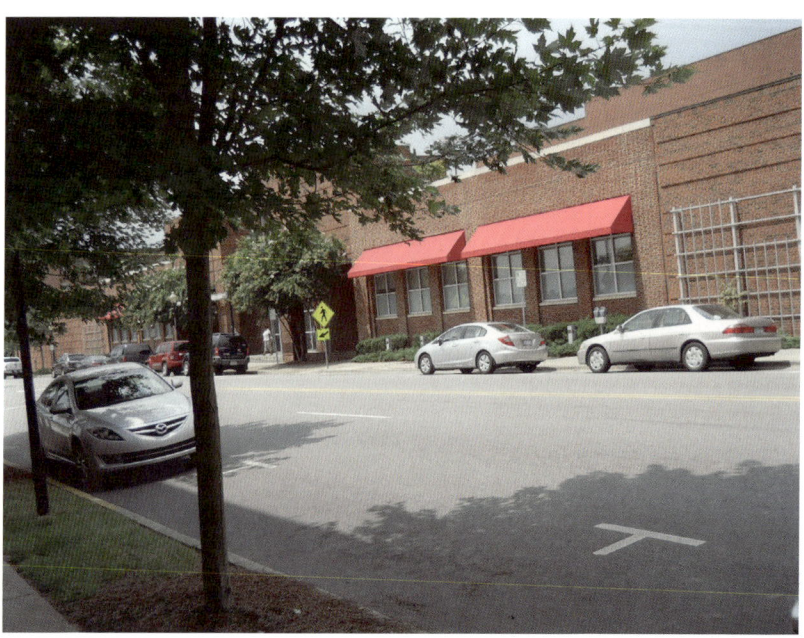

72

NORTHWEST BOULEVARD AT HAWTHORNE ROAD LOOKING WEST:

As the citizens of the newly merged Winston-Salem (1913) moved further west, they erected the effluent neighborhoods of West Highland and Buena Vista. With this effluence brought larger and greater teaching facilities. The Calvin H. Wiley Grammar School grades 1-8, opened in 1923, named for a local resident, educator, and superintendent of modern North Carolina schools. Today the school, in all of its grandeur, overlooks Hanes Park and Athletic fields in 2013.

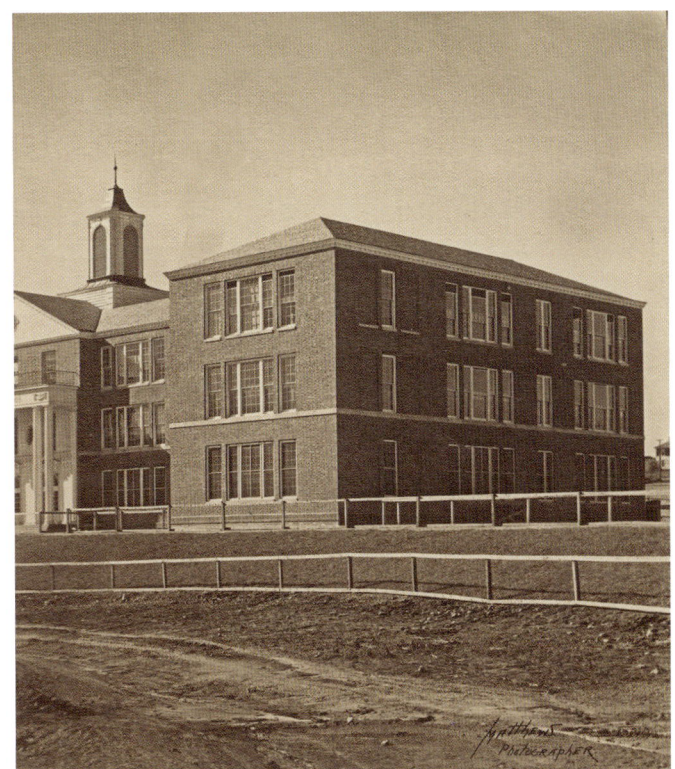

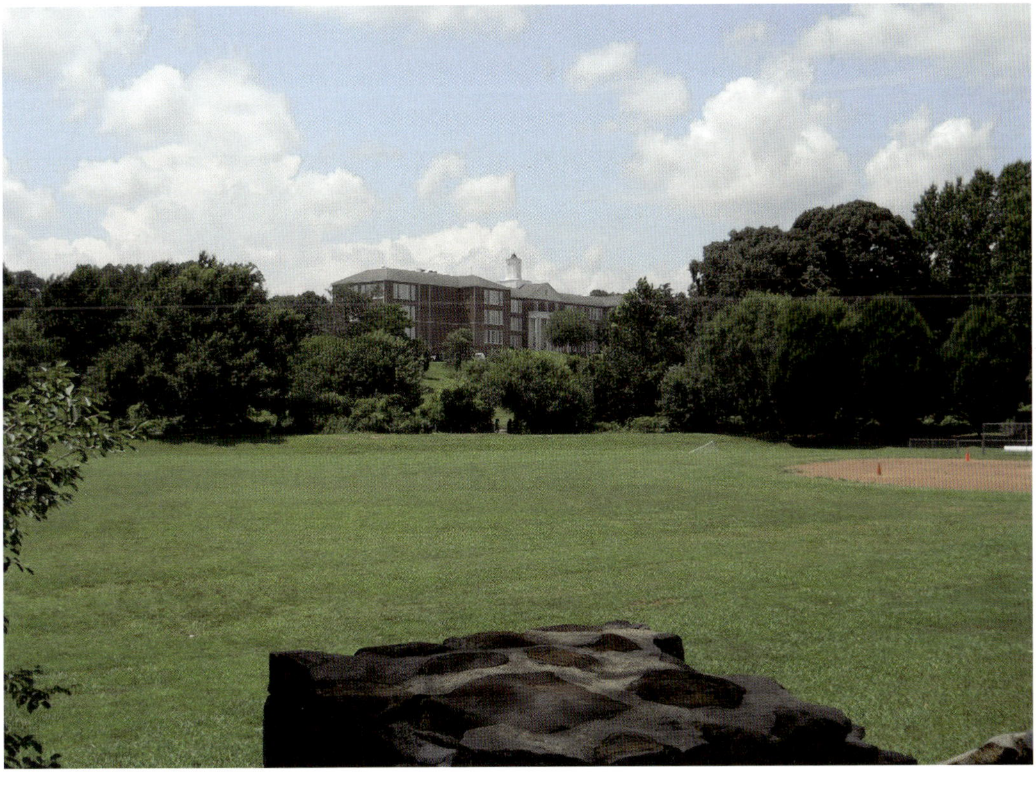

73

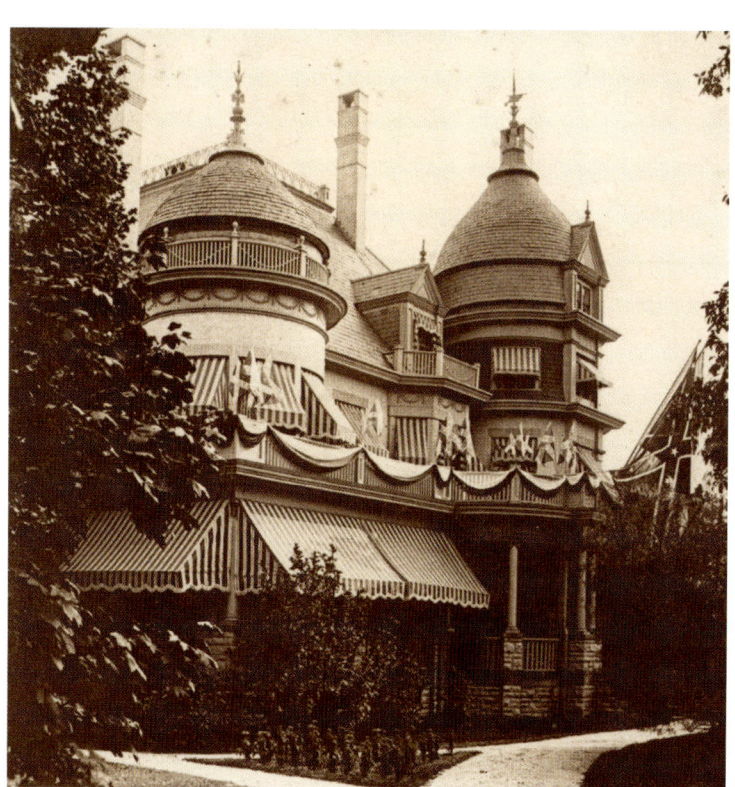

FIFTH STREET AND SPRING STREET LOOKING SOUTH: Richard J. Reynolds, founder of one of the most prominent tobacco industries in the world (R. J. R Tobacco Company) resided with his family at 666 West Fifth Street. This Victorian, antebellum mansion was one of several found on 'Millionaires' Row' at the 600 block of Fifth Street. In 2013, we find the central branch of the Forsyth County Public Library dating from 1952.

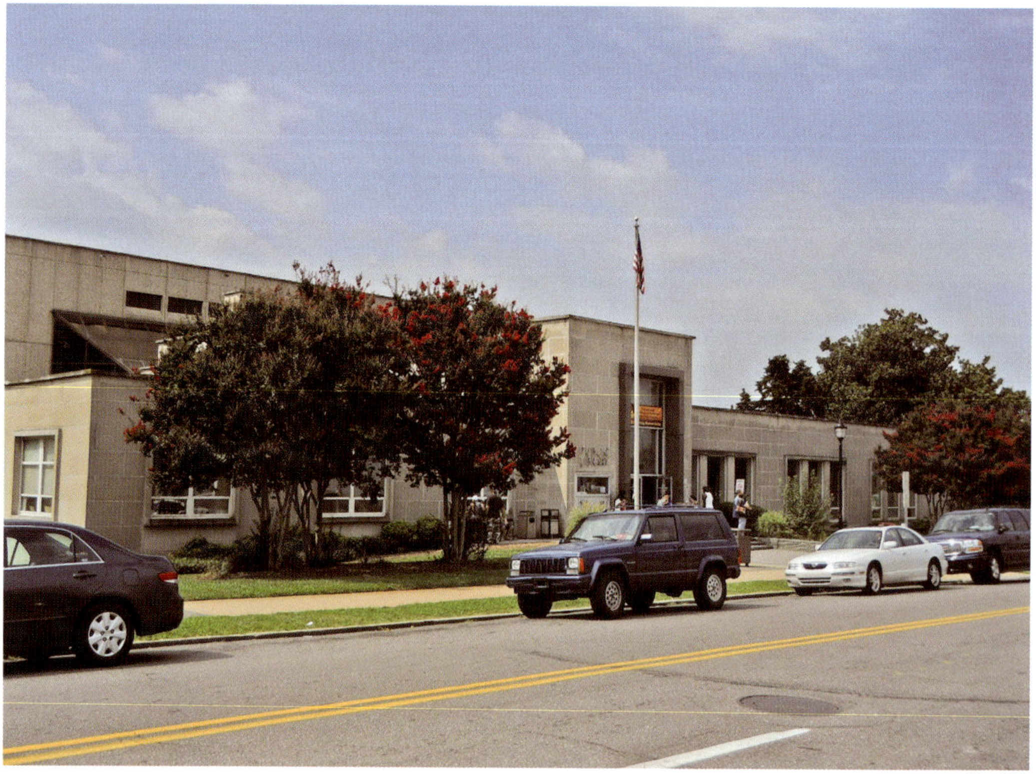

74

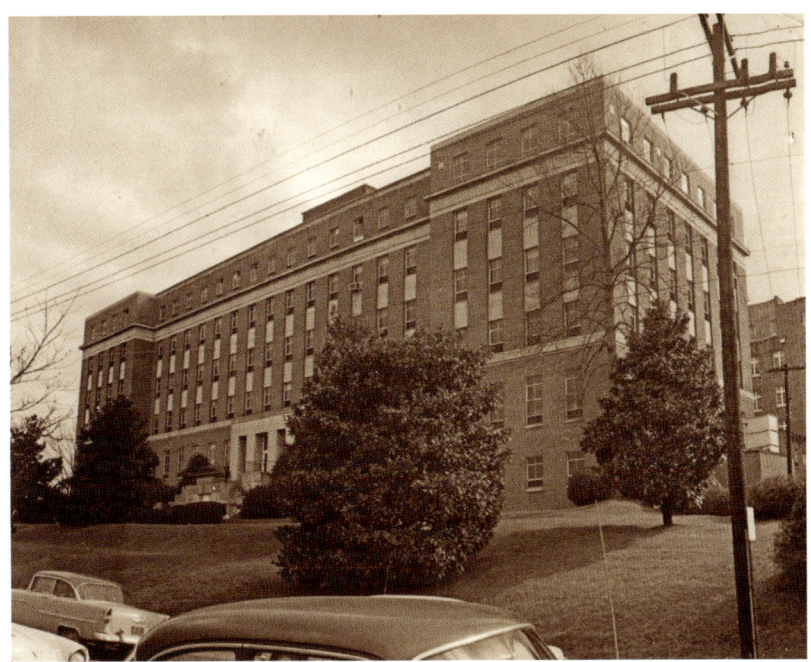

HAWTHORNE ROAD AND REYNOLDA ROAD: The North Carolina Baptist Hospital was founded in 1923 after the expansion westward by Winston-Salem residence. A large rise, 'Hawthorne Hill,' in the Ardmore neighborhood *c.* 1910 is shown in this 1950 photo. The hospital benefactors traced their roots to Wake Forest College *c.* 1836 in Wake Forest, North Carolina, a Baptist College. With the merger of medicine, religion, and liberal academics, Wake Forest College, now University campus, was moved to Winston-Salem in 1951 and is shown in this photograph *c.* 1956.

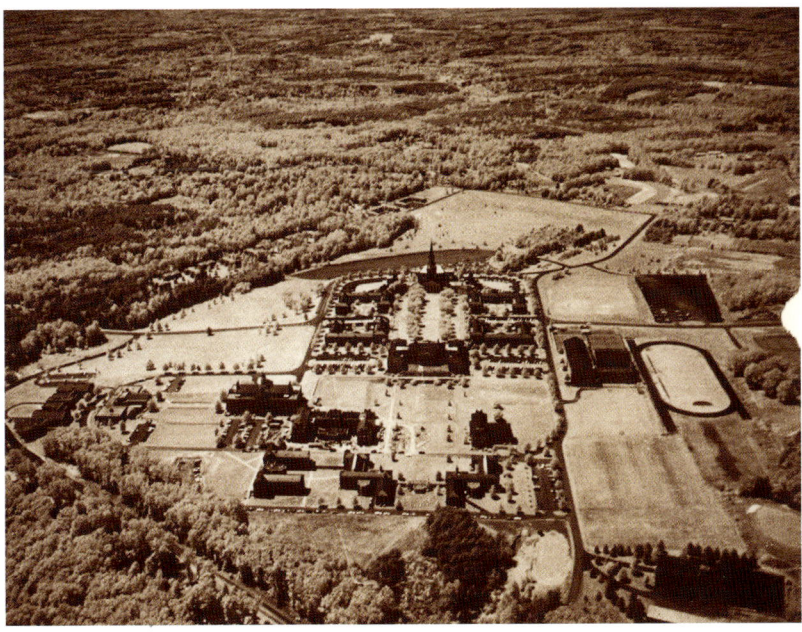

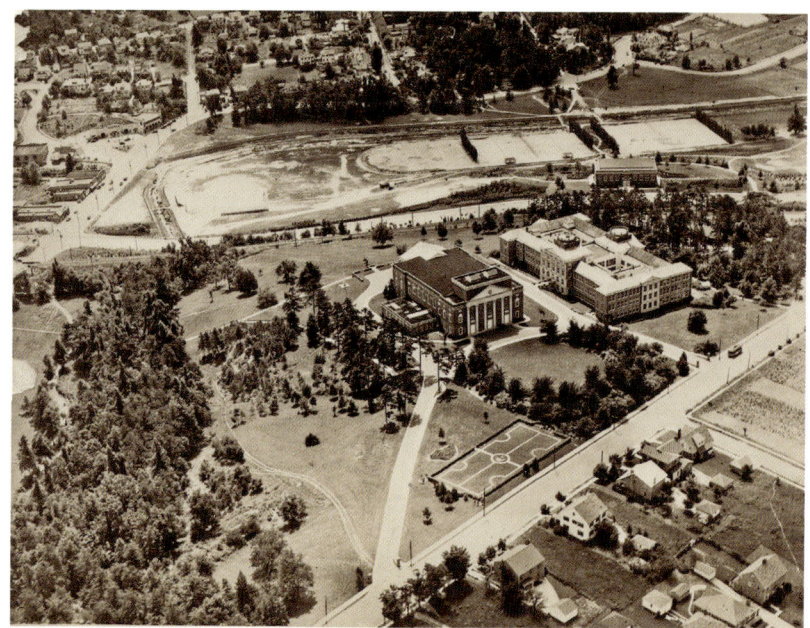

NORTHWEST BOULEVARD 'SOCIETY HILL': The 1920s saw Winston-Salem dubbed as 'A City of Industry' in 1917, adding to its résumé academic, medical, and religious excellence. Reynolds High School and Auditorium named for R. J. Reynolds is shown in 1924 as a brand new structure. The effluent Buena Vista neighborhood in the foreground and Hanes Park and Recreation area named for P. H. Hanes, R. J. R's equal in textiles in the background. Reynolds, Hanes, Gray, and Atkins High Schools were all named for 'Movers and Shakers' of Winston-Salem. Thomas Holcomb, a 1955 graduate of Reynolds High School is shown with the main campus *c.* 1978.

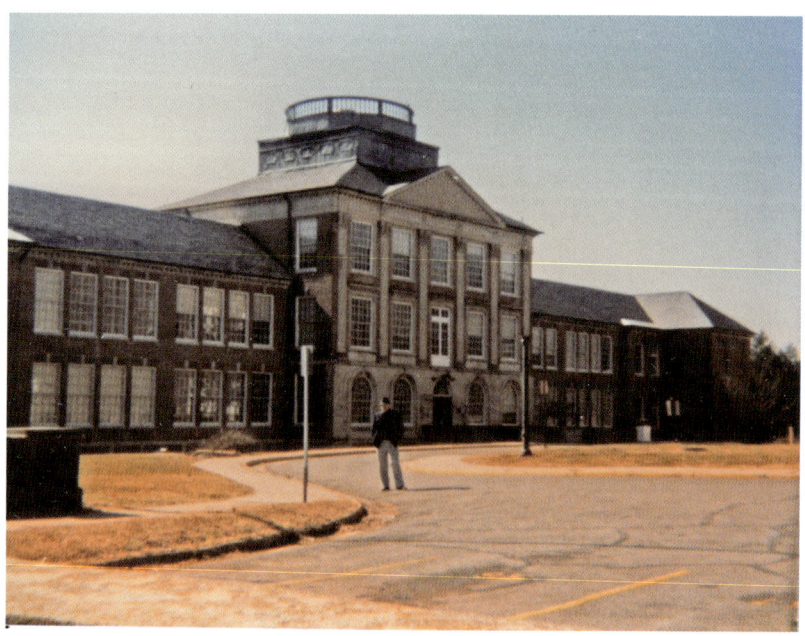

SILAS CREEK PARKWAY AT HAWTHORNE ROAD: R. J. Reynolds gave the land of his old racetrack to build the City Memorial Hospital on East Fourth Street *c.* 1914. A new hospital was needed in the late 1950s shown in this photograph from 1960. The western leg of Interstate 40 and newly constructed Silas Creek Parkway are shown in their infancy as a backdrop to the new Forsyth Memorial Hospital. This current photograph shows the hospital after it has expanded into the community and is one of several medical facilities of Novant Health, a leading medical facility in the United States.

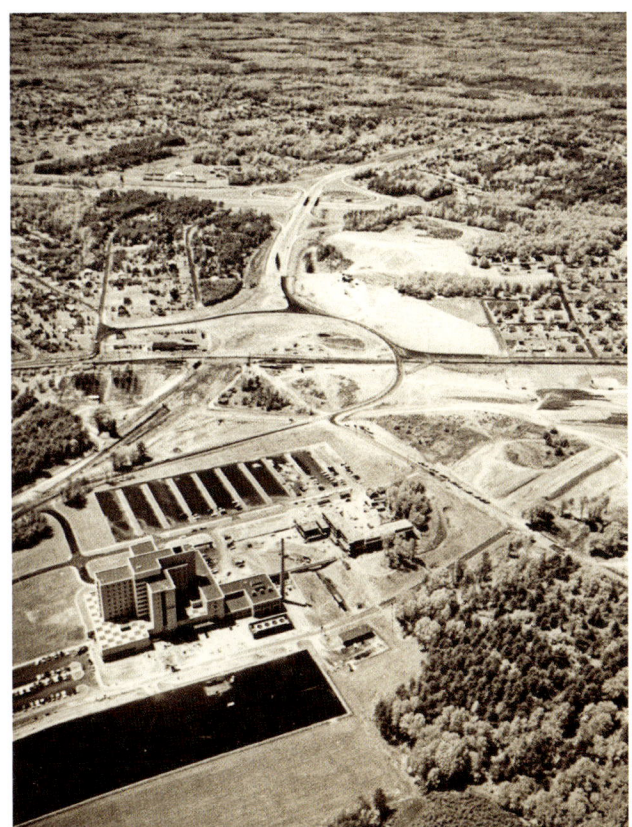

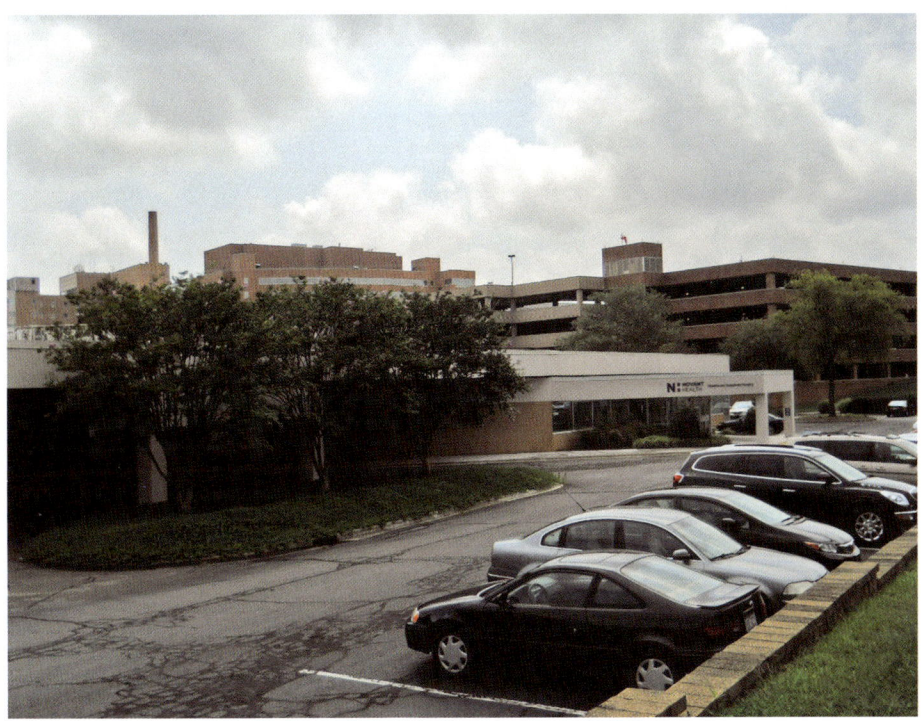

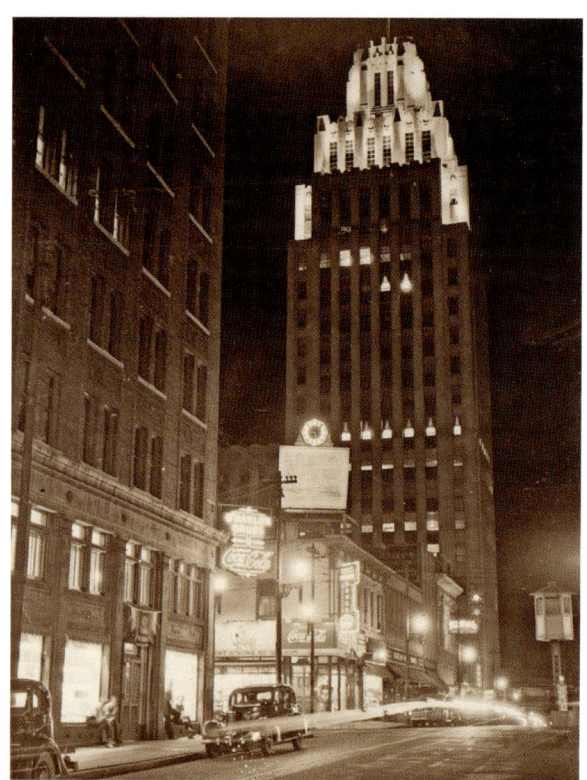

FOURTH STREET LOOKING EAST TO MAIN STREET:

The downtown at night comes alive, then and now; 'Lights, Camera, Action' in this 1930s photograph. The O'Hanlon Drug Store (left) and York Drugs (across street) was a meeting place for young and old alike. The street continues with Raylass and Kress Stores for styles of fashion. The Police Tower on the right was used to control the traffic, both auto and trolley. The Reynolds Building *c.* 1929 oversees it all. Currently, the scene is similar at night with restaurants and eateries. Although, the Reynolds executives and employees have left the Reynolds Building for the next door Reynolds Tower, the Reynolds Building will always be the prototype of the Empire State Building in New York City.

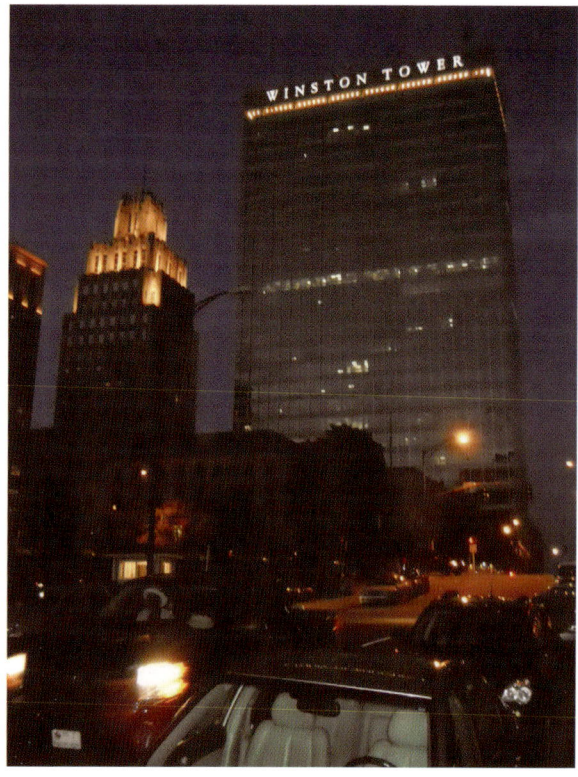

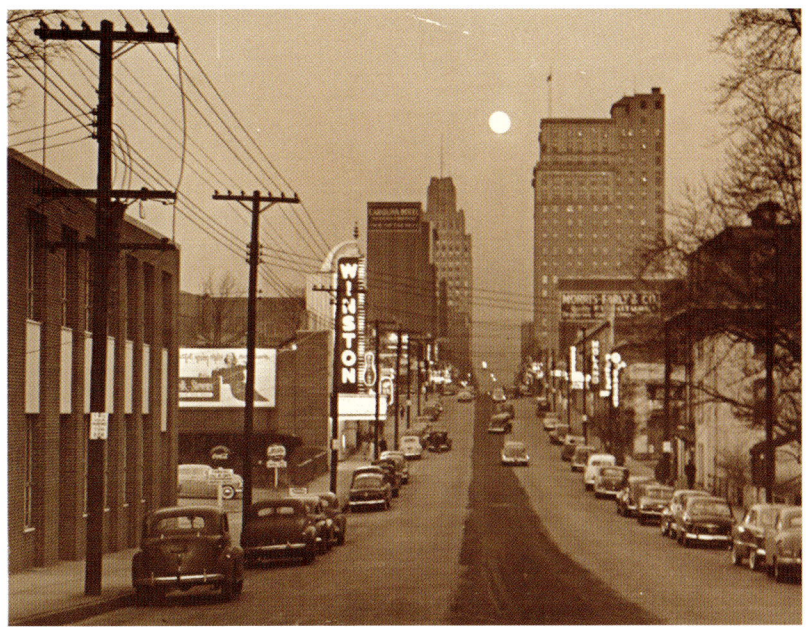

FOURTH STREET LOOKING EAST AT SPRUCE STREET: Nights in Winston-Salem changed after the trolley lines were taken up in 1936 and replaced with modern buses in this photograph from 1952. The Winston Theater, the first air-conditioned theater *c.* 1948, is shown and beyond it is the Winstonette Restaurant and the twentieth-century bowling alley. On the right side are the Alexander Apartments, Dobby's Bakery, and the Nolan Company, a heating supply company. Currently, we see on the left Step One, a non-profit organization and across the street from non-profit city parking garage. Restaurants and bars continue up Fourth Street on right side. From the Steven's Center on left and Nissen Building on right, restaurants and bars continue down Fourth toward Main Street.

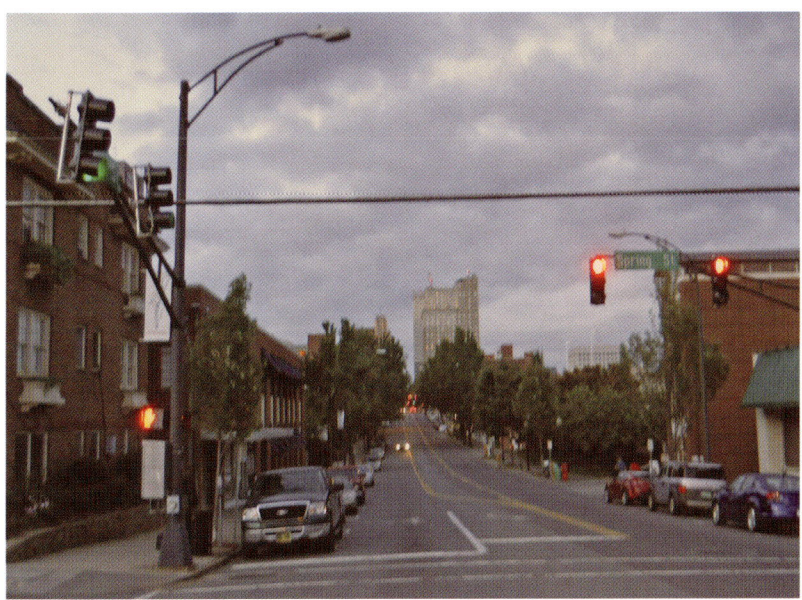

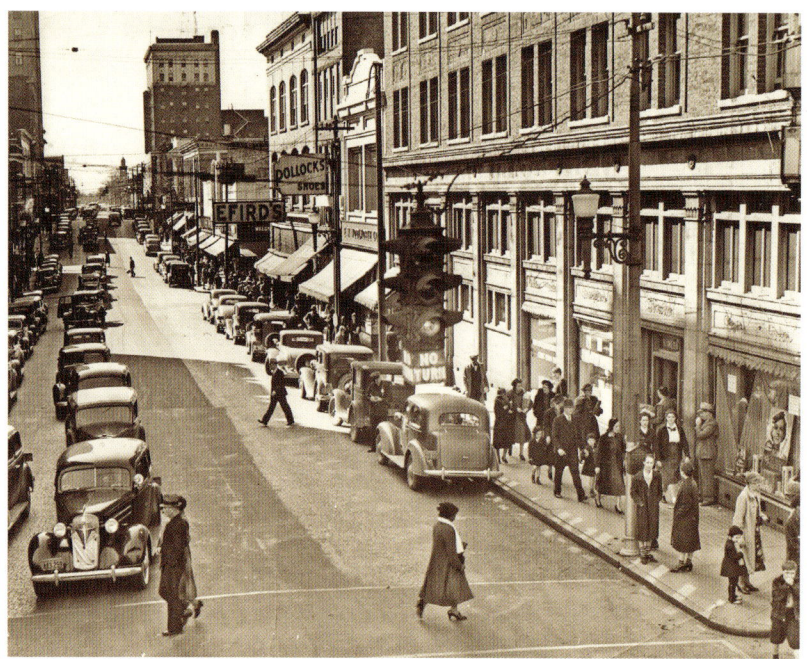

THE CHRISTMAS SEASON OF 1939: Shopping 'hustle and bustle' is shown as the old timers used to say. The Great Depression was somewhat distant and the war had not yet begun. The styles of the day can be found on the citizens and by way of Pollocks Shoes, Efird's Clothing Store, O'Hanlon Drug Store, Hines Shoes, and Mother and Daughter's Store. That year, the Carolina Theater was playing *Gone With The Wind*, *The Wizard of Oz*, and *Union Pacific*. The West End School Tower can be seen in the distance. Currently, in 2013, the Walgreens Drug Store located behind the Efird's sign and the Carolina Hotel Building are the only remaining structures from the past. Restaurants and eateries have replaced them on this Fourth Street corridor.

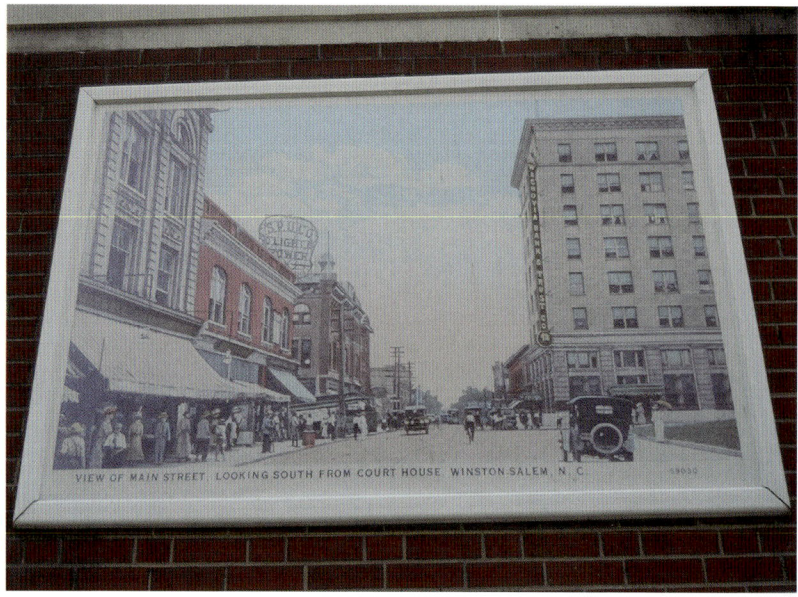

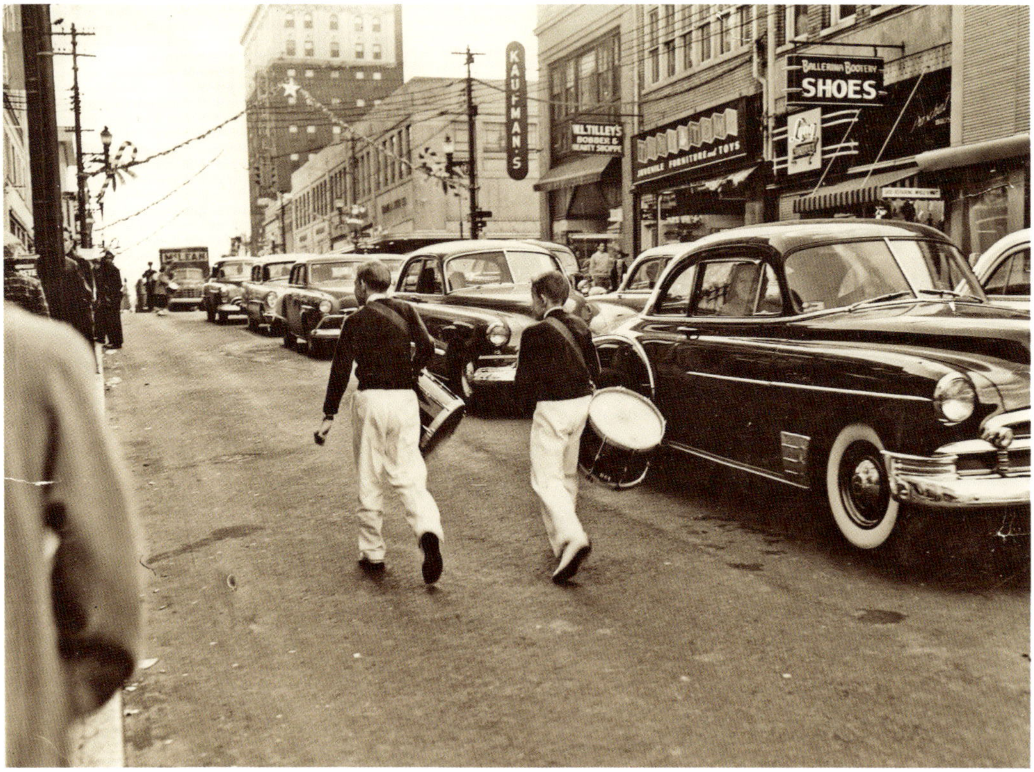

FOURTH STREET, CHERRY STREET, AND HANES MALL SHOPPING CENTER:

This 1950s photograph shows Retail Merchants Parade also known as the Winston-Salem Christmas Parade winding down and the Christmas shopping soon to begin. The two blocks of Fourth Street at Cherry and Marshall Street began business expansion in the late 1920s and early 1930s when prominent stores such as Hine Bagby, Norman Stockton, Kaufman's Ballerina Bootery and Thalheimers can be identified in photograph. Tiny Town carrying juvenile furniture and toys was the place for the kids at Christmastime. The bottom photograph shows a young lady, Tommie Howell, and Santa at the new Hanes Mall Shopping Center *c.* 1975.

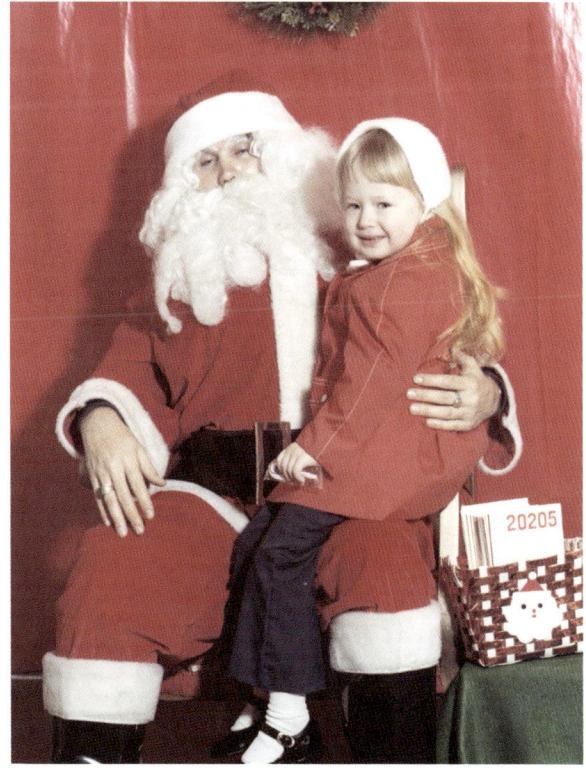

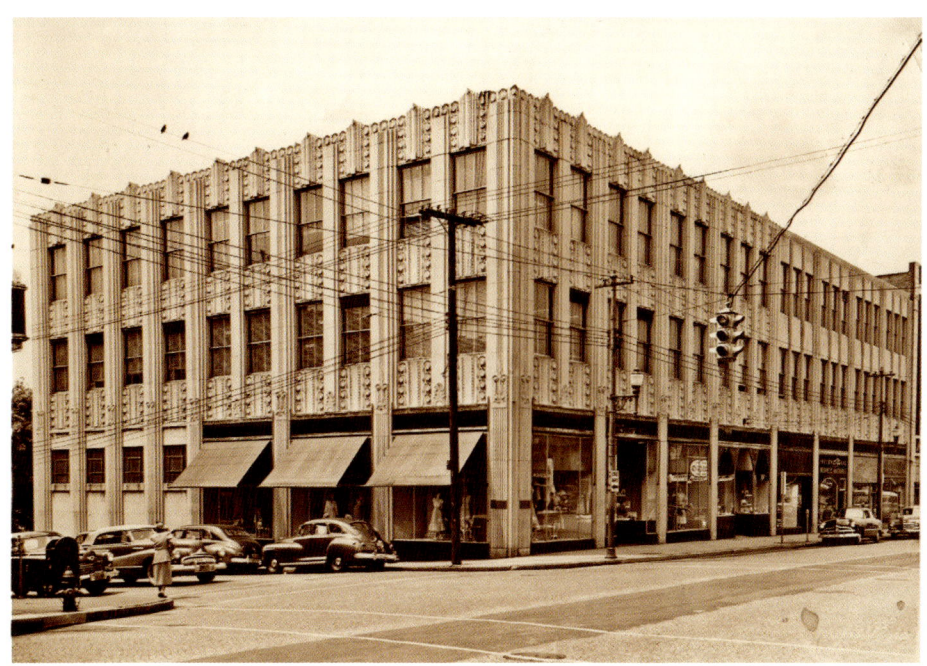

FOURTH STREET LOOKING SOUTH TO SPRUCE STREET: The Thalheimers Department Store at Fourth and Spruce was constructed in the Art Deco style. This was one of the most prominent and fashionable stores during this time period. In the 1940s and 1950s, it shared its establishment with a new and state-of-the-art business, International Business Machines (IBM). In the current photograph, the store's occupants are March of Dimes, a political center for candidates, and trendy clothing store.

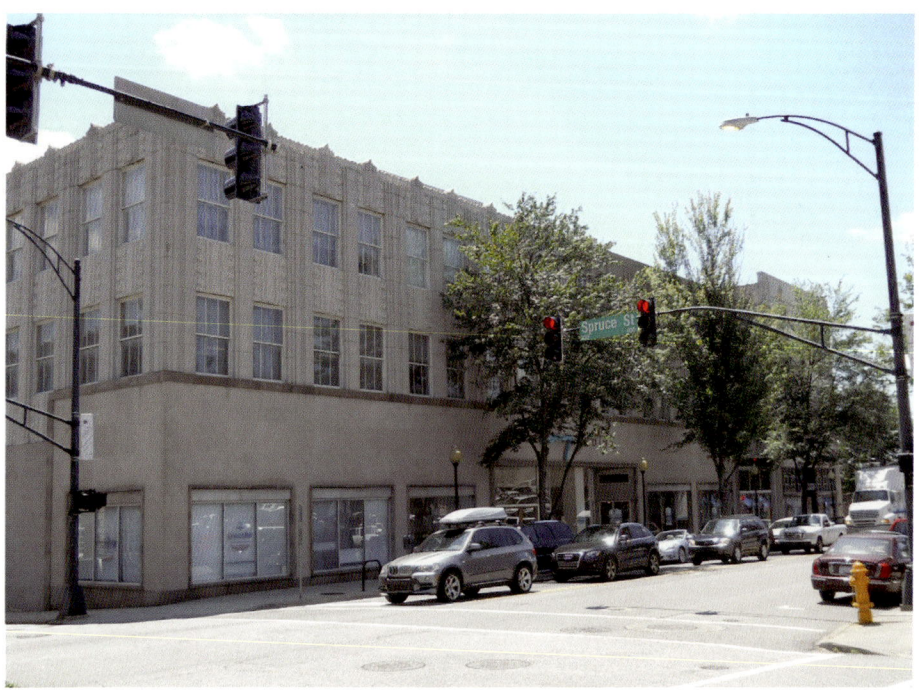

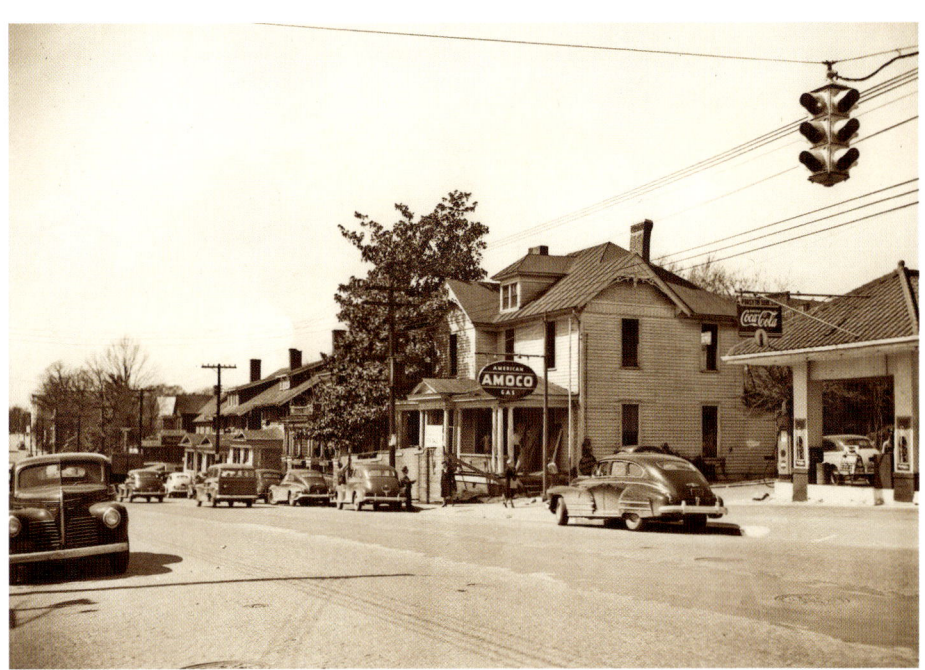

FOURTH STREET LOOKING WEST ON POPLAR STREET: Before the West End neighborhood began in the late 1890s, the natural evolution of Old Winston housing took shape: First centering around the court house block of Main Street, Liberty Street, Old Town (Trade) at Fourth Street; then branching out after Civil War Reconstruction period around 1870s. Photograph *c.* 1940s shows such a neighborhood from this early period; however, by the late 1940s, more expansion of the city's businesses westward saw a dismantling of older homes of the period. Today the city's Chamber of Commerce business center exists on this site.

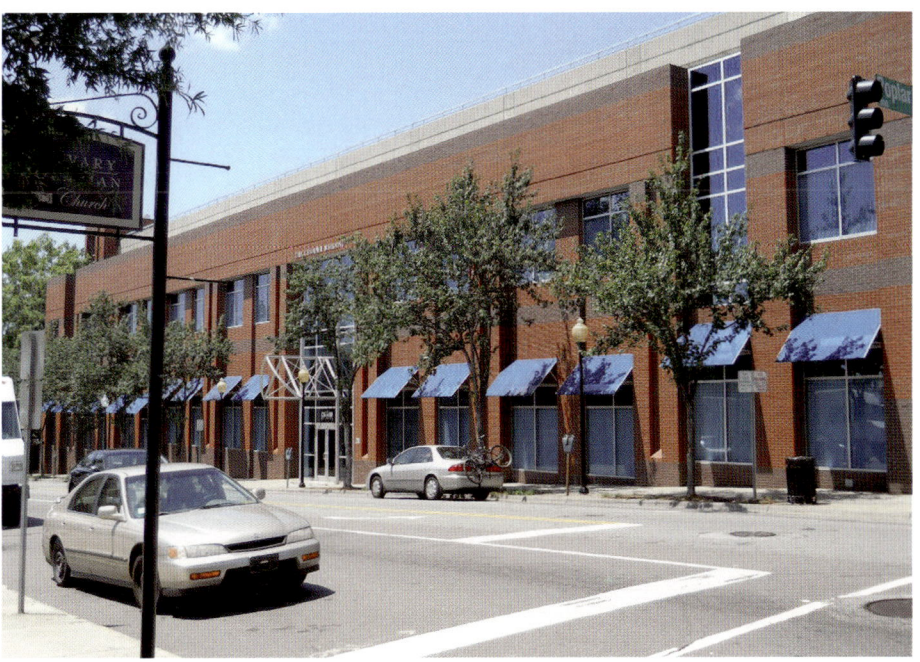

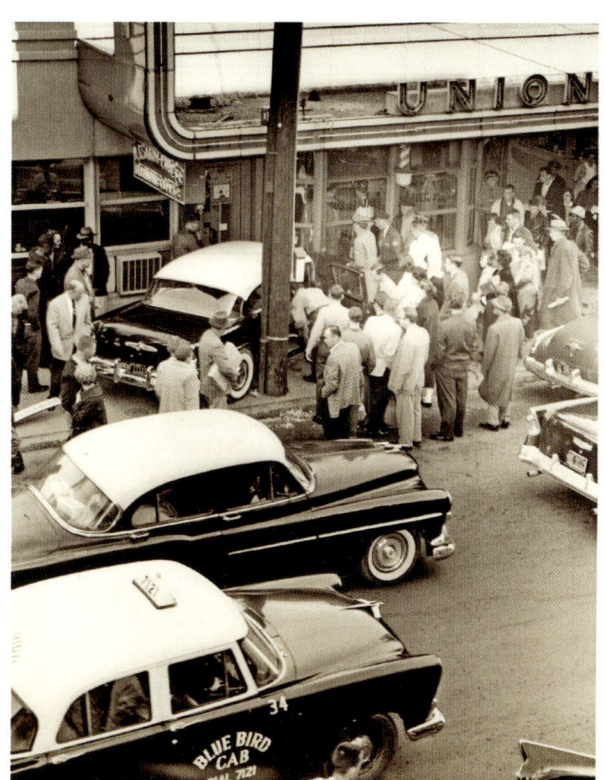

CHERRY STREET LOOKING WEST NEAR FIFTH STREET:

The Union Bus Station was always a busy hub of activity. The local buses, which had replaced the trolley cars after 1936, needed a central location. Also, the national chain of buses: Trail Ways Bus Lines and Greyhound Bus Lines needed a terminal as well. Located next to the premier hotel in this 1950 photograph is the Robert E. Lee Hotel *c.* 1923. The scene looks more like a New York City moment with all the Blue Bird Taxi Cabs assembled at one location. Thankfully, this was just a simple accident getting to close to the bus station. The postcard photograph below shows the new Union Bus Station.

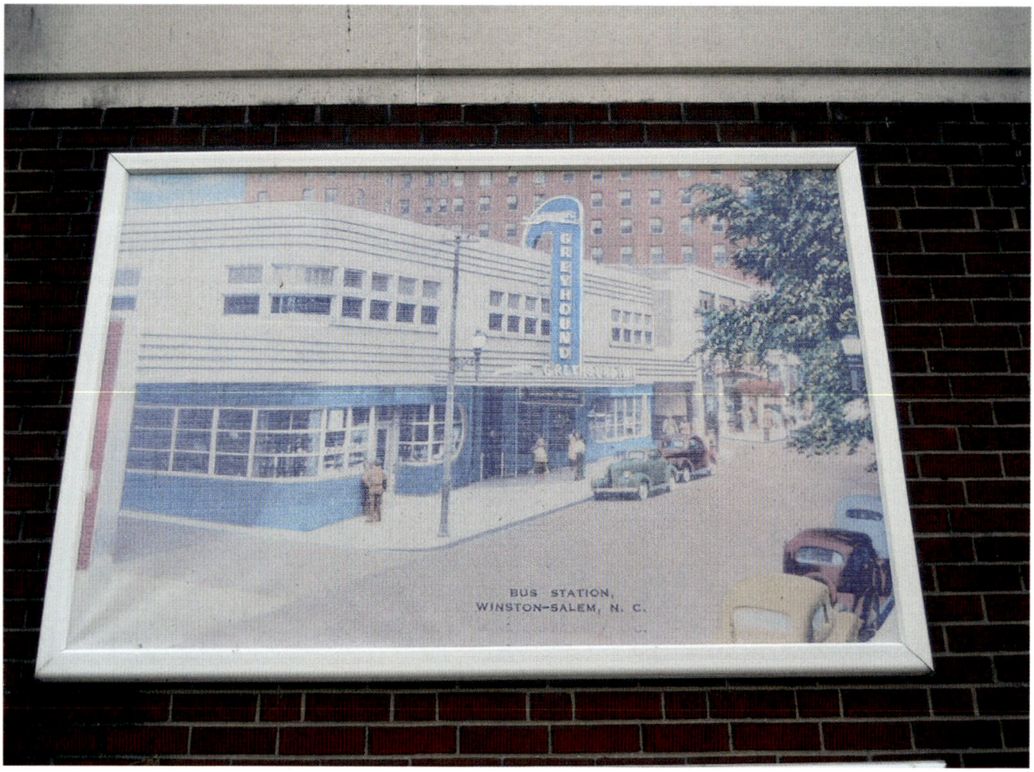

BUS STATION,
WINSTON-SALEM, N. C.

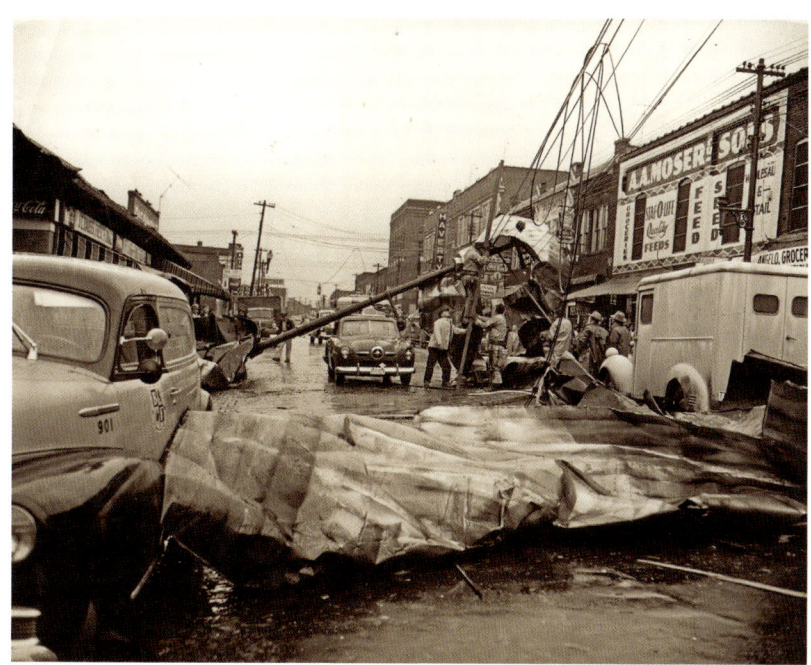

TRADE STREET LOOKING NORTH FROM FIFTH STREET: Unfortunately, another accident scene appears in this photograph, but this time by 'Mother Nature'. Old Town Street (Trade Street) in this 1950s photograph shows the businesses, which grew around the tobacco auction houses that trace their roots back to before the Civil War period. Angelo Grocery, A. A. Moser & Sons Seed & Feed Grocery Store, the Haverity Furniture Store replaced the majestic First Presbyterian Church 1850. The current landscape shows the same building structures, but with bungalows, town houses, and restaurants occupying them today.

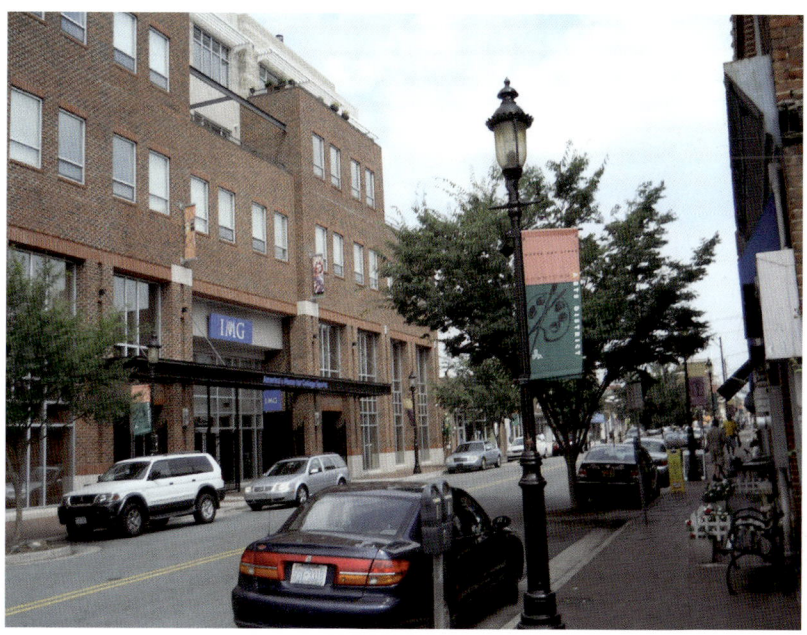

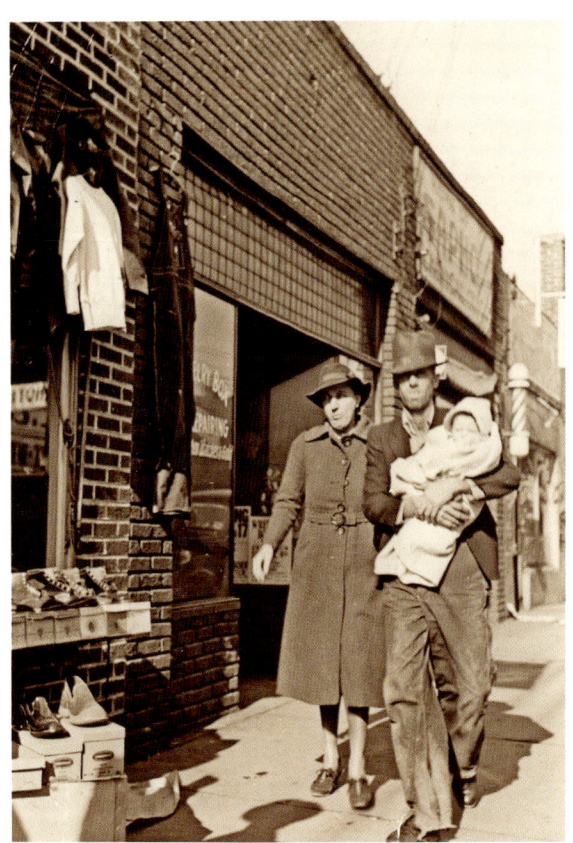

TRADE STREET LOOKING NORTH AT SIXTH STREET:

Further east on Trade Street is the area shown here in the early 1930s. The heart of the Depression had arrived and this couple epitomizes the expression, 'Brother Can You Spare a Dime?' Like many residents who were not employed at R. J. R Tobacco or Hanes Textiles, there was a lack of jobs which made life very hard. Today, the 'Trade Street Art District' has given a new face to old buildings with art and jewelry shops as shown in the 2013 photograph.

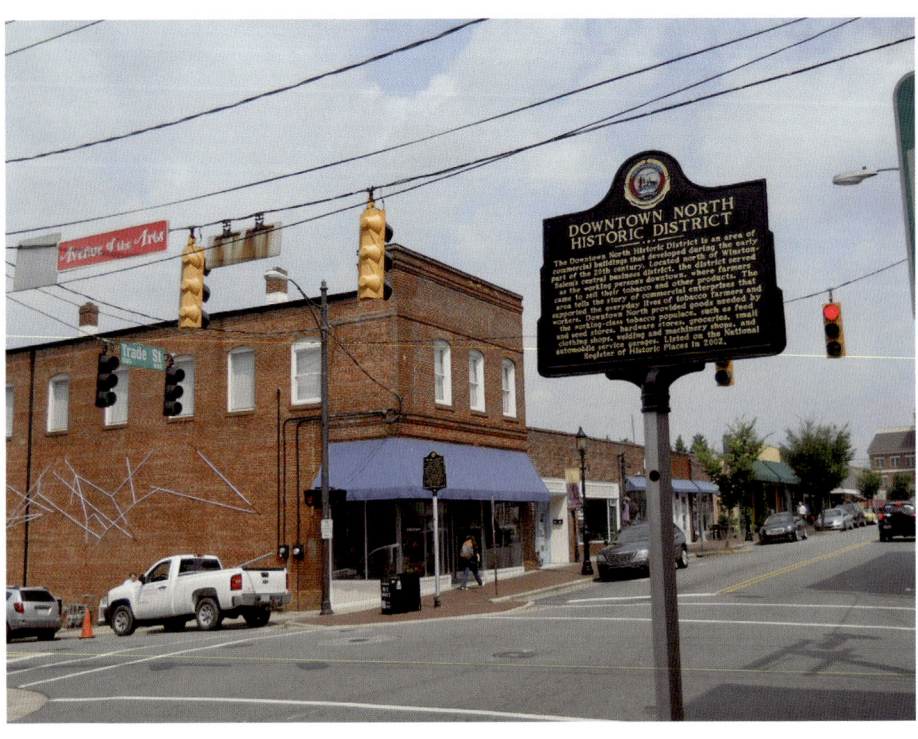

TRADE STREET NEAR SEVENTH STREET:
The late 1930s saw the Depression beginning to weaken and prosperity for the 'regular Joes' began to take shape at Planters Warehouse. Although the Tobacco Auctioneers' whistle no longer blows to sound the final words 'Sold American.' The sounds of renovation, rehabilitation, and revitalization of old tobacco warehouses blow often in the historic district of tobacco and commerce today.

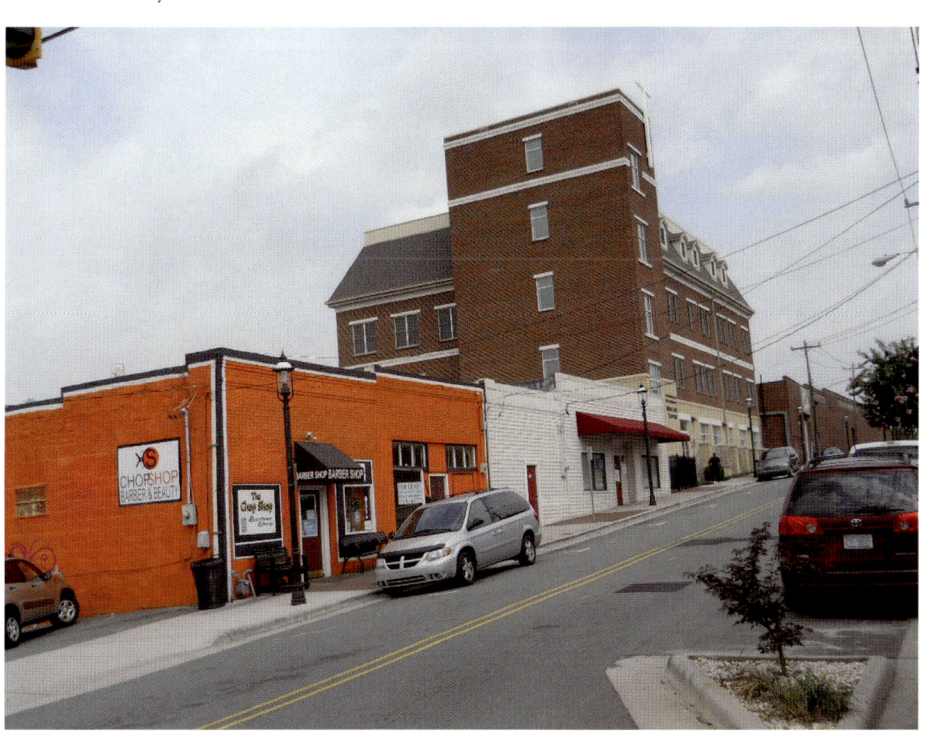

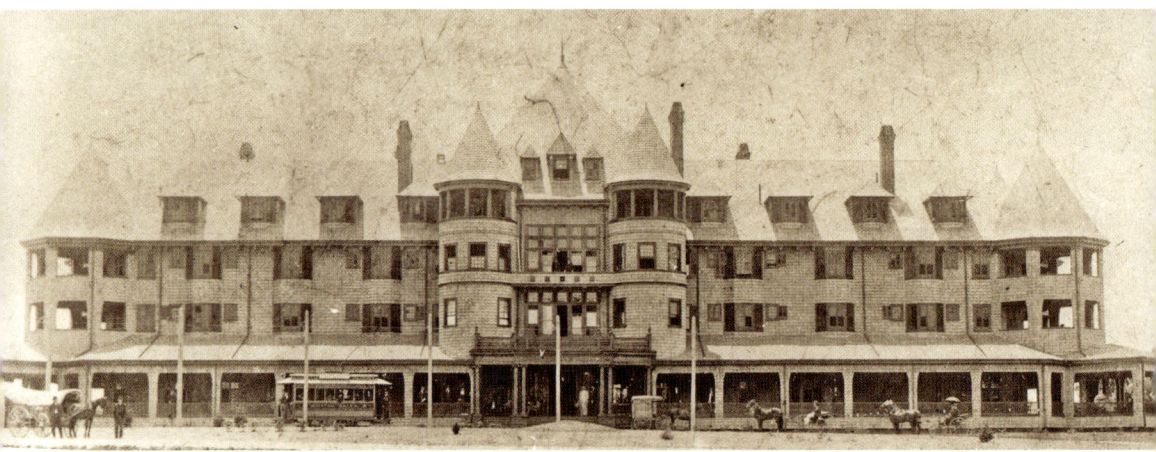

WEST END RESORT Hotel: Memories abound in this picture from 1891 of the West End Resort Hotel's arrival. The streetcar system was new and ready to bring visitors and residents alike to the hotel. When the rambling, wood framed structure burned it was said the flames could be seen from Pilot Mountain, North Carolina. Today, a much more tranquil scene from Grace Court Park and the historic marker of the 'Great Zinzendorf Hotel' is presented.

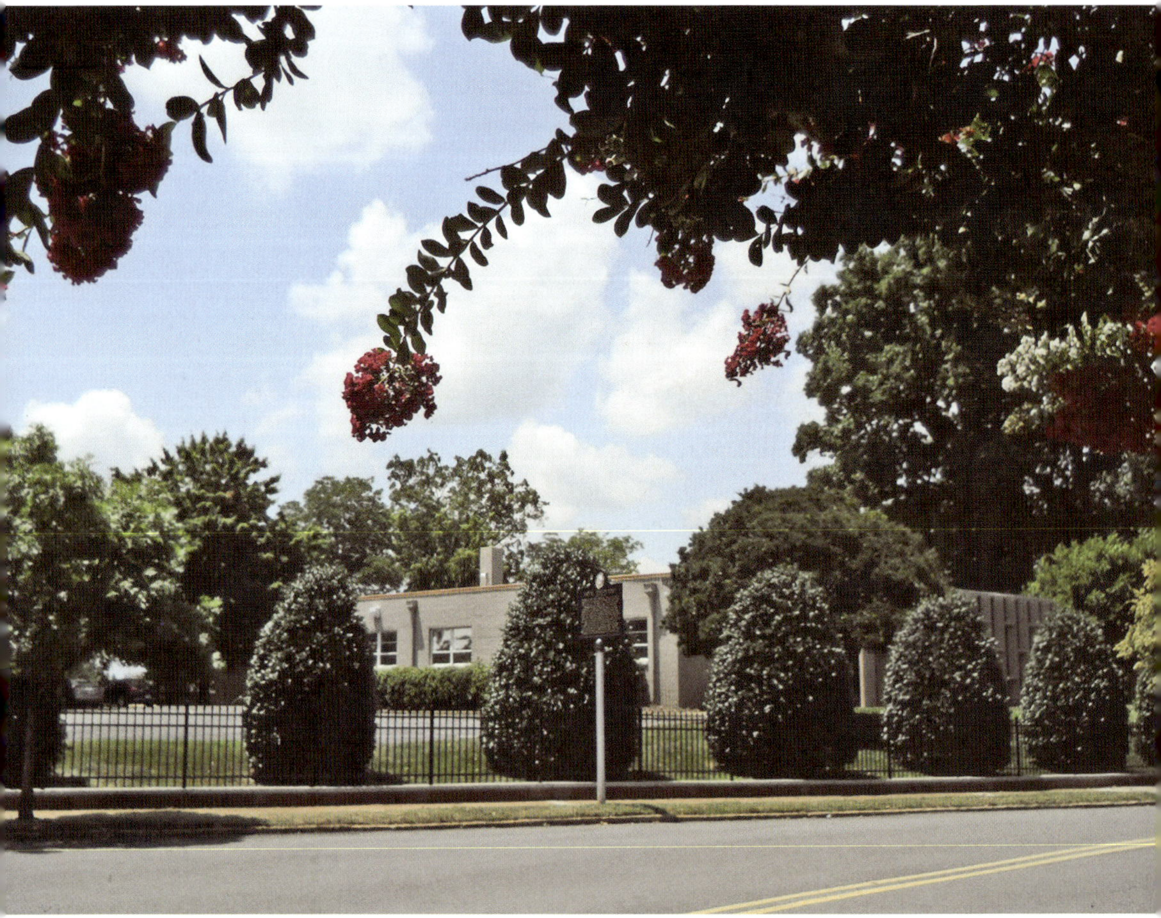

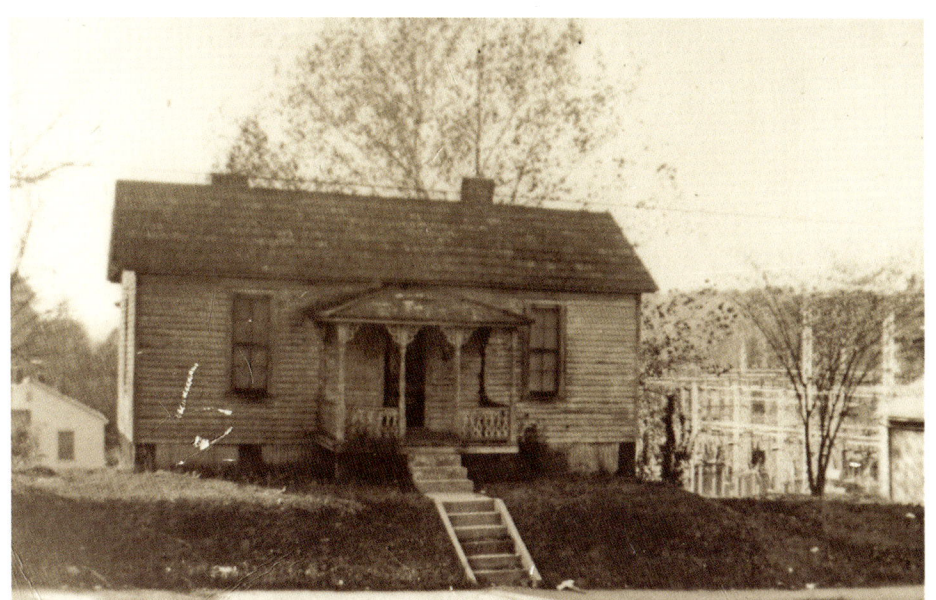

SOUTH ON BROAD STREET AT DUKE POWER STATION: Traveling south from Fourth and Broad Street downtown, one passes in the Broad Street corridor the Old West Salem neighborhood. Crossing the Salem Creek, one enters the Washington Park's neighborhood *c.* 1890s. Much like Western Winston, it had its own 'Millionaires' Row' created by Salem citizens. Ms. Lucy Johnson Branscombe resided in this Broad Street home. Today, the house has been raised by the Duke Power Energy Company and their tower along with the historic Washington Park signage is shown on this site.

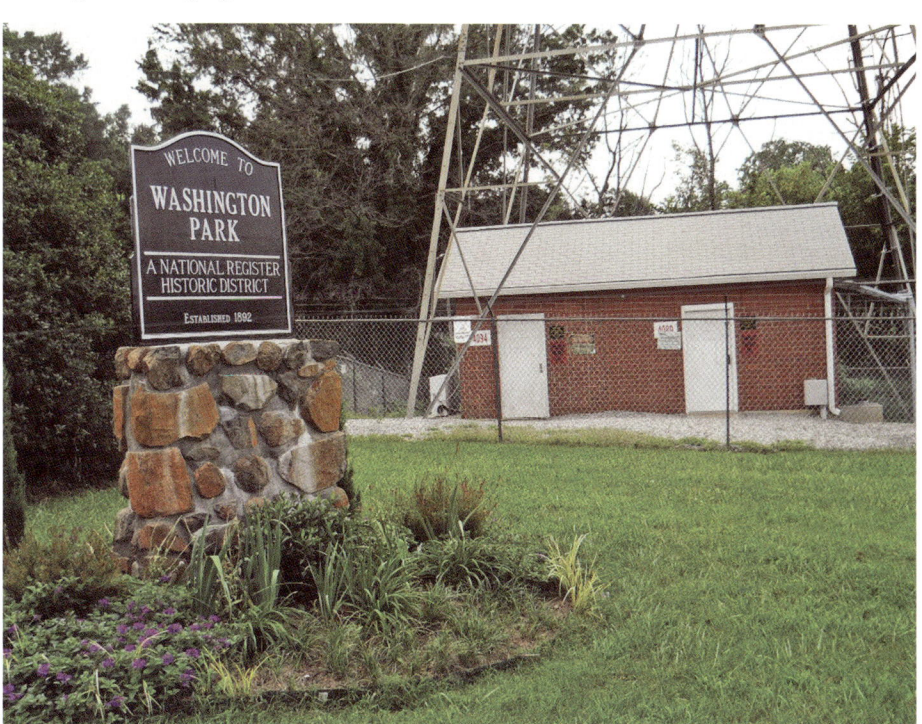

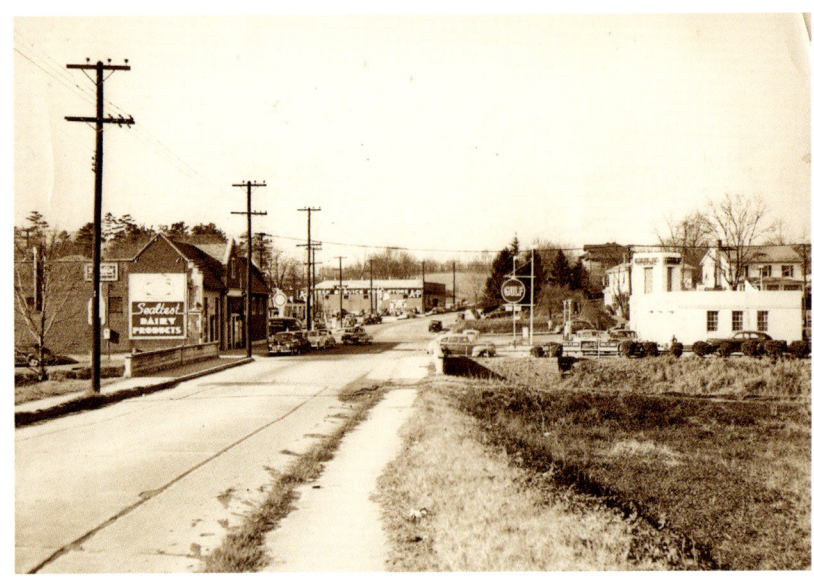

WEST FIRST STREET AND HAWTHORNE ROAD: First Street (Old Shallowford Road) was the first road cut to Salem in 1766. The street was called North Street by Old Salem and First Street by Old Winston. In this 1950s photograph, the dividing line of First Street separated the West End neighborhood on the right and the Ardmore neighborhood on the left, much like Old First Street once separated Winston and Salem. An Atlantic & Pacific National Chain Grocery Store (A & P), a Gulf Full Service Gas Station and eatery welcomed residents and visitors alike. The bridge you can see passes over Peter's Creek (Old Petersbach continuing to the Paper Mill settlement *c.* 1791 in the old days). Today, Wake Forest, Bowman Gray School of Medicine, and Baptist Hospital/Brenner's Hospital loom over Interstate 40 while the creek has been paved over for building purposes and the bridge has been removed.

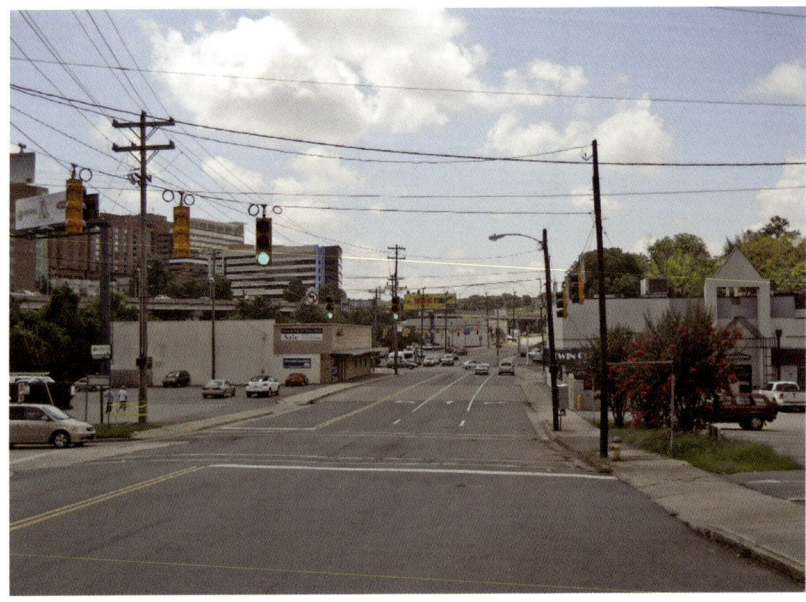

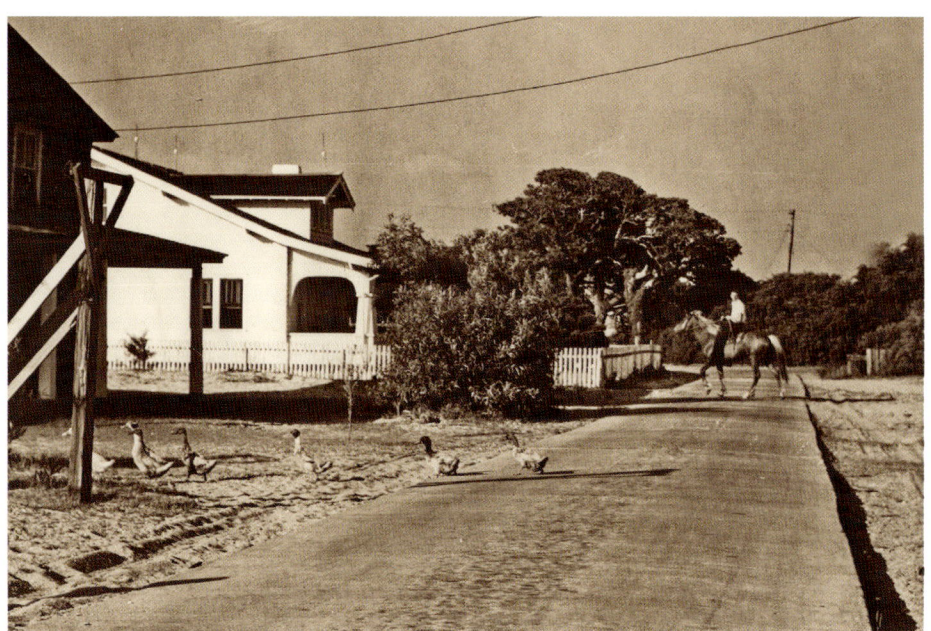

STRAFFORD ROAD AT HIGHWAY 158 LOOKING EAST: The road to Clemmonsville in the early days of Salem and Old Winston was transversed by wagons and stagecoaches. Before and after photographs are shown along this stretch of highway. In the first, the lazy days of horseback riding and an occasional duck crossing were commonplace events until the city's arm found the county. Below, is the first business to arrive and replace these humble homes above. Strafford TV Service would bring more than electricity to Strafford Road. A four lane highway producing racecar speeds between Winston-Salem and the town of Clemmons appears today.

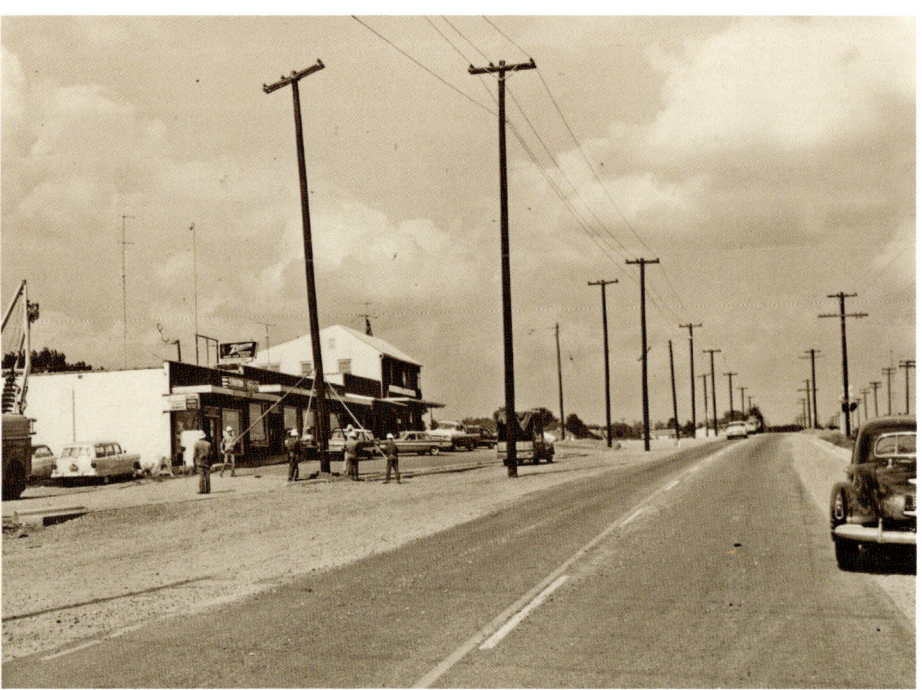

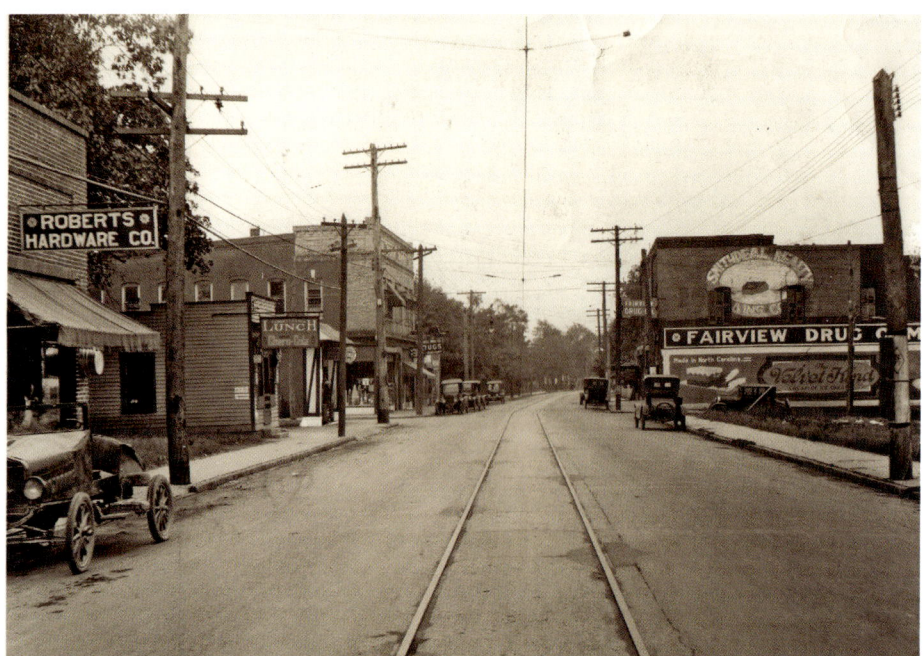

NORTH LIBERTY STREET AT FAIRVIEW STREET: The town of Liberty was founded in 1920 to the north of Salem. The Moravians sold land to fellow Moravians who did not want to live as the Moravians did in the congregational town. By the early 1900s, the Fairview Moravian Church was established. This 1910 photograph shows the businesses of Robert's Hardware and Fairview Drug Store. Beyond the streetcar tracks was a small field where Smith-Reynolds Airport had its early beginnings. The Piedmont Airline fleet of airplanes grew into a major airport throughout most of the twentieth century.

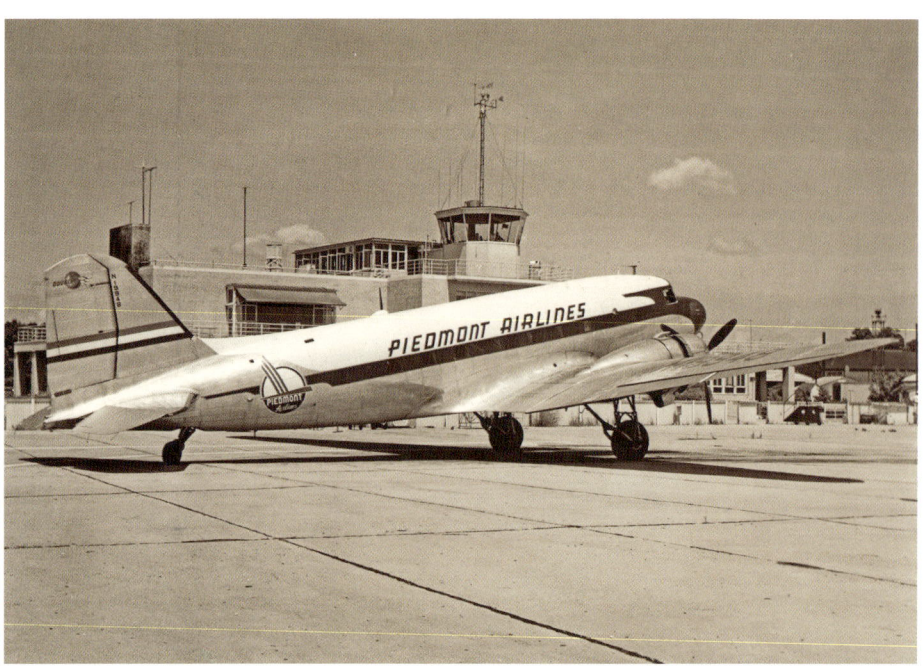

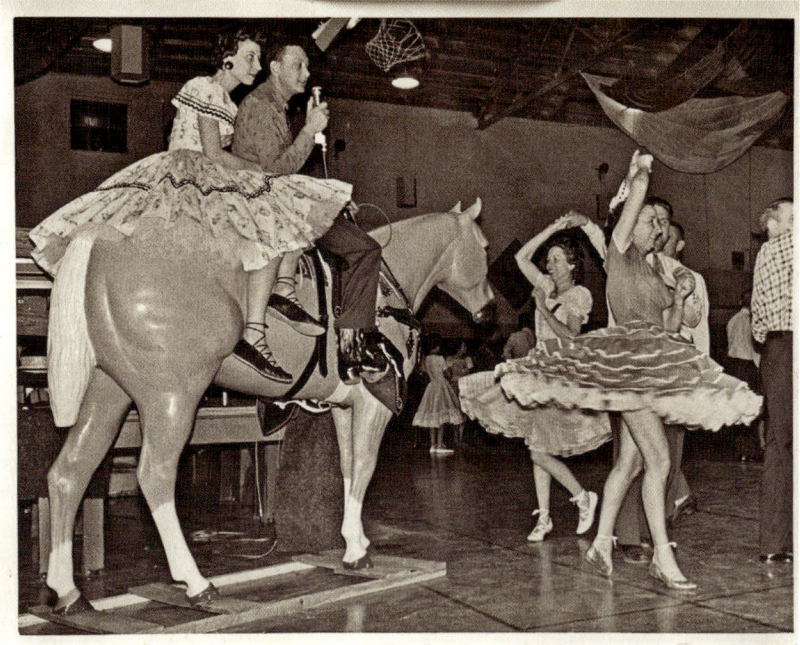

REYNOLDS PARK ROAD NEAR MARTIN LUTHER KING DRIVE: Land donated by R. J. Reynolds Tobacco Company became a playground for the young and young at heart, Reynolds Park. This older image from 1940 shows the expanse of this project. The facility included an eighteen-hole golf course; a recreational building for skating, basketball, and shindigs such as the old fashioned square dance shown in the picture.

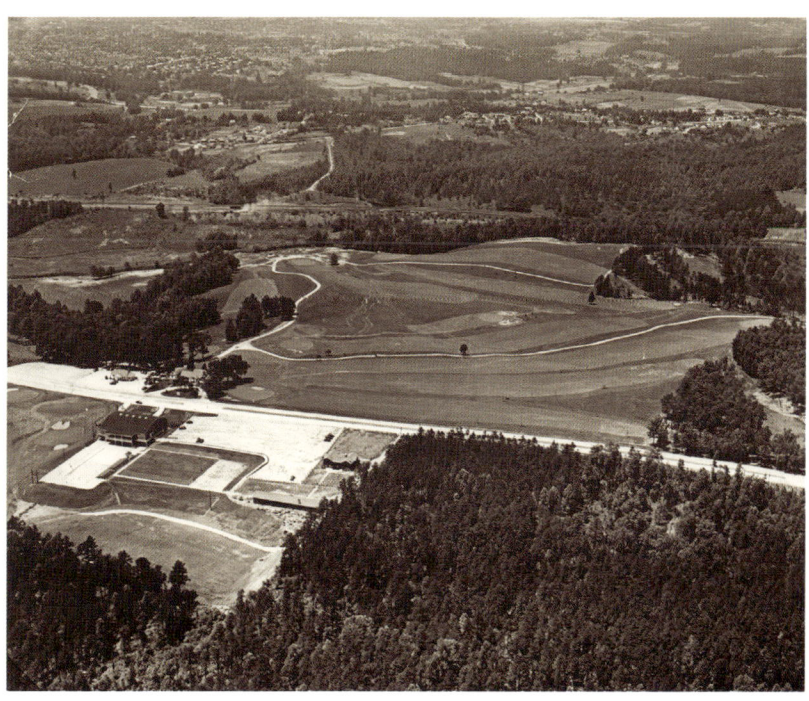

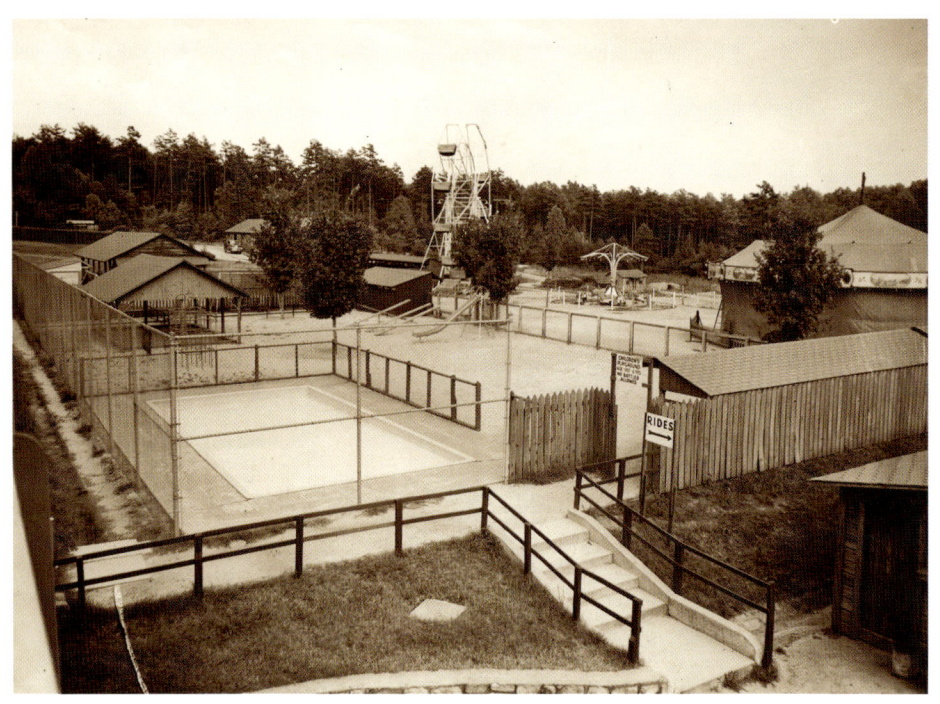

REYNOLDS PARK: Reynolds Park included a miniature amusement park: Ferris wheel, rollercoaster, merry-go-round, a miniature train complete with tunnels, a shooting gallery, a batting booth, and an Olympic size swimming pool and even a kiddy pool in the 1960s.

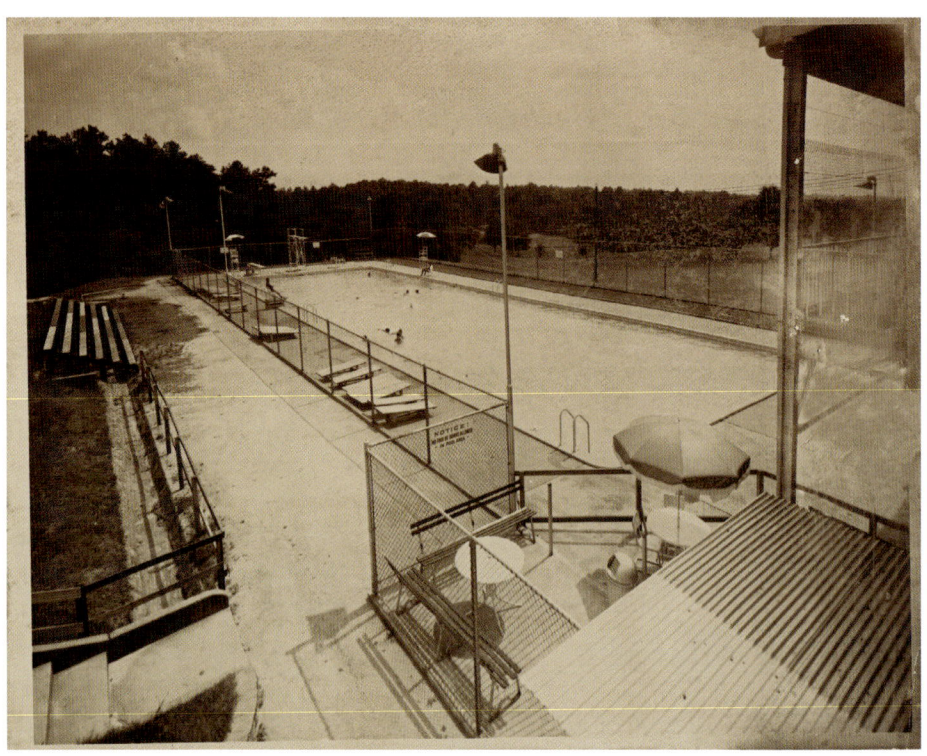

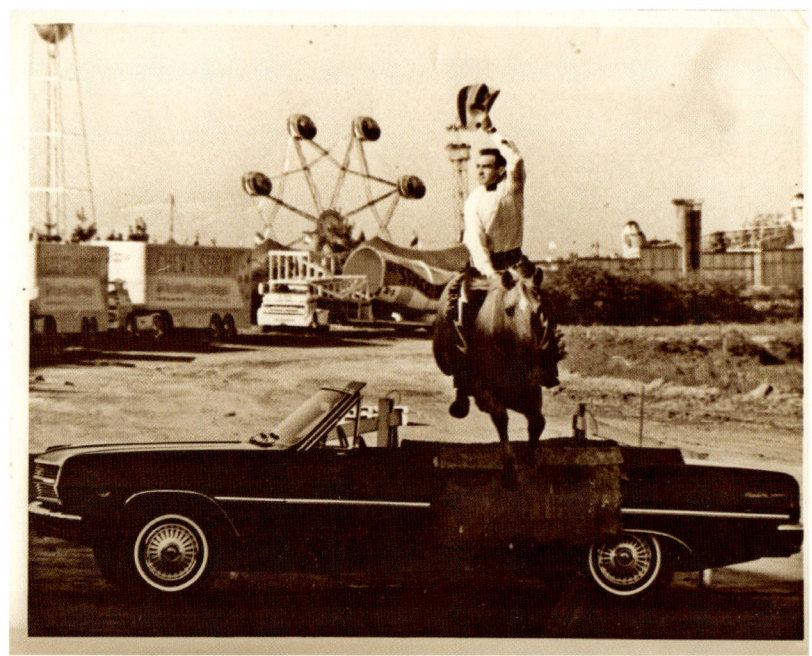

COLISEUM DRIVE AND UNIVERSITY PARKWAY NORTH: Unfortunately, Reynolds Park amusements are history. Winston-Salem has yearly fundays thanks to the second largest county fair in North Carolina, The Dixie Classic Fair. The fair traces its roots to the 1880s in Old Winston during the Tobacco Auction days. The photograph from the 1960s shows the end of another fair as the cowboy hollers 'Adios Amigos!' Another action event at the 2011 Dixie Classic Fair shows the author's children Alexandria, Sophia, and Vivian having the time of their lives on this fast rollercoaster titled the 'Wild Mouse.'

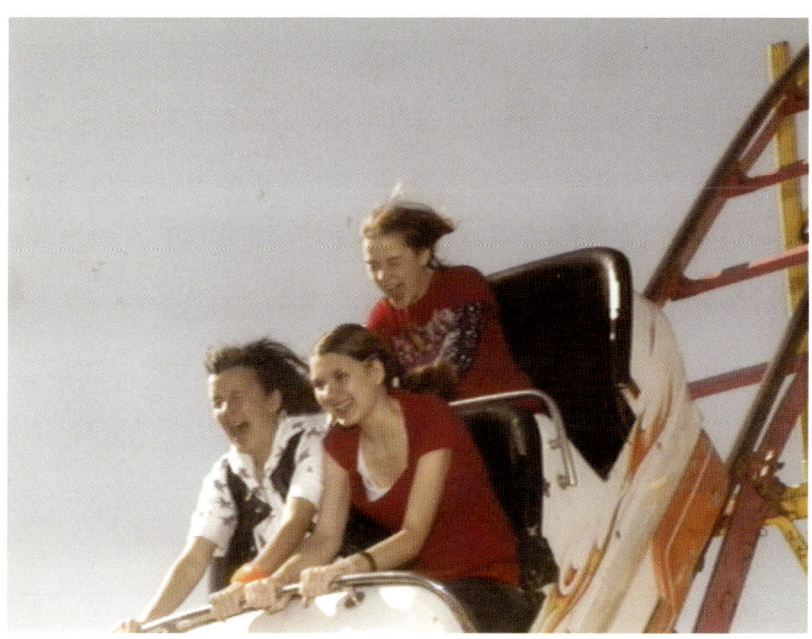

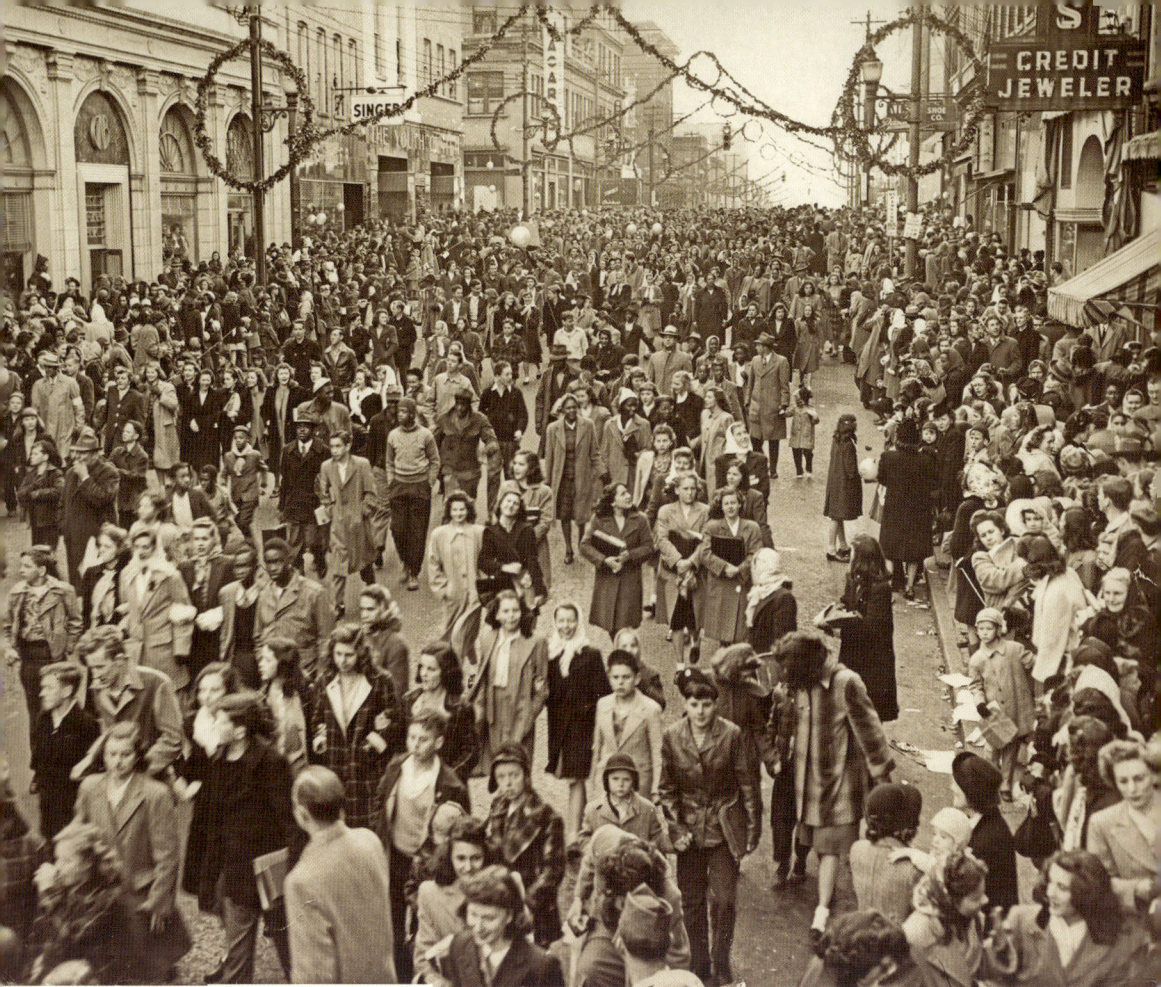

FOURTH STREET AT CHRISTMAS TIME: To acknowledge all those that have helped in bringing together this publication, *Winston-Salem Through Time* is to thank all of the people who have called Old Salem, Old West Salem, Old Winston, and Winston-Salem, the twin city, home. Special thanks go to Mr Frank Jones, Ms Adelaide Fries, Ms Miriam Brietz and Mrs Lucy Johnson Branscombe (all sadly postumously), Ms. Ann Chambers, Forsyth County Public Library, Old Salem Incorporated, Mrs LaNelle Hunter Church, Mr Thomas Holcomb, Mr Roger Willard, The West Salem Historical Association, Fonthill Publishers and their staff. Special thanks goes to my family, my wife Tommie and daughters Ali, Sophia, and Vivian. Without their help and encouragement, this publication would not have been possible. The photograph below epitomizes the strength in numbers of Winston-Salem residents at this Christmas parade celebration during the 1940s.